What American Elementary School Students Learn in Textbooks

アメリカの小学生が学ぶ
国語・算数・理科・社会
教科書

装丁————スタジオ・ギブ（川島 進）
装画————小森哲郎
挿画————高橋 満
　　　　片倉和子
編集協力————株式会社ポイントライン
　　　　OLA Co. Ltd.

What American Elementary School Students Learn in Textbooks

FROM WHAT YOUR FIRST GRADER NEEDS TO KNOW (Revised Edition)
　　　WHAT YOUR SECOND GRADER NEEDS TO KNOW (Revised Edition)
　　　WHAT YOUR THIRD GRADER NEEDS TO KNOW (Revised Edition)
　　　WHAT YOUR FOURTH GRADER NEEDS TO KNOW (Revised Edition)
　　　WHAT YOUR FOURTH GRADER NEEDS TO KNOW
　　　WHAT YOUR FIFTH GRADER NEEDS TO KNOW
AND 　WHAT YOUR SIXTH GRADER NEEDS TO KNOW
　　　By E. D. Hirsch, Jr.
Copyright © 1992, 1993, 1997, 1998, 2001, 2004, by Core Publications, Inc.
and by Core Knowledge Foundation.
Used by permission of Doubleday, a division of Random House, Inc.

Japanese Copyright © 2006 Japan Book, Inc.
All rights reserved. Printed in Japan.

アメリカの
小学生が学ぶ
国語・算数・理科・社会教科書

What American Elementary School Students Learn in Textbooks

ジェームス・M・バーダマン [編]
James M. Vardaman, Jr.

村田 薫 [編・訳]
Murata Kaoru

JapanBook

PREFACE

前　書

　英語で苦しんだ経験のある方なら、日本語を勉強している外国人に向かって、「春はあけぼの…」とか、「勝てば官軍」、あるいは「財布には一葉も諭吉もない」などと言ったりはしないでしょう。これは少し極端な例だとしても、この逆の事態を英語で経験することはよくあって、私達の思考や舌に急ブレーキがかかります。それは熟語とか会話の決まり文句の問題ではなく、その英語の文章や会話がふまえている背景的な知識を共有していないがために起こるトラブルです。文化とは特定の集団や民族においてのみ通用するものと司馬遼太郎は定義しました。ということは、他国の文化はつねに異文化であるわけですが、その異文化が共通認識として持つ知識を学ばなければその言語の習得も難しくなります。

　1991年にバージニア大学のE. D. ハーシュ教授がCore Knowledge Series（以下「シリーズ」と略す）という小学校教科書プロジェクトを発足させました。これは文化的な知識の継承や人間の相互理解に役立つような教科書を作りたいという想いから生まれた企画ですが、本書はその「シリーズ」の1～6年生用の教科書から、日本風にいえば国語・算数・理科・社会にあたる内容を選んで編集したものです。

　というと、いかにも堅苦しいお勉強の本のように聞こえますが、原著の「シリーズ」には、「へぇー」「なるほど」「あはは」が、巧みに整理・配列されていて、アメリカの小学生の知的冒険の旅への欲求に十分こたえています。本書もその原著の特長をいかして編集しましたが、日本の大人の読者のために独自の工夫も加えてあります。昨年刊行した『アメリカの小学生が学ぶ歴史教科書』を手に取ってくださった方にはもうおわかりでしょうが、本書はその姉妹篇ということになります。

　最近の中学・高校の英語教科書はずいぶん工夫されていますが、

異文化理解の面ではまだ改善の余地があるようです。むろん分量の制限のみならず特定の国の文化だけを想定して教科書を作ることはできないという事情もあります。しかし、マザー・グース、言葉遊び、世界の宗教、ことわざ、ギリシャ神話・叙事詩、アーサー王物語、演説、文学の基本、地理、そして算数や理科——こうした英語国民の血脈にあたる知識をなおざりにするわけにはいきません。そういう意味で、本書が日本の英語教科書の補完的な役割を果たすことができればというのが私達の願いです。

　本書に盛り込んだような知識を知らなければ英語ができるとは言えない、などと偉そうなお節介を言うつもりはありません。それよりも、編集を終えて改めて驚いたのですが、長い間受け継がれていく知識というものは、どうも実際上の必要性だけで生き延びてきたのではなさそうです。物語やことわざばかりでなく、直喩・隠喩などの技法にも独特の生命力やキャラクターがあって、時の流れを乗り切ってきたのも納得できます。おそらくローマ数字や幾何学でさえ例外ではありません。いわばどの知識にも「顔かたち」があって、人間のジタバタに付き合いながら歴史の時空間を悠々と歩き続けているとでもいった感じです。長い時を生き延びてきた彼らの会釈に応えて、じっくり耳を傾けてみてはいかがでしょうか。

　算数は編集の都合上、「シリーズ」の学年別配当とは異なるところがあります。また、歴史・地理関係は今回はほとんど省きましたが、日本に関しては日本紹介と近代史の章を選んでいます。Haikuの章は共編者のバーダマン教授が書き下ろしたもので、原典にはありませんが、アメリカの学校教育で幅広く取り入れられているので加えてみました。

　　2006年2月

　　　　　　　　編者　ジェームス・M・バーダマン
　　　　　　　　　　　村田　薫(記)

CONTENTS
目次

1st GRADE 1年生　　　　　13

Traditional Rhymes　古くから伝わる詩 ……14

Mother Goose　マザー・グースの唄 ……16

Playing with Words　言葉遊び ……18

How to Remember Things　いろいろなものの覚え方 ……20

Issun Boshi: One-Inch Boy　1インチの少年、一寸法師 ……22

Familiar Sayings　よく使うことわざ ……28

Religions: What Different People Believe ……30
宗教──さまざまな信仰

Judaism　ユダヤ教 ……32
The Story of Moses　モーゼの物語　32

Christianity　キリスト教 ……40
The First Christmas　最初のクリスマス　42
Jesus the Teacher: The Parable of the Good Samaritan　44
よきサマリア人について
Easter　イースター　46

Islam　イスラム教 ……48
The Five Pillars of Islam　イスラムの5柱　50

2nd GRADE 2年生

Hinduism ヒンドゥー教 ……56
Rama and Sita: A Tale from the Ramayana　58
ラーマとシータ「ラーマーヤナ」の物語

Buddhism 仏教 ……64
Buddha: The Enlightened One　ブッダ――悟りを開いた者　64
King Asoka: From War to Peace　アショーカ王――戦争から平和へ　66

Confucianism 儒教 ……70
A Wise Teacher in China: Confucius　中国の賢人――孔子　70

Paul Bunyan ポール・バニヤン ……72

Familiar Sayings よく使うことわざ ……76

Let's Visit Japan 日本を訪ねて ……78

Counting Money お金の数え方 ……80

Myths from Ancient Greece 古代ギリシャの神話 ……82

Heroes and Monsters, Gods and Goddesses ……82
英雄と怪物、神々
Greek Gods and Goddesses　ギリシャの神々　84
Prometheus Brings Fire, Pandora Brings Woe　88
火をもたらしたプロメテウス、苦悩をもたらしたパンドラ
Oedipus and the Sphinx　オイディプスとスフィンクス　90
Daedalus and Icarus　ダイダロスとイカロス　90
The Labors of Hercules　ヘラクレスの大仕事　92

3rd GRADE 3年生

    Perseus and Medusa　ペルセウスとメドゥーサ　100
    Cupid and Psyche　キューピッドとプシュケ　104
    The Sword of Damocles　ダモクレスの剣　110

Sayings and Phrases　ことわざと熟語 ……112

The Four Rules of Arithmetic　四則算（加減乗除）……114

    Addition　足し算　114
    Subtraction　引き算　115
    Multiplication　掛け算　116
    Division　割り算　116
    Fractions　分数　118

4th GRADE 4年生

Myths from Medieval England 中世イギリスの伝説 ……122

The Legend of King Arthur and the Knights of the Round Table……122
アーサー王と円卓の騎士団の物語

- How Arthur Became King: The Sword in the Stone 122
  アーサーはいかにして王となったか――石に刺さった剣
- The Sword Excalibur and the Lady of the Lake 128
  宝剣エクスカリバーと湖の姫
- Guinevere グィネビア 130
- Sir Launcelot ランスロット卿 134

Sayings and Phrases ことわざと熟語 ……140

Haiku 俳句 ……144

Pangaea: Continental Drift パンガイア：移動する大陸 ……148

Roman Numerals ローマ数字 ……150

5th GRADE 5年生

The Iliad and the Odyssey　イリアスとオデュッセイア ……154
The Iliad　イリアス ……154
- The Quarrel Between Agamemnon and Achilles　156
  アガメムノンとアキレスのいさかい
- The Arming of Achilles　アキレスの武装　162
- The Death of Hector　ヘクトルの死　168
- Epilogue to the Iliad　『イリアス』の結末　172

The Odyssey　オデュッセイア ……176
- Odysseus and the Cyclops　オデュッセウスとキュクロプス　176

The Language of Geography　地理の用語 ……188

Regions of the United States　アメリカ合衆国の地域区分 ……194

Geometry　幾何学 ……196

Reproduction　生殖 ……206

Learning About Literature　文学を学ぶ ……216
- Kinds of Literature: Tragedy and Comedy　文学の種類：悲劇と喜劇　216
- Simile and Metaphor　直喩と隠喩　218
- Personification　擬人法　224

Sayings and Phrases　ことわざと熟語 ……226

Abraham Lincoln's Gettysburg Address ……230
エイブラハム・リンカーンのゲティスバーグ演説

6th GRADE 6年生

John F. Kennedy: Inaugural Address ……234
ジョン・F・ケネディ「大統領就任演説」

Martin Luther King, Jr.: "I Have a Dream" ……238
マーティン・ルーサー・キング牧師「わたしには夢がある」

Japan: The Opening of Japan 日本の開国 ……244
- The Meiji Restoration and the Modernizing of Japan   246
  明治維新と日本の近代化
- Japan Becomes a World Power   日本が世界の強国になる   250

Capitalism and Socialism   資本主義と社会主義 ……254

Large and Small Numbers   大きな数と小さな数 ……260
- Numbers Through Millions   億までの数   260
- Decimals   小数   263
- Way of Writing Multiplication   掛け算の書き表し方   265
- Exponents   指数   266
- Powers of Ten   10の累乗   267

Can You Analyze a Poem and Enjoy It Too? ……268
分析しても詩は楽しめる?
- Structure in Poetry   詩の構造   270

Sayings and Phrases   ことわざと熟語 ……278

1 What American 1st GRADERS Learn in Textbooks

LANGUAGE ARTS • 国語

Traditional Rhymes 古くから伝わる詩

Early to Bed
By Benjamin Franklin from *Poor Richard's Almanac*

Early to bed and early to rise
Makes a man healthy, wealthy, and wise.

「早寝」
ベンジャミン・フランクリン『貧しい農夫リチャードの暦』より

早寝に早起き続けていれば、
丈夫で金持ち、賢い人に。

Star Light, Star Bright

Star light, star bright,
First star I see tonight,
I wish I may, I wish I might,
Have the wish I wish tonight.

Rain, Rain, Go Away

Rain, rain, go away
Come again another day
Little Johnny wants to play.

Rain, rain, go to Spain,
Never show your face again.

「きらきら光る　お星さま」

きらきら光る　お星さま
最初に見つけた　お星さま
願おうかな　願うのやめよかな
今夜の　わたしの　ひそかな願い

「あめ、あめ、ふりやめ」

雨　雨　行っちまえ
また　こんどに　しておくれ
リトル・ジョニーの　おでましだ。

雨　雨　スペインまで　行っちまえ
おまえの顔など　見たくもない。

1st GRADE

Time to Rise
by Robert Louis Stevenson

A birdie with a yellow bill
Hopped upon the window-sill.
Cocked his shining eye and said:
"Ain't you 'shamed, you sleepy-head?"

「起きる時間」
ロバート・ルイス・スティーブンソン

黄色いくちばしの鳥が
窓にぴょんと飛んできた。
眼をキッと光らせてこちらを見ると、
「よお、寝坊助、だめじゃねえか」

*Ain't=Aren't 日常会話などで用いられる非標準的な言い方。
 'shamed= ashamed 弱く発音されるaが抜け落ちたもの。

Roses Are Red

Roses are red,
Violets are blue,
Sugar is sweet,
And so are you.

「バラは赤く」

バラは　赤く
すみれは　青い
お砂糖は　あまく
あなたと　おなじ

Now I Lay Me

Now I lay me down to sleep,
I pray the Lord my soul to keep.
If I should die before I wake,
I pray the Lord my soul to take.

「おやすみの祈り」

これから　おやすみの床につきます
どうか　かみさま　わたしのたましいを　お守りください
もしも　めざめるまえに　死んでしまったときには
どうか　かみさま　たましいは　あなたのおそばに

NOTE
これはこどもの就寝のお祈りで、植民地時代の1680年代に出た初等教育の教科書 The New England Primer（19世紀までに約500万部印刷）に収められた。以後、数世紀にわたってアメリカのこどもたちはこの詩を覚えてきた。

LANGUAGE ARTS • 国語

Mother Goose　マザー・グースの唄

"Humpty Dumpty Sat on a Wall"

Humpty Dumpty sat on a wall,
Humpty Dumpty had a great fall;
All the King's horses and all the King's men
Couldn't put Humpty together again.

「ハンプティ・ダンプティ」

ハンプティ・ダンプティが、塀にすわる。
ハンプティ・ダンプティが、ドンと落ちる。
王様の馬も家来も全員集まり、
ハンプティをくっつけたがもどらない。

"Baa, Baa, Black Sheep"

Baa, baa, black sheep,
Have you any wool?
Yes, sir, yes, sir,
Three bags full.
One for the master,
And one for the dame,
And one for the little boy
Who lives down the lane.

「メェー、メェー、黒い綿羊さん」

メェー、メェー、黒い綿羊さん、
羊毛はあるかい？
はい、はい、おまかせ、
袋に三つ分。
ひとつはご主人、
ひとつは奥様、
残るひとつは、向うの家の
坊やの分。

NOTE

現代英語にもっとも影響を与えたものは聖書とシェイクスピアだ。しかし、マザーグースも忘れることはできない。その数は800篇を超え、ほぼ全英語国民が何らかの形で記憶しているマザーグースは、語呂のよさ、ナンセンスの楽しさで心の深層に入り込む。英語のリズム、発想を知る上でこれほど貴重なものはない。

"Three Wise Men of Gotham"

Three wise men of Gotham
Went to sea in a bowl;
If the bowl had been stronger
My song had been longer.

「ゴサムの三賢人」

ゴサムの町の三賢人
お椀を漕いで、海に出た。
お椀がもっと頑丈だったら、
この歌ここで終わりゃしない。

"Hickory, Dickory, Dock"

Hickory, dickory, dock,
The mouse ran up the clock.
The clock struck one,
The mouse ran down,
Hickory, dickory, dock.

「チック、タック、トック」

チック、タック、トックと鳴る時計、
ネズミがたったと駆けあがる。
時計がボーンと一時を打てば、
ネズミはとっとと駆けおりる、
チック、タック、トックと鳴る時計。

"Tom, Tom, the Piper's Son"

Tom, Tom, the piper's son,
Stole a pig and away he run;
The pig was eat,
And Tom was beat,
And Tom went howling down the street.

「トムや、トムや、笛吹きのせがれ」

トムや、トム、笛吹きのせがれ、
豚を盗んでとんずらし、
豚は食べられ、
トムぶたれ、
通りをトムは泣き泣き走る。

LANGUAGE ARTS • 国語

Playing with Words 言葉遊び

Riddle Rhymes　なぞなぞ

Riddle me, riddle me, what is that
Over the head, and under the hat?　*(hair)*
さあ、なぞなぞです、答えてください。
頭の上にあって帽子の下にあるもの、なあに？　(髪)

The longer she stands,
the lower she grows.　*(a candle)*
長く立っていればいるほど
背が低くなります。　(ろうそく)

House full, room full
But can't get a spoonful.　*(smoke)*
家中にいっぱい、部屋にもいっぱい、
でも、スプーン一杯分もすくえない。　(煙)

Look me in the eye, I am somebody;
But stand behind me and
I am nobody at all.　*(a mirror)*
私の目を見てごらん。私は誰かさんです。
でも、私の後ろに立ってみてごらん。
私はまったく誰でもない。　(鏡)

Why is six afraid of seven?　*(Because seven ate(eight) nine.)*
どうして6は7が恐いのか？　(7が9を食べてしまうから。)

What building has the most stories?　*(the library)*
いちばん階数の多い建物は？　(図書館)
story には「物語」のほかに「階」という意味もある。

1st GRADE

Tongue Twisters　早口言葉

Some shun sunshine—Do you shun sunshine?
人によっては陽射しを避ける——あなたは陽射しを避ける？
shun「避ける」。

A skunk sat on a stump and thunk the stump stunk, but the stump thunk the skunk stunk.
スカンク君、木株に腰かけ、木株君は木株くさいと気になった。ところが木株君のほうも、スカンク君か、こりゃスカンクくさくて好かんわ、だと。
stumpは「木の切り株」。thunkはthinkの過去形で方言。
stinkの過去形はstankが一般的だが、stunkという形もある。

She's so selfish she should sell shellfish shells.
But shell of shellfish seldom sell.
貝の貝殻を買ってもらおうなんて、あの子はなんともわがまま勝手。
でも貝の貝殻なんて売れるのかいな。

Pangrams　パングラム

The quick brown fox jumps over a lazy dog.
動きのすばやい茶色のキツネがぐうたら犬を飛び越える。

Spoonerisms　スプーナリズム

(誤) I'll shake a tower.
　　俺がタワーを揺さぶってみせる。
(正) I'll take a shower.
　　シャワーを浴びてくるね。

(誤) He's a sheep in wolf's clothing.
　　彼はオオカミの衣を着たヒツジだ。
(正) He's a wolf in sheep's clothing.
　　あいつはヒツジの衣を着たオオカミだ。

NOTE
早口言葉はtongue twisters。舌をもつれさせる言葉ということ。左の例を見るとわかるように、発音しにくい音の繰り返しによって、読むリズムがうまく作れない。

NOTE
パングラム
パングラムとはアルファベットのすべての文字を使い、なおかつ同じ文字をできるだけ少なくして文章を作るという文字遊び。いろは歌の英語版。これはいちばん有名なパングラムだが、o、a、uのような母音はどうしても何度か使うことになる。

NOTE
スプーナリズム
スプーナリズムとは愉快な言い間違いのこと。オクスフォード大学の学寮長で言い間違いをよくしたといわれるWilliam Archibald Spooner(1844–1930)の名前に由来する。

LANGUAGE ARTS • 国語

How to Remember Things
いろいろなものの覚え方

Number of days in the months　月の日数

Thirty days hath September,
April, June, and November.
All the rest have thirty-one,
But February has twenty-eight alone,
Except in leap year, that's the time
When February's days are twenty-nine.

9月は30日、
4月、6月、11月も。
残りの月は31日、されど
2月ばかりは28日、
ただし閏年なぞあって、
そのときは2月も29日。

各月の日数の覚え方を詩にしたもの。1、2行、3、4行、5、6行は、行末で韻を踏んでいる。日本では『西向く士（二、四、六、九、十一）、小の月』と覚える。leap year は閏年。

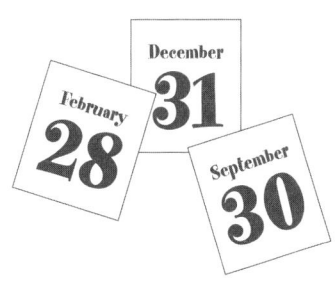

The year Columbus found America　アメリカ発見の年

In fourteen hundred and ninety-two,
Columbus sailed the ocean blue.

1492年、この年に
コロンブスは青海原を渡った。

コロンブスのアメリカ発見の年号1492を詩にしたもの。blue の韻をたよりに two を覚える。

The spelling of "arithmetic"　「算数」のつづりの覚え方

A rat in Tommy's house may eat Tommy's ice cream.

トミーんちのネズミはトミーのアイスクリームを食べてしまうかも。

単語の最初の文字をつなぎ合わせると、arithmetic になる。

The ratio of the circumference of a circle to its diameter
円周率

Yes, I know a number.
はい、私は数を知っている。

単語の文字数が順番に、3.1416（5の次の9を切り上げて6）となっている。

1st GRADE

The order of the colors of the rainbow (British)
イギリス風虹の色の順番

Richard of York gave battle in vain.
ヨークのリチャードはむなしい戦をした。

r = red（赤）
o = orange（オレンジ）
y = yellow（黄）
g = green（緑）
b = blue（青）
i = indigo（藍色）
v = violet（スミレ色）

Counting with a Tally　タリーで数える

| = 1　|| = 2　||| = 3　|||| = 4　𝍤 = 5

日本では数や回数を記録するときに5画の「正」という字を使うが、欧米ではこのようなタリーという記号を使う。タリーの歴史は古く、古代ギリシャ、中国でも用いられていた。

Telephone Numbers　電話番号

1	ABC 2	DEF 3
GHI 4	JKL 5	MNO 6
PRS 7	TUV 8	WXY 9
＊	Operator 0	#

＊ = "the star key"　# = "the pound key"

NOTE

英米の電話には数字の上にアルファベットがついている。これはかつて局番に数字ではなく地名の最初の2文字を使っていたからである。現在ではこれを利用して、電話番号の数字を記憶しやすいように言葉に置きかえている。たとえば、1-800-HELP NOWは数字では1-800-4357669となる。
　QとZがないが、Qは7にZは9に入れられたり、0のところにQとZが入ったりというバリエーションもある。

Examples:
1-800-HELP NOW (Red Cross donations for Katerina Hurricane relief)
（カトリーナ台風の義援金を募る赤十字の番号）
×-×××-GYM TO GO （フィットネス・センターの番号）

LANGUAGE ARTS • 国語

Issun Boshi: One-Inch Boy

Long ago in a village in Japan, there lived an old man and his wife who more than anything wanted a child. They hoped and they wished and they prayed. "May we be blessed with a child," they said, "even if it is no larger than a fingertip."

And then their prayers were answered. A fine baby boy was born to the old couple. They called him Issun Boshi,* which means "One-Inch Boy," for he was no taller than his father's thumb.

Issun Boshi grew up strong, smart, and helpful, though he grew no bigger. When twelve years had passed, Issun Boshi came to his parents and said, "Father and Mother, please give me your permission to go to the capital city, for I wish to see the world, and learn many things, and make a name for myself."

His parents were very worried, but they knew their boy was smart and strong, so they agreed to let him go. They made for him a tiny sword out of a sewing needle. They also gave him a rice bowl and some chopsticks.

In the rice bowl he floated down the river, using one of the chopsticks as a paddle. In a few days he arrived at the city of Kyoto. "My, what a busy city this is!" he thought. "So many feet and legs!" He walked carefully through the streets, dodging feet and cart wheels. He kept walking until he came to a beautiful house, the largest in the city. At the foot of the steps sat a pair of shiny black wooden shoes. They belonged to the owner of the house, who was the wealthiest lord in the city.

1st GRADE

1インチの少年、一寸法師

　昔々、日本のある村に、何よりも子どもがほしいと思っている老夫婦が暮らしていた。2人は、願をかけ、お祈りをして望みを託した。「どうか子宝に恵まれますように。たとえ指先くらいの大きさでもかまいません」

　そして、2人の祈りはかなえられた。年老いた夫婦に、元気な男の子が生まれたのだ。2人は赤ん坊を一寸法師と名づけた。一寸法師とは「1インチの男の子」という意味だが、赤ん坊は父親の親指くらいの大きさしかなかったのだ。

　一寸法師はたくましく、賢く、親切な男の子に育ったが、背丈は大きくならなかった。12歳になると一寸法師は両親にこう願い出た。「お父さん、お母さん、どうかわたしが都に行くことをお許しください。ぜひ世間というものを見てみたいのです。たくさんのことを学んで、ひとかどの人物になりたいのです」

　両親はたいへん心配しながらも、息子が強く賢いことを知っていたので、旅に出してやることにした。縫い針で小さな剣を作り、ご飯のお碗と箸を持たせてやった。

　一寸法師はお碗に乗り、箸を櫂のようにして漕ぎながら川を下った。数日のうちに彼は京都に着いた。「わあ、なんとにぎやかな町だこと！」と一寸法師は感嘆した。「足がこんなにもたくさん！」彼は人の足や荷車の車輪をよけながら、よく注意して通りを歩いていった。すると、立派な屋敷の前にたどり着いた。町でいちばん大きな屋敷だ。踏み段のところにはぴかぴかの黒塗りの下駄が一足置かれていた。その下駄は、町でもっとも裕福な領主であるこの屋敷の主人の履き物だった。

　大きな屋敷の扉が開いた。中から男が出てきて、ぴかぴかの黒い下駄を履いた。一寸法師は大声で言った「もしもし！　すみません！」。男はあたりを見回したが、だれもいないので、屋敷の中にもどろうとした。一寸法師は大声で「下です、足元にいるのです！　踏みつぶさないでください」と言った。屋敷の主人は、かがみこんで一寸法師の姿を見つけるとたいそう驚いた。一寸法師は

> **NOTE**
> とくに低学年の教科書ではアメリカ先住民や黒人の民話のほかに世界各国の民話が数多く紹介されていて、多民族国家アメリカらしい。日本の民話からは「一寸法師」と「舌切り雀」が選ばれている。

＊Issun Boshi
「一寸法師」と「鬼」はそのままIssun Boshi, oniとなっているが、原文にはそれぞれ[IH-soon BOH-she]、[OH-nee]という発音表示がある。
　これはアメリカの新聞・雑誌などが固有名詞の発音などに用いる独特の表記法で、大文字のところにアクセントがある。

23

The door of the great house opened. Out walked a man who slipped on the shiny black shoes. Issun Boshi called out, "Hello! Hello there!" The man looked around and, seeing no one, began to go back in. But Issun Boshi called out, "Down here, I'm down here, near your shoes! Please be careful you don't step on me." The man, who was the lord of the house, leaned down and was very surprised when he saw Issun Boshi. Issun Boshi bowed and politely introduced himself. "My name," he said, "is Issun Boshi. I am new here and I would like to work for you."

The lord picked up Issun Boshi in the palm of his hand. In a friendly voice he asked, "But what can a little fellow like you do?"

A fly was buzzing around and bothering the lord, so Issun Boshi drew out his sewing-needle sword. With a quick *swit-swat*, down went the fly. Then Issun Boshi did an energetic little dance on the lord's hand.

"You are quite an amazing little fellow," laughed the lord. "Come, you may work for me and live in my house."

And so Issun Boshi went to live in the big beautiful house. He made friends with everyone there, especially the princess, the lord's lovely daughter. It seemed that he was always at her side, helping her in whatever way he could, whether by holding down the paper when she wrote a letter or simply by riding on her shoulder and keeping her company while she walked through the beautiful gardens around the house.

In the spring Issun Boshi traveled with the princess and her companions to the cherry blossom festival. On their way home they began to hear strange noises behind them on the narrow road. They could see nothing in the shadows, when suddenly a huge monster leaped into their path. Everyone screamed and ran—everyone except Issun Boshi and the princess.

"Who are you, and what do you want?" cried Issun Boshi.

"I am an *oni*," growled the monster. An *oni*! Everyone feared the

お辞儀をして、作法に従って自己紹介をした。「わたくしは」と彼は言った。「一寸法師と申します。この町は初めてですが、こちらで働かせていただけないでしょうか」
　主人は一寸法師をつまみ上げ、手のひらに乗せると、やさしい声で訊いた。「だが、おまえのような小さな者にできるようなことがあるかね」
　うるさいハエが主人のまわりをぶんぶん飛び回っていた。そこで、一寸法師は縫い針の剣を抜いた。すばやくシュッ、パシッと剣を振るうと、ハエは地面に落ちた。一寸法師は主人の手のひらで元気にちょいと踊ってみせた。
「小さいながらなかなかやるもんじゃのう」と主人は笑った。「よし、わしのもとで働き、屋敷で暮らすがよい」
　こうして一寸法師は大きく立派な屋敷で暮らすことになった。彼は屋敷のみんなと友達になったが、とりわけ主人の美しい娘である姫とは親しくなった。いつも姫のそばについていて、できることならなんでもお手伝いをしていた。手紙を書くときに紙が動かないよう押さえていることもあれば、肩の上に乗ったまま、屋敷の美しい庭を散歩するお供をすることもあった。
　春になり、一寸法師は姫と付き添いの者たちといっしょに花見に出かけた。その帰りに、細道を歩いていると、うしろから異様な声が聞こえてきた。物陰にはなにも見えなかったが、突然、大きな化け物が彼らの前におどり出た。これにはみな悲鳴を上げて逃げだした――が、一寸法師と姫だけは逃げなかった。
「おまえは何者だ、何がほしいのだ」と一寸法師は叫んだ。
「おれは鬼だ」と化け物はうなり声を上げた。なんと鬼！　鬼は魔物や悪鬼のようにだれもが恐れる残酷かつ凶暴な怪物である。
　しかし、一寸法師は前に進み出て叫んだ「道を開けるんだ、この魔物め！　姫様はこのわたしがお守りする、手を出そうものなら、きっと後悔することになるぞ！」
「ふん！　まあ、見ておれ！」と鬼はうなり声を上げた。鬼は一寸法師をさっとつかむと、口の中にほうり込み、ごくんと呑みこんでしまった。どんどん一寸法師は滑り落ちていって、ポトンと鬼の胃袋に着地した。
「このでくの坊め、もっと考えてから口に入れるもんだ」と一寸法師は言った。彼は縫い針の剣を抜き、鬼の胃の壁を力いっぱい突き刺し始めた。

oni, who were fierce and terrible creatures, like demons or goblins.

But Issun Boshi stepped forward and shouted, "Get out of the way, you demon! I am here to guard the princess, and if you try anything, you will regret it!"

"Ha! We'll see about that!" growled the *oni*. Then he snatched up Issun Boshi, popped him into his mouth, and, *gulp*, swallowed him whole. Down, down Issun Boshi slid until he landed, *plop*, in the *oni*'s stomach.

"This big oaf should be more careful about what he eats," said Issun Boshi. He pulled out his sewing-needle sword and began to jab it as hard as he could into the walls of the *oni*'s stomach.

"Ow! Ooh! Agh!" shouted the *oni*. Then he gave a loud "Burp!" and out popped Issun Boshi. In pain, the *oni* ran away whining and crying.

Issun Boshi ran over to the princess. She was bending down and picking up something from the ground. With great excitement she said, "Look, Issun Boshi, the *oni* was so scared that he dropped this magic hammer. If you make a wish on it, it will come true."

Issun Boshi bowed to the princess and said, "My lady, I would ask that you make a wish."

"No, Issun Boshi," said the princess. "You won this because of your bravery. You should be the first one to wish on it."

So Issun Boshi took the hammer and said, "I already have my greatest wish, which is to serve you. But if I could have another wish, I would wish to be as tall as other men."

Then he gave the hammer to the princess, who made a silent wish on it herself. Then and there, Issun Boshi began to grow taller... until beside the princess stood a handsome young man.

That night, when the princess told her father how brave Issun Boshi had been, and how he had risked his life to save her, the lord was so happy that he gave permission for Issun Boshi to marry the princess. And so, you see, the princess's wish came true, too.

Issun Boshi's brave deeds were celebrated throughout the land. He and the princess lived happily together, along with Issun Boshi's proud and happy parents, whom Issun Boshi had brought to the lord's house to be part of the family.

「おお、うう、痛い！」と鬼は悲鳴を上げた。そして、ゲエッと大きな音を立て、一寸法師を吐き出した。痛みに苦しみながら、鬼はめそめそ泣いて逃げていった。

　一寸法師が駆け寄ると、姫はかがみ込んで何かを地面から拾い上げているところだった。姫はとてもうれしそうに言った。「見て、一寸法師。鬼はすっかりおびえて打出の小槌を落としていったわ。この小槌に願いごとをすると、かなえられるのよ」

　一寸法師は姫にお辞儀をして「姫様、どうか姫様が願いごとをなさってください」と言った。

「いいえ、一寸法師」と姫はさえぎった。「おまえの勇敢な行いでこれが手に入ったのです。まずおまえが願いごとをしなさい」

　そこで一寸法師は小槌を手に取って言った。「わたくしはすでに、姫様にお仕えするという最高の望みを手に入れております。しかしながら、もしもう１つ望みがかなえられるなら、人並みの大きさになってみたいと思います」

　そう言って一寸法師が小槌を手渡すと、今度は姫が静かに黙ったまま自分の願いごとをした。するとたちまち一寸法師は大きくなり──姫のそばに、美しい青年の姿が現れた。

　その夜、姫が父親に一寸法師がいかに勇敢に命を危険にさらして自分を救おうとしてくれたかを話して聞かせると、主人はたいそう喜んで、一寸法師に姫との結婚を許した。かくして、姫の願いごともまたかなったというわけである。

　一寸法師の勇敢な行為は都中の評判になった。一寸法師と姫は幸せに暮らし、息子のことを誇りに思って喜ぶ両親も、一寸法師の計らいで主人の屋敷に招かれ、仲良くいっしょに暮らしたのだった。

LANGUAGE ARTS • 国語

Familiar Sayings よく使うことわざ

An apple a day keeps the doctor away
「1日リンゴ1個で医者いらず」

People use this saying to mean that eating apples helps keep you healthy.

このことわざは、リンゴは健康に良いという意味で使われる。

Do unto others as you would have them do unto you
「自分がしてもらいたいと思うようなことを人にしてあげなさい」

This saying is called the Golden Rule. People use it to mean: treat people as you would like to be treated yourself. It comes from the Bible.

このことわざを「黄金律」という。意味は、「わたしならこうしてもらいたいと思うことを他の人にもしてあげなさい」ということで、聖書にある言葉だ。

Hit the nail on the head
「しっかりくぎの頭を打つ」

When you use a hammer, you have to hit the nail right on its head to make it go in straight. So, when someone says that you "hit the nail on the head," they mean that you have said or done something just right.

金槌でくぎを打つときには、まっすぐにくぎが刺さるように正確にくぎの頭をたたかなければならない。だから、「しっかりとくぎの頭を打ってるね」と誰かがあなたに言ったとすれば、あなたが的を射たことを言ったか、あるいはした、という意味なのだ。

Practice makes perfect
「練習が完璧を生む」

People use this saying to mean: doing something over and over makes you good at it.

このことわざは、「なんでも繰り返し練習しているうちにうまくなるものだ」という意味で使う。

1st GRADE

Let the cat out of the bag
「猫を袋から出してしまう」

If you "let the cat out of the bag," you tell something that was meant to be a secret.

「猫を袋から出してしまう」というのは、秘密にしておくはずだったことを人にしゃべってしまうということだ。

The more the merrier
「多ければ多いほど楽しい」

People use this saying to welcome newcomers to a group. They say this because it means: the more people who take part, the more fun it can be.

➡ The house was full of kids playing. Still, when the doorbell rang, Mr. DeNiro opened the door and waved in more children, saying, "Come in, come in, the more the merrier."

このことわざは新しい仲間をグループに迎え入れるようなときに使う。なぜこんなふうに言うかというと、「参加する人が多ければ多いほど楽しみは多くなる」からだ。

➡家の中は遊ぶ子どもたちでいっぱいだった。でも、玄関のチャイムが鳴ると、扉をあけたご主人のデニーロさんは、やってきた子供たちを招きいれ、「ようこそ、いらっしゃい。多ければ多いほど楽しいもんね」と言った。

Never leave till tomorrow what you can do today
「今日できることを明日に延ばすな」

People use this saying to mean: don't put off things you have to do.

このことわざは、「しなければならないことを後に延ばすな」という意味で使う。

Land of Nod
「ノドの国」

To be in the "land of Nod" means to be asleep.

「ノドの国にいる」というのは、眠っているという意味。(注：Nodは、旧約聖書の「創世記」に出てくる、エデンの東にある土地でカインが住んだところ。「居眠りをする」のnodとかけたしゃれ)

WORLD CIVILIZATION • 世界史

Religions: What Different People Believe

For thousands of years, different religions have helped many different people try to answer some big questions. These are not just questions that people asked long ago in ancient times. People still ask these questions today, questions like: How did the world begin? Where did people and animals come from? Why is the world the way it is? How should people behave?

Today there are many religions in the world. Let's find out more about three religions that have been important to many people for thousands of years. These three religions are called Judaism, Christianity, and Islam. Today these religions have millions of followers. But thousands of years ago, each of these religions was just getting started. We're going to look back to these long-ago times and learn about how Judaism, Christianity, and Islam began.

But first, think about this: do you remember that people in ancient Mesopotamia and ancient Egypt believed in many gods? They believed in gods of nature, such as a sun god and an earth god. They believed in many other gods, such as a god of the dead and a god to protect the city. Well, there's a big difference in the religions you're going to learn about now. Judaism, Christianity, and Islam do not believe in many gods. Instead, all of these religions believe in just one God. (When you refer to just one God, you spell the name with a capital "G," because that's how you begin a name, right?—with a capital letter.) Thousands of years ago, this belief in just one God was a new idea. And this new idea came first from the religion called Judaism.

宗教
——さまざまな信仰

　何千年もの間、人生の大きな疑問への答えを探してきた世界各地の人々のよりどころとなったのは、さまざまな宗教でした。こうした疑問をいだいたのは、はるか昔の古代の人間だけではなく、いまなお人々は同じ問いを抱えています。たとえばこんな問いを——世界はどのようにして始まったのだろうか？　人間や動物はどこから来たのだろうか？　なぜ世界はこのようなあり方をしているのだろうか？　ひとはどのように行動すべきなのだろうか？

　こんにち、世界には数多くの宗教があります。何千年ものあいだ多くの人々の心をとらえてきた3つの宗教について、もっと調べてみましょう。3つの宗教とは、ユダヤ教、キリスト教、イスラム教のことです。現在、これらの宗教には数多くの信者がいます。しかし、何千年かさかのぼれば、そのどれもまだ宗教として始まったばかりだったのです。このはるか昔の時代へともどってみて、ユダヤ教、キリスト教、イスラム教がどのように誕生したのかを見てみましょう。

　しかし、その前に1つ問題があります。古代メソポタミア、古代エジプトの人々は「多くの」神々を信じていたという話を覚えていますか。彼らは、太陽の神、大地の神といった自然の神々を信じていたのです。そのほかにも、死者の神、町の守護神など、多くの神々がいました。これからみなさんが学ぶ宗教とはずいぶん違いますね。ユダヤ教、キリスト教、イスラム教では、複数の神々を信じることはありません。そうではなく、これらの宗教では、「唯一の」神を信じるのです（唯一の神Godを書き表すときは、はじめの"G"を大文字で綴ります。名前を書くときとおなじですね——大文字で始めるでしょう？）。何千年もの昔には、唯一の神というのは新しい発想でした。この新しい発想はそもそもユダヤ教という宗教から生まれました。

NOTE

ユダヤ教、キリスト教、イスラム教は西洋の3大宗教である。ユダヤ教徒、キリスト教徒、イスラム教徒には共通するところが多い。神をなんと呼ぶかは異なるが、これらの宗教の信徒はみなおなじ神を信仰している。

　この3宗教の聖典にはいくつかおなじ物語が出てくる。コーランにはトーラや聖書に出てくる物語が数多くあり、たとえばノアと洪水、モーゼの物語などがそうだ。

WORLD CIVILIZATION • 世界史

Judaism

The followers of Judaism today are called Jews. The Jewish people believe in one God. To worship God, they go to a place called a synagogue. The holy book of the Jewish people is called the Bible, or sometimes the Hebrew Bible. It was written in Hebrew, a language that is still spoken by many Jews today. The first part of the Hebrew Bible is called the Torah: it tells the history of the Jewish people and their God. Many Jewish people believe that the Torah was written by a man named Moses.

The Story of Moses

Moses was a great leader of the Jewish people. Way back in the time of Moses, the Jewish people were known by another name: they were called Hebrews. Sometimes the Bible also calls them Israelites or the Children of Israel. Here is some of the story of Moses, as told in the Hebrew Bible.

The story of Moses begins in Egypt more than three thousand years ago. It was an awful time for the Hebrews because they were forced by the Egyptians to work as slaves. The Hebrews had to work long and hard in the hot sun, carrying the heavy rocks used to build the big monuments.

Now, the Pharaoh of Egypt noticed something that bothered him. He saw that among the Hebrews more and more children were being born every day. He began to worry that one day there might be so many Hebrews that they would rise up and fight against their Egyptian masters. And so Pharaoh gave a cruel command.

ユダヤ教

こんにちではユダヤ教を信仰する人々はユダヤ人と呼ばれています。ユダヤ民族は唯一の神を信じています。礼拝のときに、彼らはシナゴーグ（会堂）というところへ行きます。ユダヤ民族の聖典は、聖書、あるいはヘブライ聖書と呼ばれています。この聖書はヘブライ語で書かれましたが、それはいまなお多くのユダヤ人が話している言葉です。ヘブライ聖書の第1部は律法（トーラ）といって、ユダヤ民族と彼らの神の歴史が記されています。ユダヤ人の多くは、モーゼという人物が律法を書いたと考えています。

モーゼの物語

モーゼはユダヤ民族の偉大な指導者でした。はるか昔のモーゼの時代には、ユダヤ民族には別の名前がありました。彼らはヘブライ人と呼ばれていたのです。また、聖書では、イスラエル人、あるいはイスラエルの子供たち、と呼ぶこともあります。ヘブライ聖書から、モーゼの物語を少し紹介しましょう。

モーゼの物語は、3000年以上も昔のエジプトで始まります。ヘブライ人にとってはひどく苦しい時代で、彼らはエジプト人の奴隷として働かされていたのです。ヘブライ人は太陽の照りつけるなか長く厳しい労働を強いられ、巨大な建造物を造るために重い岩を運びました。

そのエジプトの王ファラオには、1つ気がかりなことがありました。生まれてくるヘブライ人の子供たちの数が、日増しに増えていったのです。ファラオが心配し始めたのは、ヘブライ人の数が増えれば、いずれ戦いのために蜂起してエジプト人の主人を倒そうとするかもしれないということでした。そこでファラオは残忍な命令を下しました。ヘブライ人に生まれた男の赤ん坊はみなナイル河で溺死させよ、と命じたのです。

ちょうどそのころ、あるヘブライ人の女性に男の赤ん坊が生まれました。彼女はファラオの恐ろしい命令を聞き知っていました。彼

ダビデの星。ユダヤ教のシンボルでイスラエルの国旗にも使われている。

NOTE

律法
ヘブライ聖書で律法と呼ばれるのは、「創世記」「出エジプト記」「レビ記」「民数記」「申命記」の5書で、これらはまた「モーゼ5書」ともいい、ユダヤ教の最初の経典となった。キリスト教徒の聖典である旧約聖書の最初の5書も内容は同じである。

NOTE

モーゼ
モーゼは紀元前13世紀の人。聖書によれば120歳まで生きた。キリスト教でイエスは新しいモーゼであり、イスラム教でもモーゼは最高の預言者とされる。シナイ山でモーゼが神から「十戒」を授かり、神と契約を結んだことによってヘブライ人は神の民となった。十戒には、唯一神信仰、姦淫・偶像崇拝の禁止などがある。

He ordered that all boy children born to the Hebrew people should be drowned in the Nile River!

Just at this time a Hebrew woman gave birth to baby boy. She knew of Pharaoh's awful command. She decided she must do something to save her boy, but what? What could she do?

For a few months she did her best to hide him, but she could not keep him hidden forever. And so this is what she did. She wove a basket out of a long grass called bulrushes. She put tar on the bottom of the basket so that it would float. Then she carried her baby down to the Nile River and put him in the basket. She left the basket, with the baby in it, floating among the long grass by the riverbank. Hidden in the distance, the baby's older sister, named Miriam, watched the basket and waited to see what would happen.

Soon a group of women came walking along the riverbank. It was Pharaoh's daughter, along with the maidens who served her, coming to bathe in the river. Pharaoh's daughter saw the basket in the bulrushes, and she sent a maid to fetch it. When she looked inside, she saw a crying baby boy! "He must be one of the Hebrew children," she said. She felt sorry for the little child, all alone. She named him Moses, which, it is said, means "drawn out of the water."

Just then the baby's older sister, Miriam, came out of her hiding place. She approached Pharaoh's daughter and asked, "Shall I go and find a Hebrew woman to help you take care of the child?"

"Yes, do," said Pharaoh's daughter. Now, who do you think Miriam went to get? Moses's own mother! So, with two mothers to take care of him, Moses was raised as a prince in the palace of his people's enemies!

When Moses grew up, he saw something that upset him. He saw an Egyptian beating a Hebrew slave. Moses fought the Egyptian, and he killed him. And now Moses was in very big trouble. He had to leave Pharaoh's palace. He left behind his comfortable life and went far away and began to live as a shepherd.

The Hebrew Bible tells us that one day, as Moses was keeping watch over the sheep, he saw an amazing sight: it was a bush covered with flames, yet the bush itself was not burned by the flames. Then a voice spoke from the burning bush and said to Moses, "I am the God of your fathers. I have seen the suffering of my people who are in Egypt. I will

女はなんとかして赤ん坊を救おうと決心しました。でもどうやって？　自分に何ができるというのか？
　数ヵ月のあいだ母親は赤ん坊を必死に隠しましたが、ずっと隠し通せるはずもありません。そこで彼女はこうしたのです。まずパピルスという細長い草でかごを編み、水に浮かぶようにかごの底にタールを塗りました。それから赤ん坊をナイル河に連れて行き、かごの中に寝かせました。そして赤ん坊を乗せたかごを、高い草の生い茂る河岸に浮かべたのです。赤ん坊の姉のミリアムが、遠くからこっそりかごの行方を目で追い、成り行きをじっと見守っていました。
　まもなく数人の女性たちが河岸を歩いてやってきました。それはファラオの娘とその侍女たちで、水浴をするために河にきたのです。パピルスの茂みにかごを見つけたファラオの娘は、すぐに侍女に取りに行かせました。中をのぞいてみると、男の赤ん坊が泣いているではありませんか。「きっとヘブライ人の子供だわ」と彼女は言いました。彼女はひとりぼっちの小さな子供をかわいそうに思いました。その子を彼女はモーゼと名づけましたが、「水から引き上げられた者」という意味だといわれています。
　ちょうどそのとき、赤ん坊の姉ミリアムが隠れていたところから出てきました。彼女はファラオの娘のそばへ寄って、「赤ん坊の世話をするヘブライ人の女を探してまいりましょうか？」と申し出ました。
　「よろしい、まかせましょう」とファラオの娘は言いました。さて、ミリアムは誰を探しに行ったと思いますか？　そう、モーゼの実の母親です。なんとモーゼは、2人の母親に養われて、自分の民族の敵の王宮で王子として育てられることになったのです。
　成長したモーゼは、ある出来事を目撃して、気が動転してしまいます。エジプト人がヘブライ人の奴隷を鞭打っていたのです。争ううちにモーゼはそのエジプト人を殺してしまい、大変な窮地におちいります。もはや王の宮殿にとどまるわけにはいきません。彼はそれまでの何不自由ない暮らしを後にし、王宮から遠く離れたところで、羊飼いに身をやつして暮らすことにしました。
　ヘブライ聖書によれば、ある日モーゼは羊の番をしていて、驚くべき光景を目にしました。木の繁みが炎に包まれているのですが、それでいて繁みそのものは燃えていないのです。そのとき、炎の立つ繁みからモーゼに呼びかける声が聞こえました。「わたしはおまえの先祖たちの神である。わたしはわが民がエジプトで苦しんでい

send you to Pharaoh that you may bring forth my people out of Egypt to a good and broad land, a land flowing with milk and honey."

Moses was afraid. He said, "O Lord, who am I to do this? Pharaoh will not listen to me. I am not a man of words. I do not speak well." Then God became angry and asked Moses who had given him the power to speak in the first place; and God told Moses, "I will teach you what to say."

So Moses, together with his brother, named Aaron, went to Pharaoh and said, "God has commanded you: 'Let my people go.'" But Pharaoh said, "I do not know your God, and I will not let your people go." And Pharaoh made the Hebrews work even harder.

Then, says the Hebrew Bible, God punished the Egyptians. He sent a plague of frogs: the Nile River was filled with frogs, and the people found frogs in their beds and in their food bowls. Still, Pharaoh refused to let the Hebrews go. So God sent more punishments. The land was covered with gnats, and flies, and locusts. The crops died, and the cattle died. The people of Egypt found their skin covered with terrible sores. Thunder crashed in the sky as a terrible hail battered the earth.

Finally, Pharaoh had had enough. He let the Hebrews leave Egypt. They gathered their few belongings and set off to the land that God had promised to Moses and his people, the promised land "flowing with milk and honey."

神から、エジプトに行きヘブライ人を救い出すように命じられるモーゼ。

るのを見た。おまえはファラオのもとへ行き、わが民をエジプトから脱出させ、広く豊かな大地、乳と蜜の流れる楽園へと導くのだ」

　モーゼはおそれを覚えつつ、こう言いました。「神よ、なぜこのわたしがそんな大それたことを。ファラオがわたしの言葉に耳をかすはずもありません。わたしは言葉巧みな人間ではありません。話には自信がないのです」。すると神は怒って、そもそもおまえに言葉を話す力を与えたのは誰か、と言いました。そして、モーゼに向かって、「言うべき言葉は、わたしが授けよう」と告げたのです。

　モーゼはアーロンという名の兄とともにファラオに謁見し、「神が『わたしの民を解放せよ』と命じたのです」と言いました。ところがファラオは「わたしはおまえの神など知らぬし、おまえの民は解放しない」とはねつけました。それから、ファラオはヘブライ人たちをいっそう厳しく働かせました。

　それで神はエジプト人を罰したのだ、とヘブライ聖書には書かれています。神は蛙の災いをもってエジプトに報いました。ナイル河には蛙があふれ、エジプト人のベッドや食器の中にも蛙が入りこみました。それでもファラオはヘブライ人を解放しようとしません。そこで神はさらに罰を加えたのです。ぶよ、はえ、いなごが大地を覆いました。作物は枯れ、家畜は死に、エジプト人の肌にはひどい腫れ物ができました。空には雷鳴がとどろき、雹が激しくエジプトの大地をたたきました。

　ついにファラオも耐えられなくなりました。ファラオはヘブライ人をエジプトから解放したのです。彼らは荷物をまとめると、神がモーゼとその民に約束した土地、「乳と蜜の流れる」約束の地へと出発しました。

　エジプトを逃れるヘブライ人の旅は、「出エジプト」と呼ばれています。それは長くつらい旅でした。出発してまもなく、ヘブライ人たちは海岸に着き、そこで休むことにしました。ところが、彼らの知らないうちに、ファラオはヘブライ人を解放するという考えを翻していました。ファラオは彼らを奴隷として働かせるために取り戻そうと思い兵に後を追わせました。

　ファラオの大軍が迫ってくるのを見て、ヘブライ人たちは恐怖におののきました。背後からは兵士が軍馬に引かせた戦車を駆って、ぐんぐんやってきます。目の前は海です。どうすればいいのだろう？　彼らは大声でモーゼに救いを求めました。「われわれをエジプトから連れ出しておいて、こんな砂漠で死ねというのですか？」

NOTE

エジプト脱出

モーゼがヘブライ人を率いてエジプトから脱出したのは紀元前1280年頃とされるが、聖書の記述は多くの伝説を含むと考えられている。モーゼらのエジプト脱出については、旧約聖書の第2巻「出エジプト記」に詳しい。

The journey of the Hebrews out of Egypt is called the Exodus. It was a long, hard journey. Soon after they started, the Hebrews came to the shore of a sea, where they stopped to rest. They didn't know, however, that Pharaoh had changed his mind about letting the Hebrews leave. He wanted them back to work as slaves. So he sent his soldiers after them.

When the Hebrews saw Pharaoh's mighty troops approaching, they were terrified. The soldiers, riding fast in their horse-drawn chariots, were coming at them from one side. On the other side was the sea. What could they do? They turned to Moses and cried out, "Have you brought us out of Egypt only to die here in the desert?"

But Moses raised his staff and a great wind began to blow. It blew so hard and so strong that the waters of the sea parted in two. The Hebrews were amazed to see a dry path between two walls of water! Moses led his people across this path through the sea. Not far behind came the soldiers of Pharaoh. But as they came across, the walls of water came crashing down, and all of Pharaoh's men were drowned.

The Hebrews were safe. Moses led them to their promised homeland, which is now called Israel. The escape of the Hebrews from Egypt is still celebrated by Jewish people today as an important holiday in the Jewish religion. It is called Passover.

エルサレムにある嘆きの壁。古代イスラエルの神殿の遺構とされ、ユダヤ教徒の聖地になっている。またイスラム教徒も、この壁を聖地とみなしている。

ヘブライ人が海を渡り終ったとき、水の壁は崩れ、ファラオの軍勢を飲み込んだ。

　ところが、モーゼが杖を掲げると、強風が巻き起こったのです。そして、強く激しく吹く風の力で、海の水が2つに分かれました。水の壁のあいだの乾いた道を見て、ヘブライ人たちは驚嘆しました。モーゼはこの道を通って、海の向こう側へと彼の民を導きました。すぐ後ろにはファラオの軍勢が迫っていましたが、彼らが渡ろうとすると水の壁は崩れ落ち、兵隊たちはみな溺れてしまいました。

　ヘブライ人たちは助かりました。モーゼは彼らを現在イスラエルと呼ばれる約束の祖国へと導きました。ヘブライ人たちのエジプト脱出は、いまなおユダヤ教の重要な祭日として祝われています。その祭日は「過ぎ越しの祭」といいます。

(NOTE)
宮清めの祭
もう1つ、ユダヤ教には宮清めの祭(ハヌカー)という祭日がある。通常は12月に祝われ、「光の祭」と呼ばれることもある。8日間にわたって、毎晩、メノーラという特別な燭台に蝋燭が灯される。

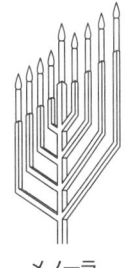

メノーラ

1st GRADE

WORLD CIVILIZATION • 世界史

Christianity

The religion called Christianity began about two thousand years ago. It grew out of the religion you've just learned about, Judaism. It happened like this.

As you know, Moses led the Hebrews to their promised homeland, called Israel. But there were still many hard times ahead. More than once, the Jewish people were conquered and ruled over, as they had been by the Egyptians.

The Jewish people, as well as many other people, were conquered by the powerful Romans. The Romans had strong armies with thousands and thousands of soldiers. It was hard for the Jewish people to be ruled by the Romans. Many people in Israel hoped for a savior—a person who would come and save them. The Jewish people called this savior they hoped for the Messiah. Many Jewish people thought that when the Messiah came, he would lead the Jews against their Roman conquerors and make them free.

Into this world was born Jesus of Nazareth. Many people believe that Jesus was the Messiah the Jewish people were waiting for. These people are called Christians because Jesus was also called the Christ (which means something like "the chosen one").

Jesus was not the son of a king or a powerful warrior. His parents, named Mary and Joseph, were humble people. The story of Mary, Joseph, and the birth of Jesus is told in the holy book of Christians, called the Bible.

1st GRADE

キリスト教

　キリスト教はおよそ2000年ほど前に誕生しました。キリスト教は、いまみなさんが学んだユダヤ教から派生した宗教で、こんなふうに始まりました。

　ヘブライ人たちを約束の祖国イスラエルへと導いたのはモーゼでした。しかし、彼らにはなお困難な時代が待ちかまえていました。エジプト人にされたような侵略・征服をユダヤ民族が受けたのは、1度にとどまりませんでした。

　ほかの多くの民族と同様、ユダヤ民族も強力なローマ軍に征服されました。ローマ人は無数の兵隊からなる強大な軍隊を持っていました。ローマ人の支配はユダヤ人にとって苦しい時代で、イスラエルの人々は救世主——彼らを救いに来る人——を待ち望みました。ユダヤ人は自分たちの待ち望むこの救世主をメシアと呼びました。メシアが来れば、ユダヤ人を率いて征服者ローマ人に立ち向かわせ、自由をもたらしてくれると信じたのです。

　こういう状況の中で、ナザレの地にイエスが生まれました。多くの人々はイエスがユダヤ民族の待ち続けていたメシアであると信じました。このような人々をキリスト教徒といいますが、それはイエスがキリスト（「神に選ばれた者」というような意味）とも呼ばれたからです。

　イエスは、王の息子でも権力を持つ戦士の息子でもありません。父ヨゼフ、母マリアは、身分の低い人たちでした。マリアとヨゼフの話、そしてイエス誕生の物語は、『聖書』と呼ばれるキリスト教の聖典に記されています。

NOTE
イエス・キリスト
イエス・キリストは紀元前7年頃に生まれ、紀元後30年頃（ともに推定）に十字架上で処刑された。イエスはユダヤ人が待望していた神の国の到来を告げ知らせた。その意味ではユダヤ教の延長上にある預言者だが、ユダヤ教の律法にそむくような教えを説いたのでユダヤ人に憎まれ、社会秩序を乱すものとしてローマ軍によって殺された。

キリスト教のシンボル、十字架。ただし十字架はキリスト教以前にもあって、古代エジプトやケルト文化などでは十字形のシンボルが使われていた。

NOTE
旧約・新約聖書
聖書には旧約と新約があるが、キリスト教徒にとっては両方が聖典である。（聖書の旧約と新約とは、キリスト教徒が唯一神ヤハウェと結んだ契約の新旧のこと）ユダヤ教にとっても旧約聖書の39書が聖典であるが、彼らは旧約聖書とは言わずにタナッハと呼ぶ。新約聖書はユダヤ教では聖典ではない。

　イスラム教は、ユダヤ教とキリスト教とをイスラム教が出現するまでの準備とみなす。

The First Christmas

Christians celebrate the birthday of Jesus on the day called Christmas. Here, from the Bible, is the story of the first Christmas.

In the city of Nazareth, there lived a young woman named Mary. She did not know that something amazing was going to happen to her.

The Bible tells us that one day Mary was visited by an angel sent by God, an angel named Gabriel. "Hail, O favored one!" Gabriel said to Mary ("Hail" means "Hello"). Mary was amazed and scared. "Do not be afraid," said the angel. But what Gabriel told her made her more afraid and very excited. The angel said that Mary would have a son, and that this son would be the Messiah, the promised one, the savior of Israel.

Then Mary asked the angel, "How can I have a son? I do not even have a husband." The angel told her that the baby would be sent from God, and that her child would be called the Son of God.

Months later, Mary prepared to go on a trip with her new husband, Joseph. It was a hard time to travel, for indeed, Mary was now expecting a child. But they had to make the trip. The ruler of the Romans, called the emperor, had sent out an order. The Roman emperor wanted to tax all the people he ruled (that means he wanted to get money from them). He ordered them to return to the town of their ancestors to pay their taxes.

So Mary and Joseph went to the town of Joseph's ancestors, the little town of Bethlehem. It was a hard journey. When they arrived, Mary could feel that it was time for her baby to be born, that very night.

But they could find nowhere to stay: there was no room at the inn. The innkeeper told them they could stay in the stable where the animals were kept. In there they would at least find some straw to rest on.

And there in the stable, with the cattle and other animals moving softly about, Mary gave birth to her baby son. And since there was no crib or bed, she placed him in a manger, which held the feed for the animals to eat.

Nearby there were shepherds in the field, keeping watch over their flock by night. An angel appeared to them and said, "Fear not: for, behold, I bring you good tidings of great joy. For unto you is born this day a Savior, which is Christ the Lord."

最初のクリスマス

　キリスト教徒はクリスマスの日に、イエスの誕生を祝います。聖書に書いてある最初のクリスマスの物語を紹介しましょう。
　ナザレの町にマリアという娘が暮らしていました。やがてわが身に驚くべきことが起こることなど、彼女には知るよしもありません。
　聖書には、ある日マリアのもとに神からガブリエルという天使が遣(つか)わされたと書かれています。「ヘイル、神様のお気に入り！」とガブリエルはマリアに言いました(「ヘイル」は「やあ」という意味です)。マリアは驚き、おびえました。「おそれることはない」と天使は言いました。しかし続けてガブリエルの告げる言葉を聞くと、彼女の不安と興奮はさらに高まりました。マリアには息子が生まれ、その息子はイスラエルの救世主、メシアになるだろうとガブリエルは言うのです。
　マリアは天使に尋ねました。「どうしてわたしに息子が生まれるのでしょう？　わたしには夫さえおりません」。天使は、その赤ん坊は神から遣わされた者で、「神の子」と呼ばれることになるだろうと答えました。
　数ヵ月が過ぎ、マリアは結婚した夫ヨゼフと旅に出る準備をしていました。マリアにとっては、旅をするのはつらい時期になっていました。もうすぐ子供が生まれようとしていたのです。しかし彼らは旅に出なくてはなりませんでした。ローマ人を支配する皇帝が、ある命令を下していたのです。ローマ皇帝は彼の支配するすべての人民に税金を課したいと考えていました(つまりお金を徴収したかったのです)。皇帝は人民に、祖先の暮らしていた町に戻って税金を収めるよう命じたのです。
　そこでマリアとヨゼフは、ヨゼフの父祖の地であるベツレヘムという小さな町に向かいました。旅は苦しいものでした。到着すると、マリアには今夜にも子供が生まれるということが分かりました。
　しかし彼らは泊まるところを見つけることができませんでした。宿には空き部屋がなかったのです。宿の主人は、家畜のいる畜舎でよければ泊まれます、と言いました。そこならば、少なくとも藁を敷いて休むことができるというのです。
　牛やいろんな動物たちがのそのそ動きまわる畜舎で、マリアは男の子を産みました。赤ん坊用の寝台も、ふつうのベッドもなかったので、マリアは家畜のえさを入れる飼葉桶(かいばおけ)に赤ん坊を寝かせました。

キリストの誕生。西暦ではこの年にBC (Before Christ)からAD(Anno Domini =in the year of Our Lord) 1年になったはずだが、後世の暦学者の誤りにより、誕生はBC (紀元前) のことになってしまった。

The shepherds were amazed. For so many years their people had waited for a savior, a mighty leader. Could it be that their savior was born here, among such plain and humble people?

The shepherds hurried to Bethlehem to see the child. They found Mary, and Joseph, and the babe, who was lying in a manger. The shepherds told Mary what the angel had said. Then they went to tell everyone the good news. But Mary remained quiet and thought deeply about all that had happened.

And that is what the Bible tells us of the first Christmas. Christians today remember and celebrate the first Christmas each year on the twenty-fifth of December by putting on special plays, by giving gifts, and by singing songs about Bethlehem, the angels, the shepherds, and the baby Jesus.

Jesus the Teacher: The Parable of the Good Samaritan

When Jesus grew to be a man, he started teaching. People flocked to listen and Jesus soon had many followers. When Jesus taught people, he often told parables. A parable is a story that teaches a lesson.

Jesus taught that you should love your neighbor as you love yourself. Once a lawyer asked Jesus, "Just exactly who is my neighbor?" To answer this question, Jesus told the parable of the Good Samaritan. (A Samaritan is a person from the region called Samaria.)

近くの草原では、羊飼いたちが羊の群れの夜番をしていました。そこに天使がやってきて、こう言いました。「おそれることはない。よいか、わたしは大いなる喜びを知らせにやって来たのだ。今日、おまえたちに救世主、主キリストが生まれたのだ」

羊飼いたちは驚きました。彼らの民族は、ほんとうに長いあいだ、救世主となる強力な指導者を待ちわびていたのですから。自分たちの救世主が、こんなところに、質素で身分の低い者のいるところに生まれるなどということがありうるのだろうか？

羊飼いたちは子供を見ようとベツレヘムへ急ぎました。彼らはマリア、ヨゼフ、そして飼葉桶に寝かされた赤ん坊を見つけました。羊飼いたちは天使から聞いたことをマリアに告げると、このよい知らせをすべての人々に広めました。しかし、マリアはじっと静かに、いっさいの出来事について深く思いをめぐらしていました。

これが聖書に出てくる最初のクリスマスです。こんにちキリスト教徒は、毎年12月25日になると、キリスト生誕の劇を演じ、プレゼントを贈り、ベツレヘム、天使たち、羊飼いたち、そして幼な子イエスにまつわる歌を歌って、最初のクリスマスを受け継ぎ、祝福するのです。

よきサマリア人について

成人したイエスは教えを広め始めました。話を聴こうとする人々が群れをなし、たちまちイエスには多くの信徒ができました。イエスは教えるときによく寓話を使いました。寓話とは教えを含む物語です。

イエスは、自分を愛するように隣人も愛さなければならないと教えました。あるとき律法学者がイエスに尋ねました。「私の隣人とは誰のことなのでしょう？」イエスはよきサマリア人の寓話を話してこの問いに答えました。（サマリア地方出身の人をサマリア人といいます）

あるとき、とイエスは言いました。1人の旅人が道を歩いていると、とつぜん盗賊が襲いかかってきました。盗賊は彼の持ち物を奪い、彼をひどく殴りつけたのです。旅人は虫の息で道のわきに倒れていました。まもなく聖職者がやって来て、男が倒れて苦しんでいるのを見ましたが、助けようとはしませんでした。さらにもう1人道を通りかかりましたが、彼も助けようとはせず、そのまま歩いて

Once, said Jesus, a man was traveling along a road. Suddenly he was attacked by thieves. They robbed the man and beat him. He lay half-dead by the side of the road. Soon a priest came along. He saw the man lying in pain, but did not stop to help him. Then another man came down the road; he, too, walked right on by without helping. Then along came a Samaritan. When the Samaritan saw the half-dead man, he went to him and took care of his wounds. He took the man to a nearby inn. He told the innkeeper that he would pay whatever it cost to take care of the man.

When Jesus had told this story, he turned and asked the lawyer, "Which now of these three was neighbor unto him that fell among the thieves?"

And that, from the Bible, is the story of the Good Samaritan. What do you think? Who was most like a neighbor to the man who was robbed and beaten? Why?

Today, people sometimes call anyone who goes out of his or her way to help someone in need a "good Samaritan."

Easter

Many people listened to Jesus and believed him. But many others got angry with Jesus. They expected a savior who would lead them in a great fight against the Romans. Instead, Jesus said that people should forgive their enemies.

Although many people began to follow Jesus, other people became his enemies. His words made them angry and scared. And so they hurt Jesus, and eventually they killed him. He was put to death on a cross, so the cross has become the main symbol of Christianity. Christians believe that on the third day after Jesus died, he rose from the dead; Christians celebrate his rising from the dead at Easter. Easter and Christmas are the two most important holidays and celebrations for Christians.

いってしまいました。それからサマリア人がやって来ました。瀕死の旅人を見つけたサマリア人は、近づいて傷の手当てをすると近くの宿まで運んでやり、治療にかかる費用はいくらでも負担しようと主人に申し出ました。

この話をすると、イエスは律法学者に向かって尋ねました。「この3人のうち、誰を盗賊に襲われた者の隣人と呼ぶべきでしょうか？」

これが聖書に書かれた「よきサマリア人」の物語です。みなさんはどう思いますか？　ひどく殴られたうえに持ち物を奪われた旅人の隣人といえるのは、どの人でしょうか？　そしてなぜ？

こんにちでも、困っている人を助けようとして力をつくす人を「よきサマリア人」と呼ぶことがあります。

イースター

多くの人々がイエスに耳を傾け、彼の言葉を信じました。しかしイエスに反発する者も少なくはありませんでした。彼らはローマ軍との大きな戦いを勝利に導いてくれる救世主を求めていました。しかしイエスは、敵を許しなさいと説いたのです。

多くの人々がイエスに従いましたが、従わない者はイエスの敵になりました。イエスの言葉は彼らに怒りと恐怖とをあたえました。だから、彼らはイエスを傷つけ、ついには殺してしまったのです。イエスが十字架に磔になって殺されたために、十字架はキリスト教の重要なシンボルになりました。死から3日後、イエスは死者たちの間からよみがえったとキリスト教徒たちは信じています。キリスト教徒はイースターにイエスの死からの復活を祝います。イースターとクリスマスという2つの行事は、キリスト教徒にとって何より大切な祭日であり、祝典なのです。

> **NOTE**
> **イースター**
> イースターという名称（日本語では復活祭）は古代ゲルマン民族の光りと春の女神、エオスターに由来。毎年、春分後の満月の後にくる日曜日にイースターを祝う。
>
> ユダヤ教徒はほぼ同じ時期に、ヘブライ人のエジプト脱出を記念して Passover（過越しの祭）を祝う。
>
> イースターや謝肉祭など、その年によって日にちが変わる祭日を a movable feast（移動祝祭日）という。

WORLD CIVILIZATION • 世界史

Islam

A long time after Jesus lived—in fact, more than five hundred years later—a man named Muhammad was born in the land then called Arabia.

The religion of Islam began in the time of Muhammad. Followers of Islam are called Muslims (sometimes spelled Moslems).

Muhammad was a merchant, a person who buys and sells things for a living. He was a respected man in his hometown of Mecca (sometimes spelled Makkah). Many people called him al-Amin, which means "the Trustworthy."

Because he was a merchant, Muhammad traveled a lot to buy and sell his goods. In his travels he met many different people. Some of them were followers of the two religions you've already learned about: Judaism and Christianity. From these Jews and Christians, Muhammad learned about the idea of one God. And from the Christians he learned about the teachings of Jesus.

Muhammad thought about what he learned during his life and travels. When he returned home, he looked around at what he saw in his own land and he became troubled. He saw that many of the people still worshiped many gods. He felt that too many people in the city of Mecca had become proud and greedy. He did not like the rich rulers of the city. He believed they fought too much and were too concerned with money.

Here is the story that Muslims tell about how their religion began. Muhammad liked to go off to sit alone in a quiet cave, where he could think about things that were worrying him. One day, when he was forty years old, he went to the cave and there he had a vision (a vision is like a dream, except you're awake). Muhammad saw an angel, the angel Gabriel. Is that name familiar to you? Gabriel is the same angel that, the Bible says, came to Mary to tell her that she would give birth to the baby Jesus.

イスラム教

　イエスの生きていた時代から長い時が流れて——500年以上も後のことです——ムハンマドという男が、当時アラビアと呼ばれていた地に生まれました。

　イスラム教はムハンマドの時代に始まりました。イスラム教の信徒はムスリム(モスレムとも綴る)と呼ばれます。

　ムハンマドは商人で、物を売買して生計を立てていました。彼は故郷のメッカ(マッカと綴ることもある)では人望の厚い人でした。多くの人々が彼のことを「信頼の置ける人物」という意味の「アミーン」の名で呼びました。

　ムハンマドは商人だったので、品物を売り買いするために頻繁に旅をしました。旅の途中で彼はさまざまな人々に出会いました。その中にはみなさんが学んだ2つの宗教、ユダヤ教とキリスト教の信徒もいました。ユダヤ教徒とキリスト教徒から、ムハンマドは唯一の神という概念を学びました。そしてキリスト教徒からはイエスの教えを学びました。

　ムハンマドは人生と旅の中で学んだことについて考えるようになりました。故郷に戻ったムハンマドは、みずからの土地のありさまを見て思い悩み、苦しむようになりました。大部分の人々はまだたくさんの神々を崇拝していました。メッカではどこにいっても傲慢で貪欲な人々ばかりが目につき、町を支配している裕福な人々を不快に思いました。彼らは争いごとと金銭の問題以外に関心がないようにムハンマドには見えました。

　イスラム教徒が、彼らの宗教の始まりとして語るのは次の話です。ムハンマドは好んで静かな洞窟に行き、1人で座っていました。そこに行けば自分が思い悩むことがらについて考えることができたのです。40歳になっていたムハンマドは、ある日、洞窟で幻夢を見ました。(幻夢というのは夢に似ていますが、目覚めて見る夢です) ムハンマドは天使のガブリエルを見たのです。どこかで聞いた名前ですね。マリアのもとにやって来て、あなたはイエスの母親となるのですと告げたと聖書に書かれている、あのガブリエルと同じ天使です。

この三日月と星のマークはイスラム教のシンボルでトルコ、アルジェリアなどの国旗に使われている。

NOTE
ムハンマド
ムハンマド(570頃–632)をマホメットMahometというのは訛り。イスラムとは「神に服従する者」の意味で、聖典コーランへの絶対服従が求められる。コーランには信仰、倫理、法的規範などが記されている。

　イスラム教では礼拝での音楽が禁じられているので、コーランの朗誦が芸術として発達した。

Muslims believe that God spoke to Muhammad through the angel Gabriel. The angel told Muhammad to tell everyone in Arabia that there was only one God, whose name is Allah. "Allah" is the Arabic word for the English word "God." So, you see, Muslims worship the same God that Jewish people and Christians worship.

Muhammad set out to tell people that they should worship only the one God, Allah. Some people listened to Muhammad's teachings and believed him. But most people were not very happy to hear what he said. He told them that their ideas about religion were wrong and that they should change what they believed and how they behaved. Some people got so mad at Muhammad that they even killed some of his followers and forced him to leave Mecca, the city that was his home.

But Muhammad was determined to spread his message. He continued to teach about Allah, and more people began to follow him. The people liked Muhammad's lessons about being kind to each other and about helping the poor. They prayed many times every day. They tried hard to live better lives.

The rulers of Mecca were still angry at Muhammad, and they were worried as more people began to follow him. More than once the rulers of Mecca sent soldiers to attack the Muslims. But the Muslims fought back, and in the end they beat the soldiers of Mecca. Muhammad returned to his home city, and his many followers came with him.

Soon all of Arabia accepted Muhammad as the messenger of God. Since the time of Muhammad, the religion of Islam has spread from Arabia to many parts of the world. Muslims everywhere study the Qur'an (sometimes spelled Koran), which is the holy book of Islam. They worship Allah in buildings called mosques.

The Five Pillars of Islam

Devoted Muslims compare their religion to a building that is supported by five pillars. The Five Pillars of Islam are five rules that form the central philosophy of the Islamic faith.

The First Pillar: Shahada in Arabic

As a statement of their faith, Muslims say, "There is no God but Allah and Muhammad is his prophet." This simple statement is the basis of all Muslim belief. It is the first thing whispered into a child's ear when

イスラム教徒は、神が天使ガブリエルを通してムハンマドに語りかけたと信じています。天使はガブリエルに、神はただ1人しか存在しないこと、その名はアラーであることをアラビアのすべての人々に知らせるようにと命じました。「アラー」は、英語の「ゴッド」に相当するアラビア語です。したがって、イスラム教徒は、ユダヤ教徒やキリスト教徒とおなじ神を信仰しているわけです。

ムハンマドは、唯一の神、アラーのみを崇拝するよう人々に説いて回りました。ムハンマドの教えに耳を傾け、彼の言うことを信じる者もいました。しかし、ほとんどの人はムハンマドの言うことを快く思いませんでした。ムハンマドが、彼らの宗教に対する考え方は間違っていて、信仰も行いも改めるべきだと説いたからです。ついにムハンマドに腹を立てるあまり、彼に従う者を殺し、彼を故郷のメッカから追放してしまいました。

しかし、神からのお告げを広めようとするムハンマドの信念は揺るぎませんでした。彼はアラーの教えを説きつづけ、彼に従うものたちは増えていきました。互いに親切であれ、貧しい者を助けよというムハンマドの教えを人々は受け入れたのです。彼らは1日に何度も祈りを捧げ、よりよい生き方をしようと懸命に努力しました。

メッカの支配者たちはなおムハンマドを敵視しており、彼に従う者が増え続けるのを憂慮していました。1度ならず彼らは兵士を送ってイスラム教徒を攻撃しました。しかしイスラム教徒は反撃し、けっきょくメッカの兵士を打ち負かしてしまいました。ムハンマドは故郷の町に戻り、大勢の信徒たちも彼とともにやって来ました。

まもなくアラビア全土がムハンマドを神の預言者として認めるようになりました。ムハンマドの時代以降、イスラム教はアラビアから世界各地へと広まりました。世界のイスラム教徒たちはクルアーン（コーランとも綴る）というイスラム教の聖典を学んでいます。彼らはモスクという建物でアラーに祈りを捧げます。

イスラムの5柱

イスラム教の熱心な信者は、イスラム教を5つの柱に支えられた建物にたとえます。「イスラムの5柱」とは、イスラム信仰の根本哲学にかかわる5つの決まりごとです。

第1の柱はアラビア語でシャハーダといいます。

信仰の告白として、イスラム教徒は「アラーのほかに神はなく、

he is born and the last thing a Muslim hopes to utter at the moment of death.

The Second Pillar: Salat in Arabic

Salat means prayer. Muslims recite prayers from the Qur'an at dawn, midday, afternoon, evening, and night. At each of these five times of day, they stop what they are doing to bow down in worship in the direction of Mecca.

The Third Pillar: Zakat in Arabic

Through zakat, or giving to others, Muslims share and show kindness in a practical way to those less fortunate.

メッカにあるカーバー神殿。この四角い建物は神の象徴で、イスラム教徒は世界のどこにいても、この方角に礼拝し、巡礼はこの回りを7周する。

The Fourth Pillar: Sawm in Arabic

Sawm means fasting, or going without food and drink. Muslims fast during daylight hours throughout the holy month that they call Ramadan. Muslims believe fasting brings spiritual rewards. When the fast is over, at the end of Ramadan, Muslims celebrate with a festival.

The Fifth Pillar: Hajj in Arabic

The Hajj is a word for the pilgrimage, or religious journey, to Mecca. All healthy Muslims are expected to make a pilgrimage to Mecca at least once in their lives. Today, more than two million Muslims go to Mecca every year.

ムハンマドは神の預言者である」と唱えます。この簡潔明瞭な言葉が、すべてのイスラム教徒の信仰の基盤となっています。生まれたばかりの赤ん坊の耳に最初に囁かれるのもこの言葉であり、イスラム教徒が死の間際に唱えたいと願うのもこの言葉なのです。

　第2の柱はアラビア語でサラートといいます。

　サラートとは祈りのことです。イスラム教徒はコーランに書かれた祈りを、夜明け、正午、午後、夕方、そして夜に唱えます。1日5回行うこのお祈りのときには、イスラム教徒は活動を中断し、メッカの方向にひれ伏して礼拝を行います。

　第3の柱はアラビア語でザカートといいます。

　イスラム教徒はザカート、すなわち他者に施しをすることを通して、恵まれない生活をしている人々を親身になって助け、いたわるのです。

　第4の柱はアラビア語でソームといいます。

　ソームとは断食、つまり食べものや飲みものをとらないということです。イスラム教徒はラマダーンと呼ばれる聖なる月のあいだは、ずっと日中の飲食を断ちます。断食によって霊的な恵みが与えられると信じているのです。ラマダーンの月の最後、断食が終わるときにイスラム教徒は祝祭を行います。

　第5の柱はアラビア語でハジといいます。

　ハジとはメッカへの巡礼、すなわち宗教的な旅を意味する言葉です。健康なイスラム教徒なら誰もが、少なくとも生涯に1度はメッカへ巡礼することになっています。こんにち、メッカを訪れるイスラム教徒は毎年200万人以上にもなります。

NOTE 教室で使う英語

The Pledge of Allegiance（忠誠の誓い）
"I pledge allegiance to the flag of the United States of America and to the republic for which it stands, one nation under God, indivisible, with liberty and justice for all."
（私はアメリカ合衆国の国旗とその国旗が象徴する共和国に対して、神のもとですべての人に自由と正義を行う不可分の国家に対して、忠誠を誓います）
＊州法によってやや違いはあるが、子どもたちは「忠誠の誓い」を覚え、毎日教室で唱えることを義務づけられている。しかし、本人もしくは親や保護者が思想・宗教などの理由でこれに反対する場合は唱えなくてもよい。その生徒は黙って起立しているか、着席している。ただし、「誓い」の邪魔をしてはならない。

Good morning, everyone.（みなさん、おはよう）
＊もちろん最初は先生のこの一言から始まる。

Time to call the roll.（出席をとります）
＊take the roll ともいう。出席簿は roll book。

Present!（はい）
＊あるいは Here! という。

Tardiness（遅刻）
＊「遅刻をしてはいけません」は Don't be tardy。

Let's start our lesson now.（それでは授業を始めましょう）

Open your books to page 15.（教科書の15ページを開いて）

Read the text aloud.（教科書を朗読してください）
＊声を出して読むのは、read aloud。

Does everyone have a handout?（みんなプリントはありますか）
＊handout とは授業のために先生が作るプリント。

If you know the answer, please raise your hand.
（答えがわかる人は手を上げて）

Good job!（よくできました）

That's all for today.（今日はこれまで）

What American 2nd GRADERS Learn in Textbooks

WORLD CIVILIZATION • 世界史

Hinduism

The Ganges is the longest river in India. In ancient India, many people made their home near the Ganges. But then new people came to this region, and they did not come as friends. These new people, who came from the northwest, were called Aryans. The Aryans had large and powerful armies. They conquered and ruled over the Indian people living along the Ganges. They changed the way the Indian people lived. Let's look at some of the biggest changes, starting with their religion.

The Aryans changed the religion of the Indian people. Over many years, the gods of the Aryans combined with the gods worshiped by the Indian people. This was the beginning of Hinduism.

Hinduism is the oldest religion still practiced in the world today. Before we learn more about Hinduism, think back to the religions you've already learned about. Do you remember learning that Judaism, Christianity, and Islam all teach about one God?

Well, Hinduism is different, and may seem a little confusing at first. That's because most Hindus believe in one God and in many gods. For Hindus, the one God is called Brahman. Hindus believe Brahman is a spirit in everything in the universe—in people, animals, trees, water, the ground, the stars, everything.

So, Brahman is the one God of Hinduism. But in Hinduism there are also thousands and thousands of different gods. For Hindus, these thousands of gods are like different faces or names of Brahman.

Among the many thousands of gods in Hinduism, there are three main gods. Most Hindus believe that these three main gods are sort of in charge of all the others. They are called Brahma, Vishnu, and Shiva.

Hindus believe that Brahma is the creator god, the god who made everything. Vishnu is the god who preserves and defends life. Shiva is the god of destruction and new life. In pictures, Shiva is often shown dancing in a ring of fire. Why fire? Because fire can destroy, but it

ヒンドゥー教

ガンジス川はインドでいちばん長い川です。古代のインドでは、ガンジス川流域に多くの人々が住んでいました。ところが、あるときこの地域に新しい民族がやってきたのですが、彼らは友好的な民族ではありませんでした。北西部からやってきたこの民族はアーリア人でした。アーリア人には大きく強力な軍隊がありました。彼らはガンジス川流域に暮らすインド人を征服し、支配してしまいました。彼らによってインド人の暮らしは一変しました。特に大きな変化のいくつかを、まず宗教の面から見ていきましょう。

ブラフマー

アーリア人の進出はインド人の宗教を変えました。長い年月のうちに、アーリア人の神々は、インド人の崇拝する神々と融合していったのです。これがヒンドゥー教の始まりです。

ヒンドゥー教はこんにちまで続いている宗教の中でもとりわけ古い宗教です。ヒンドゥー教について勉強する前に、みなさんがすでに学んだ宗教を振りかえってみましょう。ユダヤ教、キリスト教、イスラム教はいずれも唯一の神を説いていたのを覚えていますか？

さて、ヒンドゥー教はこれと異なるので、はじめはちょっとわかりにくいかもしれません。というのも、ほとんどのヒンドゥー教徒は、唯一の神も多数の神々もどちらも信じているからです。ヒンドゥー教徒は唯一の神をブラフマンと呼んでいます。ブラフマンは宇宙のあらゆるものに宿る霊だとヒンドゥー教徒は考えます。人間、動物、木々、水、大地、星など、まさしくあらゆるものに宿るのです。

このように、ブラフマンはヒンドゥー教における唯一の神といえます。しかし、ヒンドゥー教にはほかにも無数の神々がいます。ヒンドゥー教徒にとって、この無数の神々というのは、ブラフマンの別の顔や名前のようなものなのです。

ヒンドゥー教の無数の神々の中に主要な3神がいて、ほとんどのヒンドゥー教徒は、その3神が、のこりの神々すべてを司るような役割をしていると考えています。3つの神とは、ブラフマー、ビシュヌ、そしてシバのことです。

can also help to cteate new things.

Besides having many gods, Hinduism is different from Judaism, Christianity, and Islam in other ways. Hinduism has no single leader or teacher. You remember that believers in Christianity follow the teachings of Jesus. And Muslims follow Muhammad. But Hinduism has no one leader or teacher that every Hindu is expected to follow.

ビシュヌ神　　シバ神

You've learned about religions that have a book of sacred writings. For Jews, the holy book is the Hebrew Bible, the first part of which is called the Torah. The holy book of Christians is the Bible. And the holy book of Muslims is the Qu'ran. Hinduism does not have one holy book —instead, it has several sacred books.

One of the oldest sacred books of Hinduism is the Rig Veda. It is filled with beautiful poems, and it tells Hindus how to celebrate weddings, funerals, and holy days. If you lived in India today, you could still hear many people saying hymns from the Rig Veda at important times in their lives.

Another important holy book for Hindus is the Ramayana. It is full of stories of great deeds and adventures. Many stories in the Ramayana tell about the hero, Prince Rama. In some of these stories, the Hindu god Vishnu takes the form of the human hero, Rama. Here is a story about Rama and Sita.

Rama and Sita: A Tale from the Ramayana

Once long ago in India, in the kingdom of Ayodhya, there lived a king called Dasaratha. He was growing old and tired, and he decided that it was time to pass on the kingdom to his favorite son, Prince Rama. But King Dasaratha's wife, who was Rama's stepmother, wanted her own son, Prince Bharat, to be king. She knew that Dasaratha loved her so much that he would give her anything she desired. So she went to him

ヒンドゥー教徒は、ブラフマーは創造神、すなわちあらゆるものを創る神であると信じています。ビシュヌは生命を維持し、守護する神です。シバは破壊と新しい生命の神です。絵に描かれたシバはたいてい炎の円の中で踊っています。なぜ炎なのでしょうか？炎は破壊する力を持つと同時に、新しいものの誕生につながるからでもあります。

　多数の神々をもつことのほかにも、ヒンドゥー教にはユダヤ教、キリスト教、イスラム教と異なる点があります。ヒンドゥー教には1人の指導者も導師もいません。イエスの教えに従うのがキリスト教徒でしたね。同じようにイスラム教徒はムハンマドに従います。ところがヒンドゥー教には、すべてのヒンドゥー教徒が従うべき指導者や導師といった人がいないのです。

　1冊の聖典によって成立している宗教についてはすでに学びました。ユダヤ教徒の聖典はヘブライ聖書で、その第1部はトーラー(律法)と呼ばれています。キリスト教徒の聖典は聖書で、イスラム教徒の聖典はコーランです。ヒンドゥー教では聖典は1冊だけというのではなく、数冊あります。

　ヒンドゥー教のもっとも古い聖典の1つが「リグ・ベーダ」です。この書には美しい詩がちりばめられ、ヒンドゥー教徒として婚礼、葬儀、聖日をどうとり行えばよいかなどが書かれています。現在のインドに暮らしていれば、人生の節目にあたる行事のときにリグ・ベーダの賛歌を唱える人がまだたくさんいることがわかります。「ラーマーヤナ」も重要な聖典の1つです。この書には偉業や冒険の物語がたくさん収められています。「ラーマーヤナ」の物語の多くはラーマ王子という英雄の話です。こうした物語の中には、ヒンドゥー教の神であるヴィシュヌが、ラーマという人間の英雄の姿となって登場するものもあります。これから紹介するのは、ラーマとシータの物語です。

ラーマとシータ──「ラーマーヤナ」の物語

　遠い昔、インドのアヨーディヤー王国にダシャラタという王がいました。年老いて体が弱ってきた王は、最愛の息子ラーマ王子に国を譲り渡そうと心に決めました。ところが、ラーマにとっては継母になるダシャラタ王の妃は、実の息子であるバーラタ王子に王位を

> **NOTE**
> **ビシュヌ神**
> 現在のヒンドゥー教で広く崇拝されているのは、ビシュヌ神とシバ神とである。ビシュヌ神はもともと太陽神で、10通りにも変身して人類を救うという。その中ではクリシュナとラーマが重要だが、仏教の開祖、釈迦もその1つで、ベーダ聖典を守るために仏教を広めたとされる。

and asked him to send Rama to the forest of Dandak for fourteen years and make Bharat king. Dasaratha was both angry and upset, but he did exactly as she asked.

The next day, Rama left his father's palace with his wife, Sita, and his brother, Lakshman, and went into the dark forest of Dandak. On their journey they met an old wise priest who warned them that demons hid within the shadows of the trees. He gave Rama a quiver of magic arrows to protect himself from the evil in the forest.

After many days traveling, Rama, Sita, and Lakshman came to a place where the old man had told them they would be safe. They built themselves a house from hardened earth and bamboo. And so they lived happily for many years.

Then one day a little fawn came running out of the forest. It was the most beautiful animal Sita had ever seen and she begged Rama to catch it for her. Leaving Lakshman to look after his wife, Rama chased the little fawn deeper and deeper into the forest.

Suddenly Sita thought she heard Rama's voice crying from the forest: "Help me, Lakshman, help me!"

Lakshman ran off into the forest to try to find his brother. No sooner was he out of sight than an ugly little old man appeared as if from nowhere. As Sita watched, the little old man grew, his face changed, and there stood Ravana, the king of the demons!

Sita screamed but there was no one to hear her. Rama and Lakshman were now both lost in the heart of the forest. Ravana had sent the little deer to draw Rama away and then tricked Lakshman with false cries for help. Now, with a wave of his hand, Ravana summoned his magic chariot and he swept Sita up and away into the sky, over the forest and across the plains and mountains beyond, until at last they crossed the sea and landed on the demon island of Lanka.

Rama and Lakshman finally found their way home. They realized that they had been tricked and that Sita had been taken away by demons. Picking up his quiver of magic arrows and his bow, Rama set out with Lakshman in search of his wife. They traveled for many miles through the forests and across the plains and mountains, but they found no sign of her.

Then one day, as they were crossing a wooded mountain pass, an

継がせたいと思っていたのです。彼女には、自分を深く愛している
ダシャラタ王ならば、なんでも望みをかなえてくれるのが分かって
いました。そこで妃は王のところに行き、ラーマをダンダカーの森
に14年間追いやり、バーラタを王にするよう頼んだのです。ダシャ
ラタ王は怒りつつもどうしていいか分からず、妃の願い通りにして
しまいました。

　あくる日、ラーマは妻のシータ、そして弟のラクシュマナととも
に父の宮殿を後にし、ダンダカーの暗い森へと分け入っていきまし
た。旅の途中で彼らは叡智にすぐれた老僧に出会ったのですが、そ
の僧は、木々の陰には悪魔が隠れていますぞ、と警告してくれまし
た。そして、森に潜む悪魔たちから身を守るようにと、彼はラーマ
に魔法の矢を入れた矢筒を持たせました。

　何日もの旅を経て、ラーマ、シータ、ラクシュマナは老僧に教え
られた安全な場所にたどり着きました。彼らは固めた土と竹を使い
自分たちで家を造り、何年も幸せに暮らしました。

　ある日、森から子鹿が飛び出してきました。シータは、これほど
美しい動物は見たことがなかったので、ラーマに捕まえてほしいと
頼みました。ラーマは妻を守っているようにとラクシュマナに言い
残し、子鹿を追って森の奥へ奥へと深く入っていきました。

　とつぜん、シータは、森の中からラーマがこう叫ぶのが聞こえた
ような気がしました。「助けてくれ、ラクシュマナ、助けてくれ！」

　ラクシュマナは兄を見つけようと急いで森に駆け込みました。そ
の姿が森の中に消えたかと思うと、醜い小柄な老人がどこからとも
なく現れました。じっと見つめるシータの目の前で、その小柄な老
人は大きくなり、顔つきが変わり、なんとそれは悪魔の王ラバーナ
だったのです。

　シータは悲鳴をあげましたが、その声を聞く者はだれもいません。
ラーマとラクシュマナはいまや２人とも森の奥深くに迷い込んでい
ました。ラバーナは、ラーマをシータから引き離すために子鹿を送
り、助けを求める偽の叫び声でラクシュマナをだましたのでした。
ラバーナは手をひと振りして魔法の馬車を呼び出すと、シータをさ
らって空に舞い上がり、森を越え、平原、はるかな山々を越え、つ
いには海を渡って悪魔の島ランカに着きました。

　一方、ラーマとラクシュマナはやっとのことで家にもどってきま
した。彼らは自分たちがだまされ、シータが悪魔に連れ去られたこ
とに気づきました。魔法の矢を入れた矢筒と弓を手に取り、ラーマ

enormous ape jumped down from a rock onto the path in front of them.

"I am Hanuman," he said, "the captain of the Vanar tribe of monkeys." He told them how he had seen Ravana's chariot flying through the sky with Sita aboard, and he promised Rama that he and his army would help in the search for Sita. He clapped his paws together and suddenly, down from the rocks, came hundreds and hundreds of monkeys.

Rama and his new army traveled on across the mountains until they reached the seashore, where the angry waves grew higher and higher, beating wildly against the rocks. Rama could not see how he would ever reach the demon island of Lanka. Then Hanuman said, "We must build a bridge to the island from trees and rocks and anything else we can find."

All the monkeys set to work. They broke off boulders from the cliffs and hurled them into the sea. When the bridge was finally finished, Rama led his army across the sea.

With a roar, Ravana and his hordes of demons came to meet them. Rama took a magic arrow from his quiver and let it fly. The arrow struck Ravana and the demon sank to the ground. A great cheer went up—Ravana was dead and Rama had won.

Rama and Sita were together again at last, and the streets of Lanka were filled with the sounds of laughter and singing as the celebrations began.

Fourteen years had passed since Rama had left his father's palace and now it was time for him to return to Ayodhya. In a magic chariot drawn by swans, Rama and Sita flew up into the clouds to begin their last journey home.

はラクシュマナとともに妻を捜す旅に出ました。彼らは森を通り抜け、平原、山を越え、何マイルも旅をしましたが、行方を知る手がかりは得られませんでした。

　ある日、木の生い茂った山道を歩いていると、巨大な猿が岩から目の前の道にひょいと飛び降りてきて、「わたしはハヌマーン、猿のバナール族の頭だ」と言いました。彼は、シータを乗せたラバーナの馬車が空を飛んでいくのを見たときのことを話し、わたしが率いる猿の大群でシータを捜す手助けをしよう、と約束してくれました。彼が両手をパンと叩くと、とつぜん、岩の上から何百頭もの猿が次から次へと降りてきました。

　ラーマと新たに加わった猿の大群がいくつもの山を越えて旅を続けると、やがて海岸にたどり着きました。海岸には荒れ狂う波がしだいに高まりながら押しよせ、はげしく岩に打ちつけていました。いったいどうすれば悪魔の島ランカにたどり着けるのか。ラーマは途方にくれました。すると、ハヌマーンがこう言いました。「木でも岩でも、手に入るものは何でも使って、島に渡る橋を造らなくてはなりません」

　猿たちはみないっせいに仕事に取りかかりました。彼らは崖の大きな岩を砕き、ぽんぽん海に投げ入れました。橋ができ上がると、ラーマは猿の大群を率いて海を渡りました。

　ラバーナと悪魔の群れが、うなり声をあげながらラーマたちを迎え撃つためにやって来ました。ラーマは矢筒から取り出した魔法の矢で、ピュッと射かけました。矢はラバーナに命中し、悪魔は地面に崩れ落ちました。どっと大きな歓声が沸き起こりました——ラバーナは死に、ラーマが勝ったのです。

　ラーマとシータはついに再会を果たしました。ランカの町の通りは笑い声と歌声に包まれ、祝祭が始まりました。

　ラーマが父の宮殿をあとにしてから14年が経ち、アヨーディヤー王国へと帰る日がやってきました。白鳥の引く魔法の馬車に乗ったラーマとシータは雲の中へ高く舞い上がり、故郷へ帰る最後の旅に出たのです。

WORLD CIVILIZATION • 世界史

Buddhism

You've just learned about one great religion that began in India—Hinduism. Now let's learn about another, called Buddhism.

Buddhism began in India. Today Buddhism is the religion of millions of people, but most of them are not in India. Today many of these people live in Southeast Asia, China, and Japan. But Buddhism began in India, and it grew out of Hinduism. It began a long time ago, with a young prince named Siddhartha Gautama.

Buddha: The Enlightened One

Siddhartha was born the son of a very rich king and queen. His father ruled a kingdom in the foothills of the high Himalayan mountains. Siddhartha wore soft, beautiful clothes made of the finest silk. Colorful flowers, soft music, and sweet smells surrounded him. When he walked, servants held umbrellas over him to keep off the sun or rain. When he grew to be sixteen years old, he married a beautiful princess.

What a life! All pleasure, and no pain. Siddhartha's father, the king, tried to make sure that his son was always happy. He even ordered that no one who was sick, old, or poor should ever come near the prince. That way, thought the king, the prince would live in a world without suffering, a world filled with beautiful things and happy people.

But one day, when Siddhartha was riding in his chariot outside the palace walls, he saw an old, gray-haired man, bent over and wrinkled, leaning on a stick. Soon after, he saw a sick man lying along the side of the road, and heard his painful cries for help. Later, for the first time in his life, he saw a dead person. Finally, he saw a holy man with a shaved head and a peaceful expression on his face.

Now Siddhartha knew what his father had tried so hard to hide

2nd GRADE

仏教

　みなさんはインドで誕生した重要な宗教の1つ、ヒンドゥー教を学んだところですね。こんどはインドで生まれたもう1つの宗教、仏教について学びましょう。

　仏教はインドで起こりました。現在、仏教は数多くの信徒を抱える宗教ですが、そのほとんどはインド人ではありません。こんにち仏教徒の多くは、東南アジア、中国、そして日本に住んでいます。しかし仏教はインドで起こり、ヒンドゥー教から派生したものなのです。仏教は遠い昔に、ゴータマ・シッダールタという若い王子と共に始まりました。

ブッダ──悟りを開いた者

　シッダールタはたいへん裕福な王と王妃の息子として生まれました。彼の父親はヒマラヤ山脈の裾野にある王国を治めていました。シッダールタの着る衣は、美しく肌触りのよい、最上級の絹織物でできていました。彼は、色とりどりの花、心地よい音楽、甘い香りに包まれて育ちました。散歩をするときには、召使たちが傘をさして、日光や雨から守ってくれました。16歳になると、彼は美しい王女と結婚しました。

　なんという人生でしょう！　苦痛を知らない、快楽ばかりの人生とは。シッダールタの父である王は、息子がつねに幸福であるように気を配っていました。王は、病気の者、年老いた者、貧しい者をけっして王子に近づけてはならないと臣下に命じていました。そのようにすれば、王子は苦しみのない世界、美しいものや幸福な人々に満ちた世界で暮らすことができると王は考えたのです。

　ところがある日、シッダールタが宮殿の塀の外に出て馬車を走らせていると、背中が曲がり、顔に深い皺の刻まれた白髪の老人が、杖にすがりつくようにしているのを見ました。そのすぐあと、病気の男が道のわきに倒れているのが見え、苦しそうに助けを求める声も聞こえました。それから、生まれて初めて、シッダールタは死人

NOTE
ブッダ（仏陀）
仏陀すなわち釈迦の生没年については紀元前463–前383年説と、前565–前485年説がある。姓はゴータマで名はシッダールタだが、仏陀はサーキヤ人で、その音の漢訳で釈迦と呼ばれるようになった。

　悟りを開いたのち、45年間インド各地を説法して回り、80歳で亡くなる。

鎌倉の大仏

from him. He saw that there is pain in the world, and that people grow old and die. He was troubled by what he had seen, and he thought for a long time. Was it right that just because he was born rich, he should be comfortable and happy while other people were unhappy and miserable?

Then he made a hard decision. He made up his mind to leave his family, his home, and his easy, comfortable life. He set off to try to understand why there was suffering and what to do about it. He cut off his long hair. He gave his soft silk gowns to a poor man and put on the poor man's old, ragged clothes. He wandered for years and years, looking for answers to his questions.

Then one night he sat down under a tree to be quiet and think. He sat and thought for a long time, and in the morning when the sun rose, he felt that now he understood. He had become "enlightened," which means wise and aware. And so he was called Buddha, which means "the enlightened one, the one who knows."

What did Buddha know? He said that he now understood that suffering and death are part of life. He said that life is like a great wheel in which birth, suffering, and death come round and round again. And he said that the most important thing is to live a life of goodness. Buddha taught people how to be good, and many people, including his wife and his father, began to follow his teachings. He said, for example, that people should harm no living thing. He told his followers to be kind and merciful to humans and animals alike.

King Asoka: From War to Peace

About two hundred years after Buddha died, a king helped spread Buddha's teachings. King Asoka didn't believe in Buddha's teachings at first. You remember that Buddha said people should harm no living

を目にしました。最後に、頭を剃って穏やかな表情をたたえた聖人を彼は見ました。

こうしてシッダールタは、父親がなんとかして彼に見せまいとしていたものを知ってしまいました。この世には苦しみがあり、人間は年老いて死ぬということが分かったのです。彼は自分の見たものに深く心を乱され、長いあいだ考えにふけりました。ただ裕福な境遇に生まれたからといって、ほかの人々が不幸でみじめであるのに、自分はぬくぬくと幸せに暮らしていてもいいのだろうか？

悩み抜いた末にシッダールタは決心をしました。家族や王宮、心地よく何ひとつ不自由のない暮らしを捨て去ると決めたのです。なぜ苦しみが存在するのか、どのように苦しみに向き合えばいいのかという疑問を解くために、彼は旅に出ました。彼は長い髪を切り落としました。やわらかな絹の衣を貧しい男に与え、貧しい男の古いぼろぼろの服を身にまといました。答えを探し求めて何年も何年も放浪しました。

ある夜、彼は木の下に座り、静かに考えはじめました。彼は座ったまま長いあいだ瞑想にふけり、やがて朝陽が昇るころになって、彼はついに答えを得たと感じました。彼は「悟り」に達したのです。「悟り」とは、すぐれた叡智と認識を持っていることです。彼がブッダと呼ばれるのはそのためで、ブッダとは「悟りを開いた者、叡智を持つ者」という意味です。

ブッダには何が分かったのでしょうか？　苦しみと死は生の一部であることが分かったのだと彼は語っています。生とは、誕生、苦しみ、死が永遠に繰り返す巨大な車輪のようなものである、いちばん大切なのは善なる生き方を心がけることである、と。ブッダは人々に善を行うためにはどうすべきかを説き、彼の妻や父親を含む多くの人々がその教えに従うようになりました。ブッダは、たとえば、人は命あるものを傷つけてはならないと言っています。彼は信者たちに、人間にも動物にもひとしく優しく慈悲深くあれと説きました。

アショーカ王──戦争から平和へ

ブッダの死からおよそ200年後、ある王がブッダの教えを広めることに力をつくしました。アショーカ王は最初はブッダの教えを信じていませんでした。すでに述べたように、命あるものを傷つけて

> **NOTE**
> **アショーカ王**
> アショーカ王の生没年は不詳。マウリヤ王朝第3代の王の座にあったのは、紀元前268年–紀元前232年頃とされる。

thing. But King Asoka was a warrior. He led his soldiers in fierce battles, in which many men were hurt or killed. Through these wars he brought the northern and southern parts of India together under his rule.

But after one fierce and bloody battle, King Asoka looked around and saw the death and hardship caused by war. He remembered that Buddha had said, "Harm no living thing," and he felt ashamed. He decided to stop making war and instead to devote himself to spreading Buddha's teachings throughout his kingdom. All over India he built hospitals for both people and animals. He told his workers to plant trees and dig wells for fresh water. He even set up houses along the road for travelers who were tired from walking great distances.

King Asoka wanted the people of India to learn more about Buddha's teachings, so he had Buddha's words carved on tall pillars and put them in places where many people would see them. Even though Asoka strongly believed in Buddha's teachings, he also believed that kings should let their people worship as they wanted to. So, many Indian people felt they could worship their different gods and also listen to Buddha's words.

King Asoka sent Buddhist priests across Asia to tell people in other lands about Buddha's teachings. So Buddha's ideas spread all over Asia, and Buddhism remains one of the largest religions in the world today.

ミャンマーの寺院

はならないとブッダは説きました。ところが、アショーカ王は戦士だったのです。彼は兵士を率いて壮烈に戦い、戦場では多くの人が負傷したり、命を落としたりしました。こうした戦争を経て、彼はインドの北部と南部をともに支配下に置きました。

しかし、あるすさまじい血みどろの戦いの後、アショーカ王はあたりを見回して、戦争がもたらした死と苦しみに気づきました。彼はブッダが「命あるものを傷つけてはならない」と説いたことを思い出し、自分のしてきたことを悔いました。戦争を放棄して、そのかわりに王国にブッダの教えを広めることに力をつくそうと決心しました。彼はインドの各地に人間と動物の両方のための病院を建てました。家来たちに、木を植えきれいな水の出る井戸を掘るように命じました。長い道のりを歩いてくたびれた旅人たちのために、街道沿いに宿も造りました。

アショーカ王はインドの人々にブッダの教えをもっと知ってほしかったので、ブッダの言葉を大きな石柱に刻み、多くの人々の目の触れる場所に立てました。彼はブッダの教えを深く信じていましたが、王たるものは人々に自由な信仰を許すべきだと考えました。それで、インド人の多くは、自分たちの信じる神々を自由に崇めながら、ブッダの言葉にも耳を傾けたのでした。

アショーカ王は仏教の僧侶たちをアジア各地に派遣して、よその土地の人々にブッダの教えを伝えました。そのため、ブッダの思想はアジア全体に広まり、仏教はこんにち世界でもっとも大きな宗教の1つとして残っています。

ブッダがはじめて教えを説いた場所にアショーカ王がたてた石柱の頂部。4頭のライオンが背中合わせに立っている。

WORLD CIVILIZATION • 世界史

Confucianism

A Wise Teacher in China: Confucius

Long, long ago, about the same time that Buddha lived in India, another wise man was teaching in China. His name was Confucius. Confucius was a very peaceful man. But during his life, China was not a peaceful country. Instead, many groups were fighting each other. They rode around the countryside and robbed and hurt the people in the villages.

Confucius, who was wise, gentle, and thoughtful, grew tired of all this fighting. He said that the fighting should stop and that all the people should come together under a single wise ruler. The people, he said, should obey a good ruler, while a good ruler should take care of the people. He said to the rulers, "You are there to rule, not to kill. If you desire what is good, the people will be good."

Confucius said many other things about how people should live and treat each other. For example, he said that you should respect your parents and teachers, and honor your ancestors.

You know the Golden Rule, don't you? It says, "Do unto others as you would have them do unto you." Confucius was the first person we know of to teach the Golden Rule, although he put it this way: "What you do not wish for yourself, do not do to others."

Many people in China began to listen to his teachings, which became known as "Confucianism." Confucianism is not a religion, like Islam or Christianity, because Confucius did not have anything to say about God or the gods. Confucianism is a way of thinking about how to live a good life and how to treat others.

孔子

儒教

中国の賢人──孔子

　はるか遠い昔、インドでブッダが生きていたのと同じころ、もう1人の賢人が中国で教えを説いていました。彼の名前は孔子です。孔子はたいへん穏やかな人でした。しかし、孔子の生きた時代の中国は穏やかな国とはいえません。穏やかどころか、多くの集団が互いに争っていたのです。彼らは馬に乗って農村を荒らし回り、村人たちを襲い、家財を強奪したりしました。

　賢く、寛大で、思慮深い人物であった孔子は、そのような争いごとはもうたくさんだと思いました。争いごとをやめ、すべての民衆が1人の賢明な統治者の下に集わなくてはならない、と孔子は言いました。民衆はよき統治者に従い、よき統治者は民衆を大切にしなくてはならない。彼は統治者たちにこう言いました。「あなたがたの仕事は国を治めることであって、人々を殺すことではありません。あなたがたが善いことを望むなら、民衆も自然に善くなるのです」

　孔子はほかにも、人々がどのように生き、お互いどのように接すればよいのか、さまざまなことを語りました。たとえば、両親や先生を敬い、祖先を尊ぶように、と孔子は説きました。

　みなさんは〈黄金律〉を知っていますね。「自分がしてもらいたいと思うことを、他人にしてあげなさい」という戒律です。わたしたちが知るかぎり、最初に黄金律を説いた人物は孔子なのですが、彼はつぎのように表現しています。「自分がしてほしくないことを、他人にしてはならない」

　中国の多くの人々が孔子の教えに耳を傾けるようになり、その教えはやがて「儒教」として知られるようになりました。儒教はイスラム教やキリスト教のような宗教ではありません。というのも、孔子は神や神々についてはいっさい語っていないからです。儒教とは、どのように善い人生を送り、どのように他人と接すればよいかを説く思想なのです。

> **NOTE**
> **孔子**
> 孔子(前551–前479)を英語で Confucius と綴るのは、中国語の「孔夫子」の英語音訳 K'ung Fu Tzu に由来する。有名な『論語』は孔子の著書ではなく、弟子が書いた孔子の言行録である。釈迦、孔子、キリスト、いずれも自らは書物を残さず、言行録が聖典になった。

> **NOTE**
> **黄金律**
> 「黄金律」とはキリストの教えの根本的な倫理で、新約聖書にある「山上の垂訓」の1つ(マタイ伝第7章12節)。ただし、同様の教えは仏教の慈悲、ヒンドゥー教のカルマなど、世界の多くの思想・宗教に見られる。
> 　古代バビロニアのハムラビ法典や『旧約聖書』などにある「目には目を、歯には歯を」という復讐の思想と異なり、キリストは「敵を愛せよ」と言う。

LANGUAGE ARTS • 国 語

Paul Bunyan

America is a big country with a big appetite for stories about big deeds and larger-than-life heroes. These stories, called tall tales, may have a bit of truth, but they mostly serve up a heaping portion of humorous exaggeration. Now you are to meet the most favorite American tall tale character.

As a baby, Paul Bunyan was mighty big. How big? Well, when he sneezed, he blew the birds from Maine to California. When he got a bad case of the hiccups, people for miles around ran out of their houses screaming, "Earthquake! Earthquake!"

When Paul Bunyan grew up, he became a logger. There was no one who could match Paul at cutting down trees. In those days, as Americans were moving West and building the country, they had to cut down a lot of trees to make their homes, not to mention their schools, churches, boats, and furniture.

Paul made himself a giant ax, with a handle carved out of a full-grown hickory tree. With one swing, he could bring down a hundred trees. Once, when Paul was tired after a hard day of logging, he let his ax drag behind him as he walked back to the logging camp. It dug a ditch that people today call the Grand Canyon.

Sometimes, being so big and all, Paul got to feeling lonely with no one his size around. But then came the Winter of the Blue Snow. It was called that because it was so cold

ポール・バニヤン

　アメリカは国も大きいが、怪物もどきのヒーローたちの途方もない力業(ちからわざ)を伝える物語への食欲も旺盛だ。こうした物語をトール・テールというが、事実と一致するところはごくわずかで、たいていは面白おかしく誇張した話をてんこ盛りにしたごちそうである。ここに登場するのは、アメリカのトール・テールの中でももっとも愛されている人物だ。

　生まれたときから、ポール・バニヤンは途方もなく大きかった。どのくらい大きかったかって？　そうだな、くしゃみをしたら、鳥たちをメインからカリフォルニアまで吹き飛ばしてしまった。しゃっくりがひどいときには、周囲数マイルの人々が、「地震だ！　地震だ！」と悲鳴をあげながら家から飛び出したね。
　ポールは成長して木こりになった。木を切り倒すことにかけては、ポールにかなう者は1人もいなかった。その当時、アメリカ人は西に向かって進みながら国造りをしていたので、家を建てるのに多くの木を切り倒さなくてはならなかった。言うまでもなく、学校や教会、船や家具を作るのにも木は必要だった。
　ポールは自分用に大きな斧を作った。柄の部分はヒッコリーの大木を削ったものだ。彼はたった一振りで、100本もの木をなぎ倒してしまった。あるとき、ポールは1日中木を切り倒していて疲れてしまい、斧を引きずりながら小屋まで歩いて帰った。そのとき削られた溝が、こんにちグランド・キャニオンとよばれているところだ。
　ときどき、あまりにもからだが大きいので、ポールは自分と同じくらいの大きさの者が誰もいなくて寂しくなることがあった。そんなときに現れたのが〈青雪の冬〉だった。なぜ〈青雪の冬〉かというと、ひどく寒くて、雪でさえ凍えて青ざめてしまったのだ。ある日、青い雪の積もった道を歩いていると、ポールは青くて大きくて柔らかな毛の生えたものが2つ、雪からぴょんと突き出ているのに気づいた。近づいてぐいと引っぱってみると、それは2つの大きな青い耳だった。そして、耳にくっついて出てきたのは、なんともばかで

that even the snow shivered and turned blue. One day, as Paul made his way through the blue snowdrifts, he saw two big, blue, furry things sticking up out of the snow. He reached down and gave a pull. They turned out to be two big blue ears. And connected to them was a giant blue baby ox!

Paul carried the half-frozen creature home, wrapped him in blankets and fed him. And when the baby ox looked up and gave Paul a big friendly lick on the face, Paul laughed and said, "Babe, we're goin' to be great friends!"

And they were. Babe grew up to be so big that, if you were standing at his front legs, you had to use a telescope to see all the way to his back legs. Everywhere Paul went, from Maine to Minnesota to Oregon and back, Babe went too. Paul chopped down the trees and Babe hauled them to the rivers, where he would dump in the logs so they could float to the sawmills.

One day, Paul said to Babe, "What this here country needs is a canal runnin' down the middle of it to float logs in." So Paul started digging. He threw great mounds of dirt and rocks to the right and the left. On one side he made the Rocky Mountains, and on the other side he made the Appalachians. And when Babe kicked over a huge bucket of water to fill the canal, well, that there became the Mississippi River.

Wherever there was logging to be done, Paul and Babe were ready to work. The last place they were seen, people say, was up in Alaska, where you can still hear the echoes when Paul shouts, *"T-i-m-b-e-r!"*

ミネソタ州ビミジ市にあるポール・バニヤンとベイブの像。普通の人間の3倍くらいの大きさになっている。

かい青い雄牛の赤ん坊！

　ポールはそのほとんど凍りついた動物を家に連れて帰り、毛布にくるんで食べものを与えてやった。子牛はポールを見上げると、うれしそうに顔をペロペロなめるので、ポールは笑いながら言った。「ベイブ、俺たち、最高の友達になれそうだな！」

　そのとおり、2人は最高の友達になった。ベイブはやがて途方もない大きさになり、前足のところからずっと向こうにある後ろ足を見るのには望遠鏡が必要なくらいだった。ポールが行くところならどこにだって、メインからミネソタへ、オレゴンへ、またその帰り道も、ベイブはついて行った。ポールが切り倒した木をベイブが川まで引っぱっていき、丸太のまま川へ落として製材所まで流すのだ。

　ある日、ポールはベイブに言った。「国の真ん中に、丸太を流して運べるような運河があるといいな」。そこでポールは運河を掘り始めた。彼は大量の土や岩を右へ左へと振り飛ばした。こうして片方にはロッキー山脈が、もう片方にはアパラチア山脈ができあがった。そしてベイブが水の入った巨大なバケツを蹴飛ばして運河に水を流したんだが、そう、それでミシシッピ川ができたというわけだ。

　木こりの仕事があるところならどこへでも、ポールとベイブは喜んで働きに行った。2人の姿が最後に目撃されたのは、言い伝えによると、北のアラスカだという。そこではいまでもポールの叫び声がこだましているのだ。「木が倒れるぞう！」

NOTE　「トール・テール」

アメリカのほら話は、新大陸の珍聞奇聞に夢中になったヨーロッパ人の好奇心が源泉のようだ。1765年、ベンジャミン・フランクリンは、今年の夏はナイアガラで滝登りする鯨が見ものですよ、と新聞に書いてヨーロッパ人をからかった。

　この伝統が19世紀の西部で一挙に開花する。開拓者たちは大自然に苦闘を強いられたからこそ、その大自然を呑みこむような滑稽話を仕立てあげ、厳しい現実に耐えたのであろう。

　ほら話を文学に取り込んで作家となったマーク・トウェインの作品には筏（いかだ）乗りのほら話が紹介されていて、「俺様がその気になれば、緯度と経度の線を網にして、大西洋で鯨をすくう」と始まって、「寒いときには熱いメキシコ湾の湯につかる」と続く。ここまでくるとポール・バニヤンもかわいい。ほら話はアメリカ産の神話だ。

LANGUAGE ARTS • 国語

Familiar Sayings　よく使うことわざ

Better late than never
「遅れても、しないよりはまし」

People use this saying to mean that it's better that something happens late than not at all.

このことわざは、何もしないよりは遅れてもした方がよいという意味で使う。

Cold feet
「足が冷たくなる（怖気づく）」

People say that someone gets "cold feet" when that person decides not to do something because he or she is afraid.

不安におびえて何かをやめてしまうようなときに、だれそれは「怖気づいた」という。

Two heads are better than one
「2つの頭は1つに勝る」

People use this saying to mean that when one person is having trouble with a task or problem, a second person can often help out.

このことわざは、誰かが仕事や問題を抱えて困っているときに、もう1人いればその事態を切り抜けることができることが多い、という意味で使われる。

Keep your fingers crossed
「指で十字を作っておく（幸運を祈る）」

People use this expression in several ways. They say it to keep off danger. And they say it to try to help make a wish come true.

この表現には使い方がいくつかある。例えば、危険に遭いませんように、と祈るときに使う。また、望みを実現させたいと願うときにもこういう。

Easier said than done
「行うは難しく、言うは簡単（言うは易く行うは難し）」

People use this saying to mean that it's sometimes easy to say what should be done, but it's harder to do it.

このことわざは、何をすべきだと口では簡単に言えるが、それを実行に移すのは難しいものだという意味で使う。

You can't teach an old dog new tricks
「老犬に新しい芸は仕込めない」

People use this saying to mean that as you get older you get more set in your ways. Once you get used to doing something in a certain way, it becomes very hard to learn a different way to do it.

このことわざは、人間は年をとるにつれて、いつも決まったやり方をするようになるということだ。これはいつもこうするという風に慣れてしまうと、別のやり方に変えるのはとても難しくなってくる。

Get up on the wrong side of the bed
「いつもの反対側から起きる」

People use this phrase to mean someone is in a bad mood.

➨ "Boy was my mom a grouch this morning. I think she got up on the wrong side of the bed."

この表現を使うのは、誰かの機嫌が悪いということを言うときだ。

➨「いやぁ、今朝はママがひどくご機嫌ナナメでさ。知らないけど、ヘンテコな起き方したんじゃないのかな」

Turn over a new leaf
「新しいページをめくる（心を入れかえる）」

To turn over a new leaf is to make a big change in the way you act.

➨ "I've been late to school nine times already this year. But starting today I'm going to turn over a new leaf. No matter what happens, I'm going to be on time."

「新しいページをめくる」というのは、生き方を大きく変えることをいう。

➨「今年はもう9回も遅刻している。でも、今日から心を入れかえるぞ。どんなことがあっても時間に間に合うようにするんだ」

GEOGRAPHY • 地 理

Let's Visit Japan

Japan is a country far to the east in Asia. Since the sun rises in the east, Japan has long been called "the land of the rising sun." A rising sun is pictured on the flag of Japan, which has a red circle on a white background.

Compared to China, Japan is a very small country. Japan is made up of many islands. The four main islands are really the tops of a great mountain range. There are many volcanoes in Japan, and there are many earthquakes.

In Japan you'll find one of the largest cities in the world, called Tokyo. Tokyo is a busy, crowded, modern city, with many banks, stores, restaurants, museums, colleges, and apartment buildings.

If you were to visit a Japanese family living in an apartment in Tokyo, the first thing you would do when you entered their home would be to take off your shoes. You would wear socks or special slippers, but you would never wear your outside shoes indoors!

If your Japanese friends invited you to stay for dinner, you might not sit in a chair but instead kneel on a cushion around a low table. To pick up your food, you would not use a fork—and no, you wouldn't use your fingers, but two slender pieces of wood about the size of pencils, called chopsticks.

In many ways, Japan is a very modern country. It has busy factories that make cars, televisions, radios, cameras, and other products that are bought by people around the world.

But there is more to Japan than a lot of modern business and industry. In Japan the people also care about their old ways and customs. For example, children in Japan learn a very old art form called *origami*. To do *origami*, you fold paper in special ways, without cutting or pasting it, to make lovely figures such as a frog or a crane.

日本を訪ねて

　日本はアジアの東の端にある国です。太陽は東から昇るので、日本は長い間「日出づる国」と呼ばれてきました。日本の国旗は昇る太陽を図案化したもので、白地に赤い円が描かれています。

　中国と比べると日本はとても小さな国で、たくさんの島からできあがっています。特に大きな島4つは、実際には巨大な連山の尾根にあたるのです。日本には火山がたくさんあるだけに地震もよく起こります。

　日本には東京という世界でも最大級の都市があります。東京は人口の密集した活発な現代都市で、銀行、店舗、レストラン、博物館、大学、マンションなどが数多くあります。

　もし東京でマンションに住んでいる日本人の家庭を訪ねることになったら、その家に行ってまず最初にするのは靴を脱ぐことです。靴下や室内用スリッパなどはかまいませんが、まちがっても外用の靴のまま家にあがってはいけません。

　日本人の友だちに夕食に招かれると、たいていはイスに座るのではなく、低いテーブルを囲んで、クッションの上にひざまずくように座ることになります。料理をいただくときはフォークはまず使いません。かといって指で食べたりしてはいけません。箸と呼ばれる、鉛筆ほどの長さの細い棒状の木片を2本使うのです。

　多くの点で、日本はきわめて現代的な国です。日本には、自動車、テレビ、ラジオ、カメラなどの製品をさかんに作っている工場があり、世界中の人々がこうした製品を買っています。

　しかし、日本は現代的なビジネスや産業であふれるだけの国ではありません。日本人は古い伝統や習慣を大事にするという側面ももっています。たとえば、日本の子どもたちは古くから伝わる「オリガミ」という紙細工を習います。オリガミを作るには独特の方法で紙を折っていきますが、ハサミやのりを使わずにカエルやツルを模した美しい作品ができます。

MATHEMATICS ● 算数

Counting Money　お金の数え方

Here are pictures of a one dollar bill and some coins. $1.00 is worth the same as 100 cents. You can write amounts of money using the dollar sign or the cents sign.

$$\$1.00 = 100 ¢$$

When you write an amount of money with a dollar sign, the numbers to the right of the little dot (called a "decimal point") are cents. For example, $1.50 is 1 dollar and 50 cents. $2.98 is 2 dollars and 98 cents.

You can write amounts less than a dollar with a dollar sign or a cents sign.

$$\$0.89 = 89 ¢$$

You read $0.89 and 89¢ in the same way —89 cents. When you count coins, start with the coins that are worth most. For example, how much is this?

これは1ドル札と硬貨の写真だ。1ドルは金額にして100セントと同じである。金額はセントやドルの記号を使って書き表すことができる。

ドル記号を使って金額を書くときに、小さな点(「小数点」という)の右側にある数字はセントを表す。たとえば、$1.50は1ドル50セント。$2.98は2ドル98セントである。1ドル以下の金額もドル記号、あるいはセント記号を使って書き表すことができる。

読むときは$0.89も89¢も同じように89セントと読む。硬貨の金額を数えるときには、いちばん大きい額の硬貨から数え始める。たとえば、これはいくらになるだろう。

One dollar	Half dollar	Quarter dollar	Ten cents (one dime)	Five cents (one nickel)	One cent (one penny)
100セント	50セント	25セント	10セント	5セント	1セント

Those coins add up to 191 cents. That is 1 dollar and 91 cents. $1.91. And we say "One and ninety one." We sometimes use "buck" instead of "dollar."

これらの硬貨の金額を合計すると191セントになる。1ドルと91セントということだ。$1.91である。口で言うときには「1と91」という。「ドル」と言わずに「バック」ということもある。

NOTE Faces of American Government on the Bills
紙幣に描かれたアメリカ政府を代表する肖像の数々

2nd GRADE

1ドル：ジョージ・ワシントン
　　　（George Washington 1732–99）
植民地軍の総司令官として独立戦争を戦い、英雄に。アメリカの初代大統領。大統領職を2期務めた。自邸マウント・バーノンは現在もバージニア州に残る。

2ドル：トマス・ジェファソン
　　　（Thomas Jefferson 1743–1826）
第3代大統領。独立宣言（1776年）の草稿を執筆。大統領としてミシシッピ川以西の広大な土地を1500万ドルでフランスから購入、アメリカの国土を倍以上にした。

5ドル：エイブラハム・リンカーン
　　　（Abraham Lincoln 1809–65）
第16代大統領。就任してまもなく南北戦争が始まり、戦争が終結した直後に暗殺された。「奴隷解放宣言」を公布（1863年）。

10ドル：アレグザンダー・ハミルトン
　　　（Alexander Hamilton 1757–1804）
強力な中央集権政府の必要性を唱えた。新国家の憲法制定の立役者となったほか、財政基盤の確立に貢献。政敵との決闘で死亡。

20ドル：アンドルー・ジャクソン
　　　（Andrew Jackson 1767–1845）
第7代大統領。1812年の対英戦争で活躍。またインディアン（アメリカ先住民）との戦争、強制移住の執行でも知られる。自由貿易の推進者。

50ドル：ユリシーズ・グラント
　　　（Ulysses S. Grant 1822–85）
第18代大統領。南北戦争時に北軍の総司令官となり、勝利に導いた。1879年に日本を訪問。負債を返すために死の数日前に書き上げた『自伝』は自伝文学の傑作。

100ドル：ベンジャミン・フランクリン
　　　（Benjamin Franklin 1706–90）
大統領にはならなかったが、独立の気運を作り、長老として大陸諸国との交渉から独立後の憲法制定にいたるまで、長い間アメリカ政界で大活躍。

LANGUAGE ARTS • 国 語

Myths from Ancient Greece
Heroes and Monsters, Gods and Goddesses

Here are some stories that have been around for two thousand years or more. These stories come to us from ancient Greece. We call these stories "myths." Many myths tell about brave heroes, great battles, terrible monsters, or gods and goddesses. Some myths explain why we have seasons, or why there are volcanoes, or how constellations got in the sky. Of course today we know the real reasons that all these things happen. But long, long ago, many people believed the myths were true. Even though we no longer believe the old myths, we like to tell them because they're such wonderful stories.

Like the people in other ancient civilizations you've learned about, the ancient Greeks believed in many gods and goddesses. The Greeks built beautiful temples, like the Parthenon, to honor their gods. In the Greek myths, the gods and goddesses sometimes act like normal people —like you and me. They need to eat, drink, and sleep. They can be happy one moment and angry the next. They fall in love and get married. They play tricks on each other. They argue and fight with each other.

Unlike people, however, the Greek gods had magical powers. Some gods could change into an animal, or hurl lightning bolts from the sky! Also, the Greeks believed the gods were immortal—which means that they never died, but lived forever.

The ancient Greeks believed the gods and goddesses lived on a mountain that rose high above the clouds, called Mount Olympus. From there, they looked down on the earth, and they used their powers to help the people they liked or hurt the people they didn't like.

古代ギリシャの神話
英雄と怪物、神々

　ここに紹介するのは、2000年、あるいはそれ以上も昔から語り伝えられてきた物語で、その起源は古代ギリシャまでさかのぼる。私たちはこうした物語を「神話」と呼んでいる。神話の多くは、勇敢な英雄、激しい戦い、恐ろしい怪物、神や女神についての物語である。その中には、なぜ季節や火山があるのか、星座がどのようにして生まれたのかを説明する神話もある。もちろん、こんにちの私たちはこうした現象が起こる本当の理由を知っている。しかし、遠い昔、多くの人々は神話が真実であると信じていた。今の私たちは古い神話をそのまま信じてはいないが、それでも神話を好んで語るのは、とてもすばらしい物語だからだ。

　これまでに学んできたほかの古代文明の人々と同じように、古代ギリシャ人も多くの男神や女神を信じていた。ギリシャ人は神々を礼拝するためにパルテノンのような美しい神殿を建てた。ギリシャ神話では、男神と女神のすることは、ときに普通の人間——あなたや私のような——と同じだったりする。彼らも食べて飲んで眠らなければならないのだ。いっとき喜んでいたかと思うと、次の瞬間には怒っているということもある。恋に落ちることもあれば、結婚もする。騙しあいもする。言い争いになって喧嘩をすることもある。

　しかし、人間と違って、ギリシャの神々には魔法の力があった。動物に姿を変えることのできる神もいれば、空から稲妻で攻撃することのできる神までいるのだ。また、ギリシャ人は神々が不滅だと信じていた——けっして死ぬことがなく、永遠に生きるのだと。

　古代ギリシャ人は、神や女神がオリンポスという、雲の上に高くそびえる山の頂に暮らしていると考えていた。そこから神々は地上を見下ろし、神力を使って、気に入った人間は助け、気に入らない人間は傷つけたりした。

Greek Gods and Goddesses ギリシャの神々

Zeus, the king of the gods, controlled the heavens and decided arguments among the gods. He could change his shape in an instant. When he was angry, he had the power to throw lightning bolts down from the heavens!

ゼウスは神々の王であり、天を支配し、神々の間の争いを裁いた。彼は瞬時にみずからの姿を変えることができた。怒りを覚えたときには、なんと天から稲妻を投げつけることもできた。

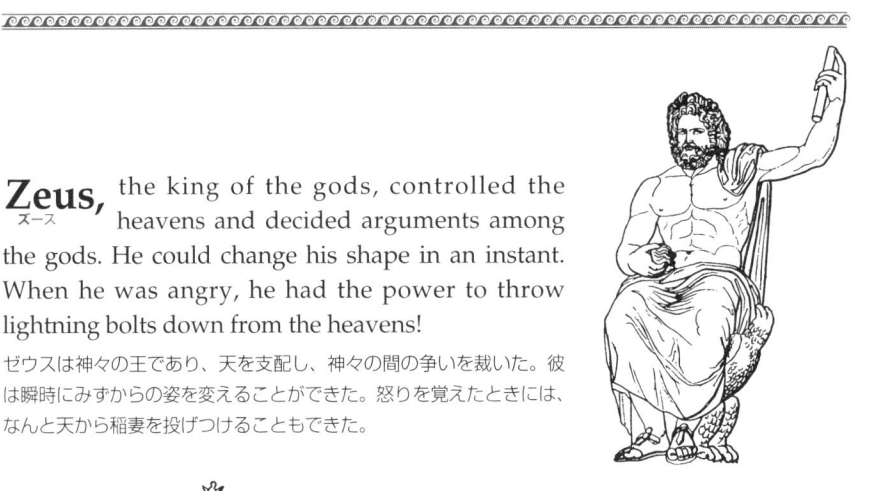

Hera, the wife of Zeus, was queen of the gods and the goddess of marriage. She could be a very jealous person. But her husband, Zeus, had a habit of falling in love with many other goddesses and women, so Hera usually had a good reason to be jealous.

ヘラはゼウスの妻、神々の女王であり、結婚を司る女神であった。彼女はひどく嫉妬深くなることがあった。しかし彼女の夫ゼウスにはしょっちゅう女神や人間の女に恋をしてしまう悪い癖があったので、ヘラが嫉妬するのも、たいていの場合はもっともなことであった。

Poseidon, the god of the sea, was an especially important god to the Greeks. Poseidon could make the oceans as calm as a sleeping baby, or he could stir up high waves to crush a ship to pieces. Poseidon has a long beard and holds a trident, a kind of long pitchfork with three prongs.

ポセイドンは海の神であり、ギリシャ人にとってとりわけ重要な神であった。ポセイドンは海を眠っている赤ん坊のように穏やかにすることもできたし、高波を起こして船を木端微塵に壊してしまうこともできた。ポセイドンは長いあごひげを生やし、三叉の矛——先端が3つに分かれた柄の長い熊手のようなもの——を持っている。

Apollo, a son of Zeus, was the god of light. He is sometimes called Phoebus Apollo. "Phoebus" means "brilliant" or "shining." He was also the god of poetry and music. No one could sing so beautifully or play so sweetly on the lyre (an instrument like a small harp). He was also the god of healing, as well as the god of archery.

アポロはゼウスの息子で、太陽の神であった。彼はポイボス・アポロと呼ばれることもある。「ポイボス」とは「輝かしい」あるいは「光り輝く」といった意味である。彼はまた詩と音楽の神でもあった。アポロのように美しく歌い、竪琴(小さなハープのような楽器)を優美に奏でる者はいなかった。彼はさらに癒しの神であり、弓術の神でもあった。

Aphrodite was the goddess of love and beauty. She had a son called Eros, though you may know him by a more familiar name, Cupid. Maybe you've seen a picture of him on Valentine's Day cards. The Greeks said that when Aphrodite wanted someone to fall in love, she ordered Eros to shoot that person with one of his magic arrows. If he hit you with an arrow, then you would fall in love with the first person you saw!

アフロディテは愛と美の女神であった。彼女にはエロスという息子がいたが、エロスよりもキューピッドという名前のほうがおなじみかもしれない。おそらくバレンタイン・デイのカードに描かれたキューピッドの絵を見たことがあるのではないだろうか。アフロディテが誰かに恋心を吹き込みたいと思ったときには、魔法の矢でその人を射るようエロスに命じるのだとギリシャ人は信じていた。エロスの矢で射られると、なんとそのあと最初に出会った人に恋をしてしまうのだ。

Hephaestus
ヘフェスタス

was the god of fire and the forge. He could cause volcanoes, making the earth spit up hot flames and lava. (The word, "volcano," comes from the Roman name for this god, Vulcan.) But most of all he used fire to make things. He used it to heat metal and make armor, swords, and spears, or beautiful cups and shining jewelry. Hephaestus was lame, and spent his time working at his fiery forge.

ヘーパイストスは炎と鍛冶の神であった。彼は火山を噴火させ、大地から熱い炎や溶岩を噴き出させることができた。(「火山 volcano」という言葉は、この神のローマ名であるウルカヌスVulcanに由来する) だが、彼が火を使ったのはなによりもまず物を作るためであった。金属を熱して鎧、剣、槍、あるいは美しい杯や輝く宝石を作ったのだ。ヘーパイストスは足が不自由だったので、自分の鍛冶場で働くのに多くの時間を費やした。

Hades
ヘイディーズ

was the grim god of the underworld, the dark and shadowy underground place that the Greeks believed people went to when they died. The Greeks often called this place Hades, the same name as the god who ruled there over the dead.

ハデスは黄泉の国の恐ろしい神であった。黄泉の国とは地下にある、暗く影におおわれた土地で、ギリシャ人は死ぬとそこへ行くのだと信じていた。ギリシャ人はこの場所のことを、そこで死者を支配する神の名前と同じように、ハデスと呼んだ。

Hermes,
ハーミーズ

the messenger god, carried commands from the gods to humans on earth. In pictures, he often has wings on his hat or sandals to show how fast he traveled.

ヘルメスは伝令の神であり、神々の命令を地上の人間に伝えた。絵の中では、彼の帽子やサンダルにはたいてい翼がついており、いかに速く移動できるかがわかる。

Athena was the goddess of wisdom. For the
アスィーナ people of the Greek city called Athens,
she was a special goddess, for they believed she protected their city. She had a most unusual birth. One day Zeus had a terrible headache. He complained to Hephaestus, who took his hammer and struck Zeus on the head! Out of Zeus's head jumped Athena, already grown-up and fully dressed in a suit of armor.

アテナは知恵の女神であった。アテナイと呼ばれるギリシャの都市に暮らす人々にとって、彼女は特別な女神であった。というのも、アテナイの人々は彼女が都市を守ってくれていると考えていたからだ。彼女はとても風変わりな生まれかたをした。ある日、ゼウスはひどい頭痛に苦しんでいた。ゼウスがヘーパイストスにそのことを訴えると、ヘーパイストスはなんと金槌を取りだし、ゼウスの頭を叩いたのだ。するとゼウスの頭から、すでに大人の姿で、鎧一式を身につけたアテナが飛び出してきた。

Same Gods, Different Names 神々の別名

The gods and goddesses of the ancient Greeks were later worshiped by the people of ancient Rome. If you look in your library for books of myths, you may find that some books use the Greek names for the gods while others use the Roman names. Here's a chart to help you keep track of who's who.

古代ギリシャの神々、女神たちは、のちに古代ローマ人たちにも崇拝された。図書館で神話関係の本を開いてみると、ギリシャ系の名前を使っている本もあればローマ系の名前を使っている本もある。そんなときのための神々の名前の対照表がこれだ。

Greek name ギリシャ名	Roman name ローマ名	Greek name ギリシャ名	Roman name ローマ名
Zeus	Jupiter (or Jove)	Artemis	Diana
Hera	Juno	Hermes	Mercury
Poseidon	Neptune	Hephaestus	Vulcan
Apollo	Apollo	Athena	Minerva
Hades	Pluto	Aphrodite	Venus

Prometheus Brings Fire, Pandora Brings Woe
プロミーシュース
バンドーラ

Once, only the gods on Mount Olympus had fire. On earth, the people had nothing to give them light in the darkness, or warm them on a cold night, or cook their food.

A brave and powerful giant named Prometheus felt sorry for mankind. He stole fire from the gods and took it to the people on earth.

When Zeus, king of the gods, found out what Prometheus had done, he was furious. To punish him, he had Prometheus tied to a rock with unbreakable chains. Day after day, a fierce eagle flew down and ripped and clawed at the body of poor Prometheus. (Much later, Prometheus was finally set free by a hero named Hercules—but that's another story.)

Now, Zeus looked down on the earth and said, "Let the people keep their fire. I will make them a hundred times more miserable than they were before they had it." And so he told Hephaestus to use his skills to make a woman at his forge. Zeus called this woman Pandora, and when he breathed life into her, she was as sweet and lovely as the flowers in spring. He sent Pandora to earth, and he gave her a closed box and told her never to open it.

But Pandora was very, very curious. Every time she looked at the box she wanted to know what was in it. She knew very well that Zeus had told her not to open it. But, she said to herself, what harm could it do to take just one little peek inside? And so she lifted the lid. Out from the box flew all the bad things in the world—pain, disease, disaster, sorrow, jealousy, and hatred.

But some people say there was one more thing in Pandora's box—hope. Hope is what keeps people going despite all the bad things in the world.

LANGUAGE ARTS • 国 語

火をもたらしたプロメテウス、
苦悩をもたらしたパンドラ

　かつて、オリンポス山の神々だけが火を持っていた。地上の人間には暗闇を照らしたり、寒い夜に暖をとったり、食物を調理したりするすべはなかった。

　プロメテウスという名の勇敢で力強い巨人は、人間をかわいそうに思った。彼は神々から火を盗むと、それを地上の人間たちにもたらした。

　神々の王であるゼウスは、プロメテウスの行いを知って激怒した。罰として、ゼウスはプロメテウスを切断できない鎖でもって岩に縛りつけた。くる日もくる日も、獰猛な鷲が舞い降りては、あわれなプロメテウスの体をくちばしでついばみ、爪で引き裂いた。（ずっと後になって、プロメテウスはついにヘラクレスという英雄によって鎖を解かれる──が、それはまた別の話だ）

　ゼウスは地上を見下ろして言った。「人間には火を持たせておこう。そのかわり持っていなかったころより、100倍もみじめな思いを味わわせてやる」。ゼウスはヘーパイストスに、鍛冶の作業場で腕によりをかけて女を1人作るよう命じた。ゼウスはこの女をパンドラと名づけて命を吹き込むと、彼女は春に咲く花のようにしとやかで美しい女となった。ゼウスは、パンドラを地上に送りこむときにふたの閉まった箱を持たせ、けっして開けてはならないぞと言い聞かせた。

　ところが、パンドラはどうしても箱のことが気になってしかたがない。箱を見るたびに、パンドラは中に何が入っているのか知りたくなった。ゼウスに開けてはならないと言われていたことはよく承知していた。でも、と彼女は思った。ほんのちょっとなら、覗いてみたって悪くはないわ。こうして彼女はふたを持ち上げた。箱の中から飛び出してきたのは、この世のありとあらゆる悪だった──苦痛、病気、災い、悲しみ、嫉妬、そして憎しみ。

　ただし、パンドラの箱にはもう1つ、「希望」が入っていたとも言われている。希望とは、あらゆる悪の存在にもかかわらず、人々の生きる支えとなるものだ。

Oedipus and the Sphinx

Long ago, near the Greek city of Thebes, there lived a terrible creature called the Sphinx. She had the face of a woman but the body of a lion with wings. When travelers came to the city, she would swoop down upon them. Then she would ask them a riddle. If they could answer the riddle, she would let them go. But if they couldn't, she would eat them! So far, no one could answer the riddle. Everyone in Thebes lived in fear of the monster.

Then one day a very smart and brave young man named Oedipus was on his way to Thebes. When the Sphinx saw him, she smiled, for she thought she would soon have a tasty lunch.

"Answer this riddle," she said to Oedipus, "or meet your doom. What creature goes on four feet in the morning, on two feet at noon, and on three feet in the evening?"

Oedipus looked up at the Sphinx and said, "Man. In childhood he crawls on his hands and knees, which is like four feet. In the middle of his life, when he is grown up, he walks on two feet. And in the evening of his life, when he is old, he uses a cane, which is like walking on three feet."

Oedipus had solved the riddle! The Sphinx was so angry that she threw herself in the ocean and drowned. And the people of Thebes were so grateful to Oedipus that they made him their new king.

Daedalus and Icarus

As you know, the master inventor Daedalus designed the Labyrinth for King Minos. Daedalus also showed Ariadne how Theseus could escape from the Labyrinth. When King Minos found this out, he was so angry that he threw Daedalus in the Labyrinth, along with his young son, Icarus.

Not even the man who invented the Labyrinth could find his way out of it. Would the father and son die there? No—for when Daedalus saw the seagulls flying overhead, he got an idea.

オイディプスとスフィンクス

　遠い昔、ギリシャの町テーベの近くに、スフィンクスというおそろしい怪物がいた。スフィンクスは人間の女の顔を持ち、からだはライオンで、翼が生えていた。旅人が町にやってくると、スフィンクスは空から舞い降りてきて謎かけをするのだ。謎を解くことができたら、旅人は通してもらえる。しかし、もし解くことができなかったら、食べられてしまうのだ。これまで謎を解いた者はいなかった。テーベの人々はみな怪物におびえながら暮らしていた。

　あるとき、オイディプスというたいへん聡明で勇敢な青年がテーベに向かっていた。スフィンクスは彼を見るとにやりとした。これでおいしい昼食にありつけそうだと思ったのだ。

「謎を解いてみよ」とスフィンクスはオイディプスに言った。「さもなければ死だ。朝は4本足、昼は2本足、夕方は3本足で歩く生き物とは？」

　オイディプスはスフィンクスを見上げて言った。「人間だ。小さいころは両手と両膝をついて這いまわるから、これは4本足のようなものだ。人生の半ば、成長したときには、2本の足で立って歩く。そして晩年になって年をとると、人は杖をついて歩くから、これは3本足のようなものだ」

　オイディプスはみごとに謎を解いてみせたのだ。スフィンクスは怒りのあまり、海に身を投げて溺れてしまった。テーベの人々はオイディプスに感謝して、彼を新しい王として迎え入れた。

NOTE
スフィンクス
エジプトのスフィンクスは腹ばいのライオンで、頭部はファラオの顔をかたどっている。最大にしてもっとも有名なものはナイル川西岸にあるギザのスフィンクス。紀元前2700年–紀元前2500年頃造られたらしい。
　一方、紀元前6–7世紀頃の絵や彫刻に残っている古代ギリシャのスフィンクスは、体はライオンだが女の顔を持ち、翼が生えていて、起き上がっている姿が特徴的だ。悪霊、死者の世界などを体現していたが、そのために魔よけにもなると考えられた。
　なお、スフィンクスはギリシャ語である。エジプトのスフィンクスの方が古いが、名称がなかったために、ギリシャ語で呼ばれるようになった。

ダイダロスとイカロス

　ミノス王のために迷宮を設計したのは、あの発明の達人ダイダロスであった。彼はまた、どうすればテセウスが迷宮を脱出できるかをアリアドネに教えてあげた。これを知ったミノス王は激怒して、ダイダロスを息子のイカロスとともに迷宮にほうりこんでしまった。

　迷宮を設計した本人でさえ出口を見つけることはできなかった。父と息子は迷宮の中で死んでしまうのだろうか？　そうではなかっ

Little by little, he gathered many feathers. He fastened them together with wax, and so made two pairs of wings like those of a bird. He put one pair on himself and the other pair on Icarus. He showed his son how to move his arms and catch the wind with his wings.

"Now, son," he said, "let us fly away from here. But listen carefully. Do not fly too high, or you will get too close to the sun, and the wax on your wings will melt."

Daedalus and Icarus flew up out of the Labyrinth, over the sea, away from the island of Crete. "Oh," cried Icarus, "it's wonderful to be free and flying through the air!"

"Yes," said Daedalus, "but do not fly too close to the sun."

A puff of wind lifted Icarus up. He was so excited that he forgot what his father told him. Higher and higher he flew, toward the highest heavens.

The warm sun began to melt the wax, and one by one the feathers fell from his wings. Then down, down, down fell Icarus into the sea. Daedalus cried out in grief as he saw the waters close over his son far below.

The Labors of Hercules
ハーキャリーズ

Hercules was the strongest man on earth. But he did not always use his strength wisely. Once, in a fit of anger, he struck and killed someone, though he did not mean to. He went to the temple of Apollo to ask what he could do to make up for his terrible mistake. He was told to go to the home of his cousin, a king named Eurystheus, and do whatever the king asked him to do.

King Eurystheus was a weak, mean man, and he was jealous of his big, strong cousin. So when Hercules came to serve him, he tried to think of the most difficult and dangerous tasks he could.

"Hercules," said the king, "for your first labor, go to the land of Nemea. A terrible lion has been killing both cattle and people there. He

た。頭上を飛ぶカモメを見て、ダイダロスはあるアイディアを思いついたのだ。

　少しずつだが、ダイダロスはたくさんの羽根を集めた。その羽根を蝋で固めて、鳥のような翼を2組作ると、その1つを自分の体につけ、もう1つをイカロスにつけさせた。彼は息子に、どのように腕を動かし、翼で風を捉えるかを教えた。

「いいか、息子よ」とダイダロスは言った。「ここから飛んで逃げ出そう。だが、よく聞きなさい。あまり高く飛びすぎてはいけない。太陽に近づきすぎると、翼を固めている蝋が溶けてしまう」

　ダイダロスとイカロスは迷宮から飛び立ち、海を越えてクレタ島を後にした。「ああ」イカロスは叫んだ。「自由に大空を飛ぶのはなんてすばらしいんだろう！」

「そうとも」ダイダロスは言った。「だが、太陽に近づきすぎてはいけない」

　風が吹いてきて、イカロスを高く舞い上がらせた。イカロスは興奮のあまり、父親の言いつけを忘れてしまった。イカロスはどんどん高く飛び、天頂へと近づいていった。

　太陽の熱が蝋を溶かしはじめ、羽根が1枚、また1枚と翼から剥がれ落ちていった。するとイカロスはどんどん海へと落下していくのだった。はるか下方で息子が水の中に消えるのを見て、ダイダロスは悲痛な叫び声をあげた。

ヘラクレスの大仕事

　ヘラクレスは地上でもっとも力の強い男だった。しかし、彼はその力を常に正しいことに使ったわけではない。あるとき、ヘラクレスは、殺すつもりはなかったのに、怒りに駆られて人をなぐり殺してしまった。このおそろしい過ちを償うための神託を仰ぐため、ヘラクレスはアポロン神殿に向かった。彼は従兄であるエウリュステウス王のもとに行き、王の言うことに従うようにとの神託を受けた。

　エウリュステウス王は力もなく根性の悪い男で、大きくてたくましい従弟のヘラクレスを妬ましく思っていた。ヘラクレスが自分のもとにやってくると、王はできるだけ困難で危険な仕事を与えようと知恵をしぼった。

「ヘラクレスよ」と王は言った。「最初の大仕事として、ネメアの

NOTE
ヘラクレスの12の大仕事
12の功業とも難業とも訳されるが、そのうち4つはここに描かれている。他には、聖獣である黄金の角をもつ大鹿の捕獲、イノシシの生け捕り、青銅の爪やくちばしを持つ鳥退治、クレタの牡牛退治などあるが、最後の大仕事は、死者の世界の番犬ケルベロスを地獄から連れてくることであった。

is so strong that he can kill a man with one blow of his huge paw. His hide is so tough that no sword, spear, or arrow can pierce it. You are to kill the Nemean lion, and bring its skin back to me."

"Well," thought the king to himself, "that should be the end of Hercules." But he did not know his cousin's strength. When Hercules found the lion, he jumped on the beast and grabbed him. Then he squeezed with all his might until at last the lion was dead. But how could he take off the lion's skin? When he tried to use his knife, the blade broke into pieces. Then Hercules got an idea: he used one of the lion's own sharp claws, and sure enough it cut the skin. After he had cleaned the skin, he wrapped it around him like a coat, with the head as a hood.

When Hercules returned, looking like a lion walking on two legs, the king was frightened. "Stay outside the palace," he said, "and I will call out my orders to you."

The king ordered Hercules to kill a fire-breathing, nine-headed monster called the Hydra. Hercules used his huge club to knock off one of the monster's heads, but then two heads grew back in its place! So he grabbed a large stick and set one end on fire. Then, as he swung his club to knock off each head, he held the fire to the neck to keep any other heads from growing back.

When King Eurystheus heard that Hercules had killed the Hydra, he thought, "He kills beasts and monsters so easily that I must think of another kind of labor. Ah, I know! I will send him across the mountains to clean the stables of King Augeas. They are the biggest and dirtiest stables in the world, filled with the waste of thousands of oxen and cattle."

When Hercules reached the Augean stables, he saw that it would take many years for a single man to clean them, even a man as strong as himself. But as he looked around he saw a river that ran nearby. "Why not use that?" he thought. So he asked King Augeas to have all the animals taken out of the stable for a day. Then he dug a ditch from

地に行け。獰猛なライオンが牛や土地の人々を殺しているのだ。恐るべき力の持ち主で、大きな前足で叩かれたら命はない。皮も丈夫で、どんな剣も槍も弓矢も歯が立たない。そのネメアのライオンを退治し、その皮をわたしのところに持って帰ってくるのだ」

「これでよし」と王は考えた。「ヘラクレスも終わりだな」。しかし王はヘラクレスの力をみくびっていた。ヘラクレスはライオンを見つけると、とびかかってつかんだ。そして力の限り絞めつけ、ライオンの息の根を止めた。しかし、どうやって皮を剥げばいいだろう。ナイフを使おうとしたが、刃がぼろぼろにこぼれてしまった。そのときある考えがひらめいた。ライオンのするどい爪を使ってみると、もののみごとに皮は切れた。皮を剥ぎとってしまうと、ヘラクレスはその皮を上着のように体に巻きつけ、切った首を頭にかぶった。

２本足で歩くライオンのような姿で戻ってきたヘラクレスを見て、王はぎくりとした。「宮殿には入らないでくれ」と王は言った。「命令はここから出すことにする」

王はヘラクレスに、口から炎を吹き、９つの頭を持つ怪物ヒドラを退治するよう命じた。ヘラクレスは巨大な棍棒で怪物の頭の１つを叩き落としたが、すぐさま２つの頭が生え出てきた。そこでヘラクレスは長い棒をつかむと、片方の端に火をつけた。そして、棍棒で怪物の頭を叩き落とすたびに火を怪物の首の切り口につけて、新しい頭が出てこないようにした。

ヘラクレスがヒドラを退治したと聞いて、エウリュステウス王は考えた。「猛獣も怪物もたやすく退治してしまうなら、別の大仕事を考えなくては。ああ、そうだ！　山の向こうに遠征させて、アウゲイアス王の畜舎の掃除をさせよう。何千もの牛の汚物にまみれて、あれほど大きくて汚い畜舎は２つとないからな」

アウゲイアス王の畜舎に到着すると、ヘラクレスほどたくましい男の力をもってしても、１人できれいにするには何年もかかりそうだった。しかし、あたりを見回してみると、近くに川が流れていた。「あれを利用してやろう」とヘラクレスは考えた。彼はアウゲイアス王に、すべての動物を１日、外に出してくれるよう頼んだ。それから、川から畜舎まで溝を掘り、建物の中を水が流れるようにした。水はあっという間に汚れを洗い流してしまった。ヘラクレスは溝を埋めると、川の流れを元通りにした。

「よく考えたな、ヘラクレスよ」とエウリュステウス王は言った。「だが、ほんとうに大変な仕事はここからだぞ。つぎの仕事は、３

the river to the stable, and let the water run through the building. The water washed away all the filth in no time. Hercules filled the ditch and set the river back on its normal course.

"Very clever, Hercules," said King Eurystheus. "But now it's time for a real challenge. For your next labor, I order you to bring me the golden apples guarded by those three magical maidens, the Hesperides." The king chuckled because he knew that these apples belonged to Hera, queen of the gods, and were kept in a secret garden that no one had ever found. Hercules knew that he could not find the Hesperides. But he could find their father, Atlas, the great giant who carried the heavens and earth upon his shoulders.

"Mighty Atlas," said Hercules, "will you tell me where to find the golden apples of the Hesperides?"

"I cannot tell you such a secret," said Atlas. "But I could get the apples for you myself, if only I did not have to hold the heavens and earth on my shoulders."

"Go and get the apples," said Hercules, "and I will hold the heavens and earth for you."

"I would be glad to have someone else carry this load for a while," said Atlas. So Hercules took the heavens and earth upon his own shoulders. His knees shook and he gasped, "Hurry, Atlas, for I do not know how long I can hold this."

In a short while Atlas came back with the golden apples, but he did not hand them over. "Hercules," he said, "I will take these apples to King Eurystheus myself." Hercules could see that Atlas did not plan to come back. So he said, "Thank you, Atlas, that is kind of you. But before you go, would you please hold the heavens and earth for just a moment? I'm not as strong as you so I need to put a pad on my shoulders to ease the pain."

"All right," said Atlas. He put down the apples and took the load from Hercules's shoulders.

"Thanks for the apples," said Hercules, and he hurried off.

After Hercules completed these and other labors, the gods allowed him to leave King Eurystheus. He traveled all over Greece, doing many great deeds wherever he went.

人の魔法の乙女、ヘスペリデスたちに守られた黄金のりんごをわたしのもとに持ってくることだ」。王はひそかにほくそ笑んだ。りんごは神々の女王であるヘラのもので、まだ誰も見つけたことのない秘密の園に隠されているからだ。ヘラクレスはヘスペリデスたちを見つけることなどできないことは分かっていた。しかし、彼女たちの父で天と地をその肩に背負った巨人アトラスなら見つけ出せる。
「偉大なるアトラス」とヘラクレスは言った。「ヘスペリデスたちの守る黄金のりんごはどこに行けば見つかりますか？」
「そんな秘密を教えるわけにはいかない」とアトラスは言った。「わたしがそのりんごを取ってきてやることはできるが、あいにくわたしは天と地をこの肩に背負っていなくてはならぬのだ」
「りんごを取ってきてください」とヘラクレスは言った。「わたしがあなたの代わりに天と地を支えています」
「この重荷をしばらく背負ってもらえるとはありがたい」とアトラスは言った。そこでヘラクレスは天と地をみずからの肩に背負った。彼はその重さにひざを震わせ、あえぎながらこう言った。「急いでください、アトラス、どのくらい持ちこたえられるか分かりません」
　まもなくアトラスは黄金のりんごを持ってもどってきたが、それを渡そうとはしなかった。「ヘラクレスよ」とアトラスは言った。「わたしがこれをエウリュステウス王に届けてやろう」。アトラスはもどってくるつもりなどないのだ。そこでヘラクレスはこう言った。「ありがとうございます、アトラス、わざわざご親切に。でも行く前に、天と地をちょっとのあいだ持ってもらえませんか？　わたしにはあなたほどの力はないので、痛みを和らげるために肩当てが必要です」
「いいだろう」とアトラスは言い、りんごを置いて、ヘラクレスの肩から重荷を引き受けた。
「りんごをありがとう」そう言うと、ヘラクレスは急いでその場を去った。
　ヘラクレスがこうした大仕事に加え、ほかの仕事も無事終えると、神々は彼に王のもとから離れることを許した。ヘラクレスはギリシャ中を旅して回り、行く先々で数々の偉業を行った。

NOTE スポーツの英語

Line up! (整列!)
On your mark! Get set! Go! (位置について、用意、ドン)
calisthenics (体操)
track and field (陸上競技)
long jump (幅跳び)
high jump (高跳び)
pole vault (棒高跳び)
vaulting horse (跳び箱) ＊vault は跳び越えるという意味。
push-ups (腕立て伏せ)
pull-ups (懸垂) ＊chin up ともいう。
sit-ups (腹筋運動)

> ＊以下のような日本で体育の時間に使われる号令は、アメリカでは軍隊用語で、学校では使わない。
>
> **Attention!** (気をつけ!)
> **Stand at arm's length!** (前へならえ!)
> **About face!** (回れ右!)

NOTE 遊びの英語

(play) tag (鬼ごっこ) ＊鬼は it という。
(play) hide-and-seek (かくれんぼ)
kick-the-can (缶けり)
jump rope, skip rope (縄跳び) ＊「君の番だよ」は It's your turn。
Let's race. (かけっこしよう) ＊I'll race you ともいう。
catch (キャッチボール)
＊「キャッチボールをしよう」は Let's play catch。

What American 3rd GRADERS Learn in Textbooks

LANGUAGE ARTS • 国 語

Perseus and Medusa
バースィアス　　　　メデューサ

This ancient myth describes the Gorgons, who were frightening female monsters with snakes for hair.

There was once a lovely young woman, so lovely that Zeus himself, the king of the gods, fell in love with her. Together they had a son, named Perseus. The father of the young woman was horrified, because it had been predicted that he would be killed by his own grandson. So he put his daughter and her baby boy into a chest and threw them into the sea.

They floated for many days and finally washed up on an island shore, where they made a home. Perseus grew up to be a strong and handsome young man.

Now, the king of the island was also cruel. He wanted Perseus's mother all to himself. He assigned Perseus to a great adventure, but he really intended a task so difficult that Perseus would not survive.

"Bring me the head of Medusa," said the king.

"Medusa?" asked Perseus in wonder. Medusa was a Gorgon, a hideous monster with a head full of snakes. She turned a man to stone the minute he looked her in the eye. No one could approach Medusa, let alone cut her head off! But Perseus accepted the challenge.

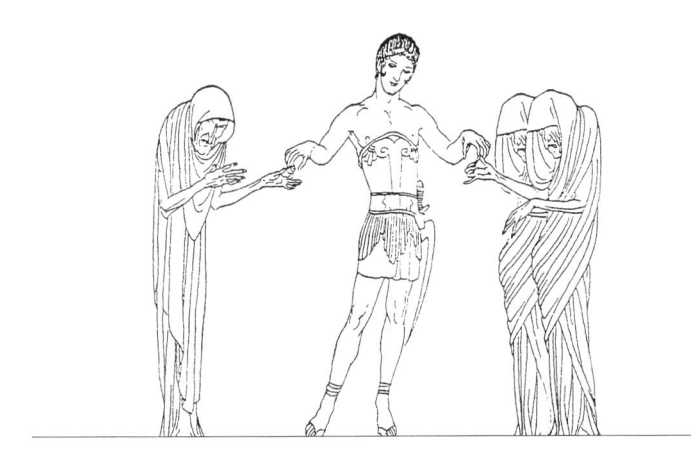

ペルセウスとメドゥーサ

　これは毛髪のように頭に蛇が巣食っている恐ろしい女の怪物ゴルゴンについての古代の神話である。

　昔、若く美しい娘がいた。あまりに美しいので、神々の王であるゼウスでさえ恋に落ちてしまった。2人の間には息子ができて、ペルセウスと名づけられた。娘の父親は恐怖におののいた。というのも、自分の孫に殺されるだろうという予言を宣告されていたからだ。そこで彼は、娘と赤ん坊を箱にいれて海に流してしまった。
　娘と赤ん坊は何日も漂流したすえ、ある島の浜辺に流れ着き、そこで暮らすことになった。ペルセウスは強く美しい若者に成長した。
　ところが、この島の王もまた非情であった。彼はペルセウスの母親をわがものにしようとした。彼はペルセウスを大冒険の旅に立たせたが、実は、ペルセウスが生還できないような困難な任務を与えようと企んだのである。
「メドゥーサの首を持ってくるのだ」と王は言った。
「メドゥーサですって？」驚いたペルセウスは訊きかえした。メドゥーサはゴルゴンの1人で、頭にたくさんの蛇が巣食っているおそろしい怪物だ。その目を見つめた者を一瞬のうちに石に変えてしまう。メドゥーサに近づける者はいないというのに、その首をはねるなんて！　しかしペルセウスはこの難題を引き受けた。
　ゼウスはヘルメスを使者に立てて、ペルセウスへの贈り物を届けさせた。
「あなたの父親に命じられて、神々の暮らすオリンポス山から、3つの品物を持ってきました」とヘルメスは言った。「知恵の女神アテナからは、くもりなく光る真鍮の楯を。冥界の神ハデスからは、かぶると姿が見えなくなる兜を。そしてわたくしからは、なんでも1振りで切ってしまう剣です」。さらにヘルメスは、翼のついたサンダルを脱ぐと、それをペルセウスに与えた。
　神々からの贈り物を得て、ペルセウスはいっそうの勇気を得た。彼はヘルメスに礼を述べ、また、偉大なるゼウスをはじめとする神々たちへの感謝を彼に託した。「ところで、メドゥーサという怪

Zeus sent his messenger, Hermes, with gifts for Perseus.

"Your father has sent me from Mount Olympus, home of the gods, with three things," said Hermes. "From Athena, the goddess of wisdom, here is a bright brass shield. From Hades, the god of the underworld, here is a helmet to make you invisible. And from me, here is a sword that cuts through anything with one stroke." Then Hermes took the winged sandals off his feet and gave them to Perseus.

With gifts from the gods, Perseus felt even braver. He thanked Hermes, and through him all the gods, including great Zeus. "But where will I find this monster Medusa?" he asked.

"You must put that question to the Three Gray Sisters," said Hermes. "These three women share a single eye. They live together in a deep, dark cave at the western edge of the world."

Perseus traveled for days and nights until he came to a twilight land. There he stood at the opening of a deep, dark cave and listened as the Three Gray Sisters mumbled among themselves.

"Someone is coming," said the first sister. "I can feel him."

"Someone is coming," said the second sister. "I can hear him."

"Someone is coming," said the third sister. "I can see him with my eye."

"Give me the eye," said the first.

"No, me," said the second, "so I can see, too!"

As they struggled over the one eye they shared, Perseus grabbed it. A howl shot up from all three sisters when they realized that not one of them had the precious eye anymore.

物はどこにいるのでしょう」と彼は訊ねた。
「それは〈3人の老婆〉に訊くといい」とヘルメスは答えた。「老婆たちは1つの目を共有していて、西の果てにある深く暗い洞窟にいっしょに暮らしている」
　ペルセウスは何日ものあいだ昼も夜も旅を続けて、たそがれの地にたどり着いた。深く暗い洞窟の入口に立ったペルセウスは、〈3人の老婆〉がひそひそ話し合う声に耳をすました。
「誰かがやってくる」と、最初の老婆が言った。「ほら、けはいがするよ」
「誰かがやってくる」と、2番目の老婆が言った。「ほら、足音が聞こえるよ」
「誰かがやってくる」と、3番目の老婆が言った。「ほら、男の姿がこの目で見えるもの」
「目をお貸し」と、最初の老婆が言った。
「いや、こっちが先だよ」と2番目の老婆が言った。「わたしも見るんだから！」
　老婆たちが1つの目を取り合っているすきに、ペルセウスはその目を奪い取ってしまった。誰も大切な眼球を持っていないと気づくと、3人は怒りの叫び声をあげた。
「おばあさんがた、怖れることはない」とペルセウスはなだめた。「ゴルゴンのメドゥーサの居どころを教えてくれれば、目は返します」
　老婆たちはペルセウスにメドゥーサの居場所を教えた。ヘルメスのサンダルを履いたペルセウスは陸を越え、海を越え、ゴルゴンの住む地へと飛んでいった。着いてみればそこに、3人の手ごわい怪物が横になって眠っていた。いちばん大きくて恐ろしいのがメドゥーサだった。
　ペルセウスは姿の見えなくなる兜をかぶって、メドゥーサに自分が近づくのを気づかれないようにした。曇りなく光る楯を持ち上げて、メドゥーサと視線を合わせずに鏡のような楯にメドゥーサの顔が映るようにした。ペルセウスは、ヘルメスの翼のついたサンダルの助けを借りてメドゥーサに近づいていき、剣を振りかざすと、一振りで恐ろしいメドゥーサの首をはねた。メドゥーサの頭に生えた蛇たちがのたうち、シューシューと音を立てた。ペルセウスはメドゥーサの首を山羊皮の袋に入れると、すぐにその場から飛び去った。
　冷酷な王が母親を捕らえている島に戻ると、ペルセウスは王座に

"Never fear, good women," said Perseus. "I will return your eye as long as you tell me where I will find the Gorgon Medusa."

The sisters told Perseus how to find Medusa. With Hermes's sandals on his feet, he flew over land and sea to the land of the Gorgons. There they were, three massive monsters, lying asleep. The biggest and most horrible one was Medusa.

Perseus put on the helmet of invisibility so that Medusa would not see him coming. He held up the bright shield so that his gaze would not meet hers and yet he could see her face, reflected as in a mirror. Aided by Hermes's winged sandals, he approached the Gorgon, raised the sword, and, with one swing, cut the head off the horrible Medusa. The snakes on her head hissed in pain. Perseus shoved her head into a goatskin pouch and instantly flew away.

Returning to the island where the cruel king kept his mother, Perseus approached the throne.

"Just as I suspected," said the king with a smile. "You have come back empty-handed."

"On the contrary," said Perseus. "I have done what you commanded." He pulled Medusa's head out of the goatskin bag. Even in death, with her eyes wide open, the Gorgon had her powers. The evil king looked her straight in the eye and turned to stone.

Cupid and Psyche
キューピッド　サイキ

Have you ever seen Cupid, that little boy with wings, on a Valentine's Day card? To the ancient Romans, Cupid was a god. Here is a myth about how he fell in love with a woman.

Once there was a king who had three daughters. The youngest, named Psyche, was the most beautiful of all—so beautiful, in fact, that people began to say she was even more beautiful than Venus, the goddess of beauty.

When Venus heard these claims, she was filled with jealousy. She went to her son, Cupid, and said, "Shoot the girl with one of your arrows and make her fall in love with the ugliest man on earth."

進み出た。
「思ったとおり」と王はにんまりと笑みを浮かべた。「手ぶらで戻ってきたのだな」
「そうではありません」とペルセウスは言った。「言われた通りに目的を達しました」。ペルセウスはメドゥーサの首を山羊皮の袋から取り出した。死んでもなお、目を大きく見開いたゴルゴンの力は失われていなかった。メドゥーサの目を見つめてしまったこの邪悪な王は、たちまち石と化してしまった。

キューピッドとプシュケ

　バレンタイン・デイのカードに、翼のある小さな男の子、キューピッドが描かれているのを見たことがあるだろうか。古代ローマの人々にとって、キューピッドは神の1人だった。これはキューピッドと人間の女の恋を描いた神話である。

　昔、ある王に3人の娘がいた。末娘のプシュケは3人の中でいちばん美しかった——あまりにも美しいので、美の女神であるビーナス以上だと評判が立つほどだった。
　これを聞いたビーナスはひどく嫉妬した。彼女は息子のキューピッドのところに行って、こう命じた。「おまえの矢であの娘を射って、地上でもっとも醜い男を恋するようにしてしまいなさい」
　言いつけに従って、キューピッドは弓矢を持って地上に舞い降りていった。プシュケを射ようと狙いを定めていると、指が滑ってしまい、矢が自分にちくりと刺さって、キューピッドはプシュケに恋をしてしまった。
　キューピッドはプシュケの家族に、神々が望んでいるのは、プシュケが山に登り、神々が夫に選んだ恐ろしい怪物と結婚することだと告げた。プシュケが勇気を出して山を登っていくと、暖かい風が彼女を包みこんだ。ふと気がつくと、彼女は壮麗な宮殿の中にいた。人の姿は見えなかったが、やさしい声が聞こえてきて、すべてはお望みのままにと言うのであった。プシュケは心地よい音楽につつまれて眠りに落ちた。眠っているあいだにキューピッドがやって来た。彼女は夢の中でしか夫に会えないのだ。彼は一晩中そばにいるのだが、夜明けが訪れる前に行ってしまう。来る夜も来る夜もプシュケ

Obediently, Cupid took his bow and arrow and flew down to earth. Just as he was taking aim to shoot Psyche, his finger slipped. He pricked himself with his own arrow and fell in love with Psyche.

Cupid sent a message to Psyche's family, saying that the gods wished her to climb a mountain and marry the husband that they had chosen for her—a terrible monster. Psyche bravely climbed the mountain, feeling a warm wind surround her. Suddenly, she found herself in a magnificent palace. She saw no one, but she heard friendly voices, promising her every desire. She fell asleep, surrounded by sweet music. While she slept, Cupid visited her. She knew her husband only in her dreams. He stayed all night, but left before morning's light. Night after night, Psyche felt her husband come to her in the darkness and leave before morning's light.

One night Psyche asked her husband why he came in darkness. "Why should you wish to see me?" he answered. "I love you, and all I ask is that you love me." Still, Psyche grew more curious. Who was her husband? What did he look like? Why did he hide? Was he indeed a terrible monster?

One night she stayed awake. She waited until she felt him lying by her side, then she lit a lamp. What she saw was no monster, but the lovely face of Cupid himself. Her hand trembled with delight, and a drop of hot oil fell from the lamp onto Cupid's shoulder and awoke him.

"I asked only for your trust," he said sadly. "When trust is gone, love must depart." And away flew Cupid, home to Venus, who scolded him for falling in love with a mere woman.

The moment Cupid flew away, the magnificent palace vanished.

は、夫が暗闇の中をやって来て、夜明け前に去って行くけはいを感じ取っていた。

　ある晩、プシュケは夫になぜ暗くなってからやってくるのか訊ねてみた。「どうしてわたしの姿が見たいんだ？」と彼は答えた。「わたしはおまえを愛している。そして、わたしがおまえに望むのは、わたしを愛してくれることだけなのだ」。しかし、プシュケはますます知りたくなるのだった。わたしの夫は誰なのだろう？　どんな顔かたちをしているんだろう？　どうして姿を隠すのだろう？　ほんとうに恐ろしい怪物なのかしら？

　ある晩、彼女は眠らずにいた。夫がとなりに横たわるのが感じられるまで待って、ランプの明かりを灯した。彼女が見たのは怪物などではなく、あのキューピッドの美しい顔だった。ランプを持つ彼女の手は喜びに震え、オイルの熱いしずくがランプからキューピッドの肩にしたたり落ちると、キューピッドは目を覚ました。
「わたしが求めていたのは信じる気持ちだけだったのに」とキューピッドは悲しそうに言った。「信じる気持ちが失われたら、愛も終わりだ」。そう言うと、キューピッドはビーナスのもとに飛び去っていった。ビーナスは、人間の女と恋に落ちるなんて、とキューピッドを叱った。

　キューピッドが飛び去っていくやいなや、壮麗な宮殿は消えてしまった。昼も夜もプシュケはさまよい歩き、失われた愛を探し求めた。そしてとうとう彼女はビーナスの神殿にやって来た。「身のほど知らずにも夫を見つけに来たのか、この醜女（しこめ）が」。ビーナスは叫んだ。彼女はプシュケに、小麦、粟、大麦、マメなどのいり混じった大きな穀物の山を見せた。「この穀物を朝までに選り分けなさい」。ビーナスは笑い、姿を消した。

　プシュケにはそんな仕事などできるはずがないと分かっていた。すると、涙に濡れる目に、穀物が1粒、また1粒、そしてつぎつぎと動き出すのが見えた。蟻の大群が彼女を助けにやって来て、粒を運んでは、それぞれ種類ごとの山に選り分けているのだった。

　ビーナスは言いつけた仕事が終わっているのを見ると、怒り狂った。「つぎの仕事はこんなに易しくないわよ」と彼女は言った。「この箱を持って地下の冥界に行き、その地の女王プロセルピナに頼んで、わたしのために美しさを少し譲ってもらってきなさい」

　冥界だって？　そこに行ってもどってこられる人間などいない。そのとき突然、声が聞こえてきた。「お金を持っていって、冥界の

Night and day Psyche wandered, searching for her lost love. At last she went to the temple of Venus herself. "You dare to come seeking a husband, you ugly girl?" Venus cried. She showed Psyche a huge pile of grain—wheat, millet, barley, and lentils. "Separate this grain by morning." Venus laughed, then disappeared.

Psyche knew the task was impossible. Then, looking through her tears, she noticed a seed moving, then another, and then many more. An army of ants had come to her aid, each carrying a seed and dividing the seeds into separate piles.

Venus was furious to find the work done. "Your next task will not be so easy," she said. "Take this box into the underworld and ask the queen of that realm, Proserpina, to send me a little of her beauty."

The underworld? No mortal could return. Suddenly, a voice spoke to her. "Take a coin to the boatman who will carry you across the river to the underworld. Take a cake to calm the mean three-headed dog who guards the underworld. And this above all: once Proserpina has placed beauty in the box, do not open it."

Following the mysterious voice, Psyche journeyed safely to the underworld, and Proserpina sent a box of beauty back with her to Venus.

But Psyche could not help wondering what was inside the box. She lifted the lid and peeked inside. A deep sleep came over her, and Psyche fell senseless to the ground.

Meanwhile, Cupid's love for Psyche had grown stronger than ever. Finding her lying on the ground, he took the sleep from her body. "See what curiosity gets you?" Cupid said, smiling, as she awoke.

While Psyche delivered the box to Venus, Cupid begged Jupiter, the king of the gods, to bless their marriage. Jupiter invited Psyche to drink ambrosia of the gods, and she became immortal. In the marriage of Cupid and Psyche, Love and the Soul (which is what the word "psyche" means today) were united at last and forever.

川を渡してくれる船頭に与えなさい。お菓子を持っていって、頭が3つある冥界の凶暴な番犬をなだめなさい。それから、これがいちばん大切なことだが、プロセルピナが美しさを箱に収めたら、決してその箱を開いてはならない」

　不思議な声に導かれたプシュケが無事に冥界にたどり着くと、プロセルピナはビーナスに届けるようにと美しさを封じ込めた箱をプシュケに託した。

　しかし、プシュケは箱の中身を知りたいという気持ちを押えきれなかった。彼女はふたを開けて中をそっとのぞいてみた。すると強い眠気に襲われて意識を失い、プシュケは地面に倒れこんでしまった。

　一方、キューピッドのプシュケへの愛はやるせないほどに高まっていた。彼女が地面に横たわっているのを見つけると、キューピッドは彼女のからだから眠気を取り去ってやった。「好奇心を抱くとどうなるか分かったかい？」目を覚ます彼女に、キューピッドはほほ笑みながら言った。

　プシュケがビーナスに箱を届けに行っているあいだ、キューピッドは神々の王であるジュピターに、2人の結婚を祝福してくれるよう頼んだ。ジュピターはプシュケに神々の飲み物であるアムブロシアを飲むようにと言い、かくしてプシュケは不死の身となった。キューピッドとプシュケの結婚によって、〈愛〉と〈魂〉——現在「プシュケ」といえば魂を意味する——は永遠に1つのものとなった。

The Sword of Damocles
ダマクリーズ

This story comes to us from ancient Rome. Many people still use the phrase "sword of Damocles" to speak of danger that is always present.

Damocles looked with envy on his friend Dionysius, the king of Syracuse. He believed that the king had a very good life—all the riches and all the power that anyone could imagine.

"You think I'm lucky?" Dionysius said to him one day. "If you think so, let's trade places. You sit here, on the throne, for just one day and see if you still think I'm lucky."

Damocles eagerly accepted his friend's invitation. He ordered servants to bring him fine robes and a great banquet of food. He ordered expensive wine and fine music as he dined. He sat back, sure that he was the happiest man in the world.

Then he looked up. He caught his breath in fear. Above his head, a sword dangled from the ceiling attached by a single strand of horse's hair. Damocles could not speak, could not eat, could not enjoy the music. He could not even move.

"What is the matter, my friend?" asked Dionysius.

"How can I conduct my life with that sword hanging above me?" Damocles said.

"How indeed?" answered Dionysius. "And now you know how it feels to be king. That sword hangs over my head every minute of every day. There is always the chance the thread will break. An advisor may turn on me or an enemy spy may attack me. Even I might make an unwise decision that brings my downfall. The privilege of power brings dangers."

ダモクレスの剣

　この物語は古代ローマから伝わるものだ。こんにちでも多くの人々が、つねに身近に迫っている危険ということに触れるときに、「ダモクレスの剣」という表現を使う。

　ダモクレスは、友人でもあるシラクサの王ディオニュソスにたいして羨望の念をいだいていた。彼は王が想像しうる限りのあらゆる富と権力を手中におさめ、とても満ち足りた人生を送っていると思ったのだ。
「わたしが幸運だと思うのか？」ある日、ディオニュソスは彼に言った。「そう思うのなら、立場を取りかえてみよう。1日だけでいいからこの王座に座ってみて、それでもわたしが幸運だと君が思うかどうか試してみようじゃないか」
　ダモクレスはよろこんで友人の提案に応じた。彼は召使たちに、立派な王衣と山のようなごちそうを持ってくるように命じた。食事をするときには、高価なワインと洗練された音楽を用意させた。椅子にゆったりと座って、自分は世界でいちばん幸せな男だと感じていた。
　そのときふと彼は上を見て、恐怖に息をのんだ。頭上には、剣が天井から、1本の馬の毛で吊るされていたのだ。ダモクレスはしゃべることも、食事も、音楽を楽しむこともできなかった。身動きさえできなかった。
「どうしたというんだい？」とディオニュソスは訊ねた。
「頭上に剣がぶら下がっていたら、ごくふつうの生活などできやしない」とダモクレスは言った。
「まったくそのとおりだ」とディオニュソスは答えた。「いまやおまえにも、王であるということがどんなものか分かっただろう。あの剣は、わたしの頭上に絶えずぶらさがっている。いつ糸が切れてもおかしくはない。参謀の1人が裏切るかもしれないし、敵のスパイに襲われるかもしれない。誤った政治的決断をして失脚することもありうる。権力という特権には危険がつきものなのだよ」

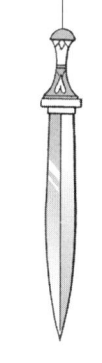

LANGUAGE ARTS・国 語

Sayings and Phrases ことわざと熟語

His bark is worse than his bite
「噛まれるよりも吠え声が恐い」

    People use this saying to describe a person who speaks angrily or threatens but may not be truly dangerous.

このことわざは、怒ったような話し方やおどすような言い方をするけれども、実際に危害を加えたりしないだろうという人のことをいうときに用いる。

Actions speak louder than words
「口よりも行いの方が声は大きい」

    This saying reminds us that what people say does not always show what they think, while what people do reveals their thoughts or beliefs more clearly.

このことわざは、口で言うことがかならずしも心に思っていることではなく、むしろ人の考えていることや思っていることは振る舞いにはっきりと現れるものだということを教えてくれる。

Beat around the bush
「やぶの外ばかりたたく」

    People use this phrase to mean that someone is avoiding direct discussion of a difficult subject by talking instead about related subjects that are less important.

関係はあってもあまり重要ではないことばかり話して、肝心の厄介な問題を正面から議論するのを避けることがあるが、そういう人に対してこの表現を使う。

One rotten apple spoils the whole barrel
「腐ったリンゴ1個が樽全部のリンゴをだめにする」

    This saying means that one bad thing can spoil everything connected with it.

このことわざは、1つの悪いことが、それに関わるすべてに悪影響をもたらすという意味である。

Last straw
「最後のひと藁」

This phrase describes the moment when things have gone too far one way and just have to change. It comes from a legend about a man who piled straw on his camel's back, one at a time. Even though each straw was light, one was the "last straw" that broke the camel's back.

この慣用句を使うのは、ものごとが一方にばかりどんどん進んでしまってなんとか方向転換しなければならないというときだ。この表現は、1本ずつラクダの背中に藁を積み上げていった男の伝説に由来する。藁1本1本は軽いけれども、積もり積もったあとの「最後のひと藁」がついにラクダの背骨を折ってしまったのである。

Beggars can't be choosers
「乞食ならえり好みはできない」

People use this saying to mean that when you are in a weak or disadvantaged position, you shouldn't be picky about the help that may be offered—even if it isn't exactly the sort of help you want.

このことわざは、自分が弱い立場や不利な立場にあるときは、たとえ自分の望みと違っていても、助けにとやかく注文はつけられない、という意味で使われる。

Let bygones be bygones
「過去は過ぎ去るにまかせよ」

People use this saying to mean letting go of whatever is bothering you so it becomes a thing of the past.

悩み事はそのまま過去のことになるのにまかせよというときに、このことわざを使う。

The show must go on
「ショーは続くのだ」

This saying means that no matter what happens, things will continue as planned.

このことわざは、どんなことが起こっても、計画通りにことを進めるという意味である。

MATHEMATICS・算数

The Four Rules of Arithmetic
四則算（加減乗除）

Addition

Addition, the + Sign and the = Sign

Addition means putting numbers together. There are 3 flowers in a glass. You pick 2 more flowers and put them in the glass also. How many flowers are in the glass?

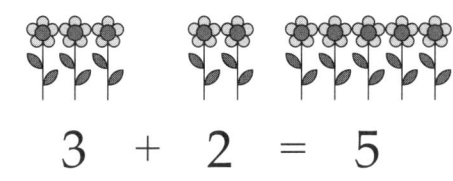

$$3 + 2 = 5$$

The Sum and Ways of Saying Addition

When you add two numbers together, the answer you get is called the sum. The sum of 3+2 is 5. The sum of 3+4 is 7.

There are different ways of saying 3+2=5. People say "three plus two equals five," or "three plus two is five," or "three and two make five." Notice that the + sign can also be read "and," and that people sometimes say "is" or "make" for the = sign.

Addends

Numbers that are added together are called addends. In 5+3=8, 5 and 3 are addends. Remember that in 5+3=8, 8 is called the sum. There can be more than two addends. In 2+3+5=10, 2, 3, and 5 are all addends.

足し算

足し算、+という記号、=という記号

足し算とは数を加えて一緒にすることである。コップの中に花が3本ある。さらに2本花をつんで、そのコップに入れるとする。コップの中にある花の数は？

和と足し算の読み方

2つの数を足して得られる答えを和という。3+2の和は5である。3+4の和は7である。

3+2=5の読み方は何通りかある。「3足す2は5に等しい」とか、「3足す2は5である」、あるいは「3と2で5になる」のようにいう。+の記号を「と」読んだり、ときには=の記号を「である」とか「になる」と言ったりすることを覚えておこう。

加数

足して一緒にする数を加数という。5+3=8では、5と3が加数である。5+3=8の計算式の8を和というが、これは覚えておこう。加数は2つ以上になることもある。2+3+5=10では、2, 3, 5はすべて加数である。

3rd GRADE

$$5 + 3 = 8$$

addend (augend) — 加数（被加数）
addend — 加数
sum — 和

Subtraction | 引き算

Subtraction Means Taking Away
引き算とは数を引くこと

Subtraction means taking a number away. Suppose, there are 5 glasses of grape juice on the table, and Pam takes 2 of the glasses away, and drinks them. How many glasses are left on the table?

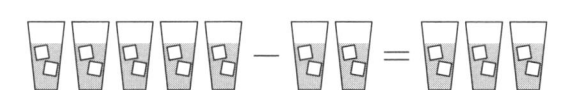

引き算とは、ある数を引くことである。テーブルの上にグレープジュースの入ったコップが5個あったとする。パムがコップ2個を持っていって飲んでしまう。テーブルに残ったコップはいくつ？

Count them. There are 3 glasses left. In numbers, this is written:

$$5 - 2 = 3$$

数えてみよう。コップは3個残っている。これを数字で書き表すとこうなる。

Or it can be spelled out: Five minus two equals three.

それを言葉で言えば、5引く2は3に等しい、となる。

The sign − means minus, and it shows that you are subtracting. You can also say, "Five take away two is three."

−の記号はマイナスの意味で、数を引いていることを示す。「5から2を引くと3」ともいう。

The Difference
差

The number you have left after you subtract is called the difference. So the difference of 7−3 is 4. What is the difference of 4−3? 1, because 4 minus 3 equals 1.

引いたあとに残る数を差という。7−3の差は4である。4−3の差はいくつになるか？ 1である。4引く3は1に等しいからだ。

$$7 - 3 = 4$$

minuend — 被減数
subtrahend — 減数
difference — 差

Multiplication

Multiplication is a quick way of doing addition when you are adding the same number over and over again.

同じ数を何度も足すような足し算をする場合、それをすばやく行うのが掛け算だ。

掛け算

Here is an example. $2+2+2+2+2=10$
You could also say: 5 twos = 10
We write this as a
multiplication problem: $5\times2=10$
We read it: Five times two equals ten.

例をあげよう。$2+2+2+2+2=10$、2が5個=10といってもよい。
掛け算の問題としては、$5\times2=10$と書く。
読み方は、5掛ける2は10に等しい、となる。

Multiplication Words

$$4 \underset{\substack{\text{factor}\\\text{(multiplicand)}\\\text{被乗数}}}{} \times \underset{\substack{\text{factor}\\\text{(multiplier)}\\\text{乗数}}}{3} = \underset{\substack{\text{product}\\\text{積}}}{12}$$

掛け算の用語

Two numbers that are being multiplied are called factors. The answer is called the product. In $5\times2=10$, 5 and 2 are factors. 10 is the product.

掛け合わせる2つの数を因数という。答えは積である。$5\times2=10$の5と2は因数で、10が積ということになる。

Division

Operations

Addition, subtraction, and multiplication are called operations. They are three of the four operations of arithmetic. The fourth operation is division.

You already know that subtraction is the opposite of addition. We say that addition

割り算

演算

足し算、引き算、掛け算を演算という。これが算数の四則算（加減乗除）のうちの3つで、4番目の演算は割り算である。

引き算は足し算を逆にしたものであることはすでに学んだ。足し算と引

and subtraction are opposite operations. The opposite operation of multiplication is division. Let's see how division works.

An Example of Division
Peter has 18 stamps. He wants to divide them into groups of 3. How many groups will he have?

$$18 \div 3 = 6$$

This is a division problem because you need to divide the 18 stamps into groups of 3 to solve it. How many groups of 3 are there in 18? There are 6 threes in 18. So Peter will have 6 groups of stamps. We write this division problem: 18÷3=6. We read it: "Eighteen divided by three equals six."

Division Words
The answer to a division problem is called the quotient. The number you are dividing is called the dividend. The number you are dividing by is called the divisor.

Learn to use these words to describe the numbers in a division problem. For example, in 12÷4=3, 12 is the dividend, 4 is the divisor, and 3 is the quotient.

There are two ways to write division. You can write it like this:

$$\underset{\substack{\text{dividend}\\ \text{被除数(割られる数)}}}{24} \div \underset{\substack{\text{divisor}\\ \text{除数(割る数)}}}{4} = \underset{\substack{\text{quotient}\\ \text{商}}}{6}$$

or like this:

$$4\overline{)24} \quad \begin{array}{l}\leftarrow \text{quotient} \\ \leftarrow \text{dividend}\end{array}$$

divisor

Remainders
Mrs. Hughes wants to divide 33 sheets of construction paper among seven students,

so that each student has the same number of sheets. If she gave each student 4 sheets, she would use 28 sheets (4×7=28). Since 33−28=5, there will be 5 sheets left over if she gives 4 to each student. Here is how you write this division problem.

Mrs. Hughes wants to divide 33 sheets of construction paper among her seven students:

$$7 \overline{)33}$$

うに配ろうとしている。生徒1人に4枚ずつ配ると28枚必要になる（4×7＝28）。33−28＝5であるから、もし1人に4枚ずつ配れば用紙は5枚残ることになる。この割り算問題は次のように書き表わす。

ヒューズ先生は、33枚の工作用紙を7人の生徒に配ろうとしている。

What is 33 divided by 7? 7 doesn't go into 33 evenly. The closest we can come is 7×4=28. So we write 4 in the ones' place for the quotient. Then we put 28 below the 33 (or the dividend), and subtract it, to show how many we have left over: 5. Our remainder is 5. So we write R5 next to the quotient 4, like this:

33を7で割るといくらか？ 7では割り切れない。もっとも近いのは、7×4＝28である。ゆえに商として4を1の位に書く。それから33（被除数）の下に28をもってきて引き算をすると、余りがいくつかわかる。5だ。ここでの余りは5だということになる。そこで商4のとなりにR5と書くと、このようになる。

$$\text{divisor} \rightarrow 7 \overline{)\begin{array}{r} 4 \text{ R5} \leftarrow \text{quotient (with remainder)} \\ 33 \leftarrow \text{dividend} \\ -28 \leftarrow \text{product of } 7 \times 4 \\ \hline 5 \leftarrow \text{remainder} \end{array}}$$

除数　商（と余り）　被除数　7×4の積　余り

Notice how you multiply the divisor and the quotient, and then subtract this product from the dividend to find the remainder.

要点は、除数に商をかけ、得られた積を被除数から引くと余りが分かるということだ。

Fractions

分数

A fraction is a part of something. A fraction can be a part of one thing, like a circle, an apple, or a pizza. A fraction can also be a part of a group.

分数は何かの一部分を示す。分数によって、円やリンゴ、ピザといったものの一部分を表すこともできる。また、ある集合の一部分を分数で表すこともできる。

In the first grade, you learned the fractions 1/2, 1/3, and 1/4. They are written out one half, one third, and one fourth (one quarter). Now you can learn the fractions 1/5, 1/6, and 1/10.

If something is divided into 5 equal parts, each part is 1/5. 1/5 is written out one fifth.

1年生のときに1/2, 1/3, 1/4といった分数を学習した。こうした分数を書き表すと、2分の1、3分の1、4分の1(四半分)となる。今度は 1/5, 1/6, 1/10といった分数を学んでみよう。

あるものを5等分すると、それぞれは1/5である。1/5は、5分の1と書き表す。

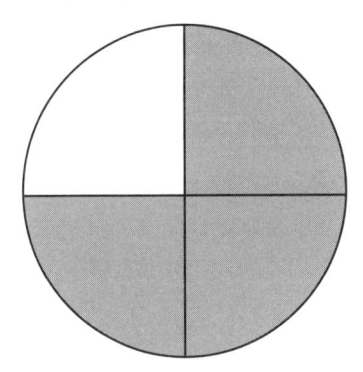

The circle has 4 equal parts. 3 of them are shaded. So 3/4 of the circle is shaded. 3/4 is written out three fourths.

この円は4等分されている。そのうち3つには影がつけてある。すなわち、この円の3/4には影がつけてあるということになる。3/4を言葉で書き表わすと4分の3となる。

Numerator and Denominator

A fraction is a part of one thing, or a part of a group. The bottom number of a fraction tells how many equal parts there are. The bottom number is called the denominator. The top number tells how many of the equal parts you are talking about. The top number is called the numerator.

In the fraction 4/8, 4 is the numerator and 8 is the denominator.

分子と分母

分数はものの一部分、あるいは集合の一部分をいう。分数の下の数字は等分のものがいくつあるかを示している。下の数字を分母という。分数の上の数字が示すのは、等分のもののうち今問題にしているのはいくつかということだ。上の数字を分子という。

分数4/8では、4が分子、8が分母である。

$$\frac{4}{8} \begin{matrix} \leftarrow \text{numerator} \\ \text{分子} \\ \leftarrow \text{denominator} \\ \text{分母} \end{matrix}$$

NOTE 教科名の英語

class schedule（時間割）

Language Arts（国語）
＊日本でいう国語の教科にあたる。

Mathematics (Math)（算数・数学）
＊加減乗除などの演算は arithmetic、幾何は geometry、代数は algebra。

Natural Science（自然科学）

Life Science（生命科学）

Physical Science（物理学）
＊日本語の理科に当たる言葉はなく、各領域ごとの科目名で呼ばれる。

Geography（地理）

World Civilization（世界史）

American Civilization（アメリカ史）
＊政治(Politics)や経済(Economics)については Social Studies という総称もある。

Fine Arts（芸術）
＊この中には音楽(music)と美術(visual arts)が含まれる。

Physical Education（体育）
＊PE という略称も使う。保健は Health 。

Home Economics（家庭科）
＊Life Skills といって、銀行口座の開設などの社会勉強をすることもある。

Recess（休み時間）
＊おもに小学校で使われる言葉で、大学などでは break 。

What American 4th GRADERS Learn in Textbooks

LANGUAGE ARTS • 国語

Myths from Medieval England
The Legend of King Arthur and the Knights of the Round Table

Have you ever heard the tales of knights in bright armor who traveled the land in search of adventure? Of magicians who cast magic spells on anyone foolish enough to oppose them? The noble knights of medieval times followed a code of chivalry: they swore oaths to serve their king and queen, to defend the helpless, and to bring honor to their land. The most famous of these knights were the Knights of the Round Table. The king they served was King Arthur, thought to be the greatest British king of those long-ago days. To promote equality and unity, he seated his knights at an enormous round table. King Arthur was probably a real leader in the early Middle Ages in the British Isles. Although we know almost nothing about the real king, we still have many stories about the legendary King Arthur and his Knights of the Round Table. Here are just a few.

How Arthur Became King: The Sword in the Stone

In days of old, Britain had many kings. One king ruled over all the others, and his name was Uther Pendragon. The dragon was his emblem and he was a mighty warrior and a great ruler. He was not only a great man in battle, but he was wise, too, for he followed the counsel of Merlin, a great magician and seer. Merlin could cast magic spells and even turn himself into animals or other people when he wished. He was called a seer because he could see the future—for everyone, that is, except himself.

Uther Pendragon had a baby son he called Arthur, and one day when Arthur

中世イギリスの伝説
アーサー王と円卓の騎士団の物語

　輝く鎧(よろい)に身をかため、冒険を求めて諸国を旅する騎士たちの物語をどこかで聞いたことはないだろうか。刃向かう愚か者をことごとく魔法にかけてしまう魔術師についてはどうだろうか。中世の高貴な騎士たちは、騎士道精神を守った。王と王妃に仕え、弱きものを守り、国に栄誉をもたらすことを誓うのが騎士道である。中でも「円卓の騎士団」はとりわけ有名である。彼らが仕えたアーサー王は、はるか昔のブリテンにおけるもっとも偉大な王といわれている。騎士たちを平等に扱いなおかつ統率を維持するために、アーサー王は巨大な円卓をかこむように騎士の座を配した。アーサー王は、中世初期のブリテン諸島を治めた指導者で、実在したと考えられている。王についての史実はほとんどわかっていないが、伝説的なアーサー王と円卓の騎士団の物語は数多く残っている。ここ紹介するのはごく一部だ。

> **NOTE**
> **アーサー王伝説**
> アーサー王は実在したケルト人の武将で、6世紀に大陸から侵入してきたサクソン人と戦った。しかし、アーサー王物語には、没落したケルト王国への郷愁・幻想が生んだ後世(6世紀–12世紀)のフィクションが多分に混じっている。
> 　アーサー王伝説は、宮廷恋愛物語、聖杯伝説、トリスタンとイゾルデの悲恋物語、ワーグナーの楽劇など、イギリスばかりでなくヨーロッパ文化全体に大きな影響を与えている。

アーサーはいかにして王となったか——石に刺さった剣

　古き世のブリテンには、数多くの王国があった。その諸国の王を支配下におさめた1人の王がいて、その名をウーゼル・ペンドラゴンといった。竜を紋章にもつこの王は、雄々しき戦士にして偉大な統治者であった。王は戦場の英雄でありまた賢者でもあったが、それはすぐれた魔術師にして預言者であるマーリンの忠言に耳をかたむけたからである。マーリンは魔法をかけたり、思うがままに獣や他の人間に変身することができた。彼は預言者と呼ばれたが、それは未来を予見できたからである。彼はすべての人間の未来を予見できた。が、おのれの未来だけは別であった。

　ウーゼル・ペンドラゴンにはアーサーという名の幼い息子がいた。まだアーサーが小さいころのこと、ある日マーリンは恐ろしい未来を幻に見た。彼の予見では、ウーゼル・ペンドラゴンはそのころ国土に蔓延(まんえん)していた疫病にかかってまもなく死ぬ運命にあった。

was still young Merlin had a terrifying vision. He foresaw that Uther Pendragon would soon die from a plague that was sweeping the land. And he saw that because Arthur was only a baby, many of the other kings would try to take Arthur's rightful place as the future leader of Britain. Some might even try to harm him, and war would break out. So Merlin secretly gave Arthur into the care of a noble knight, Sir Ector, who did not know he was protecting Britain's next king. Sir Ector raised Arthur along with his own son, Kay.

Just as Merlin had predicted, for years after Uther Pendragon died the other kings warred with each other. All of Britain was in strife, and threatened to fall apart. So Merlin placed a great marble stone in front of England's greatest cathedral. In the stone he placed a steel anvil, and into the stone and anvil he drove a glittering magic sword. On the stone was the inscription:

Whosoever pulls out this sword from this stone and anvil
Is the true-born king of all Britain.

Merlin called all the kings together to have a great feast, and afterward to see which one could pull the sword from the stone. Whoever accomplished this feat would be the king of all the kings, and bring peace to the land once more. Soon all the leaders, with their ladies and knights, assembled for the celebration. Now in those days, when there was a celebration, tournaments and contests called jousts were held in which knights proved their skill at battle. So a great tournament was held for the celebration. Arthur's stepbrother, Sir Kay, was one of the knights who competed in the tournament. Arthur, still a young man, acted as his assistant, or squire.

The horses thundered toward each other, carrying the knights in their shining armor. The knights met with a tremendous crash, and Sir Kay's sword broke in the battle. He hurried to the sidelines and shouted to Arthur to fetch him another one. While making his way back to their castle, Arthur passed the front of the church and saw the sword in the stone. Unaware of the sword's magic and in a great hurry to complete his mission, he thought to borrow the sword and easily pulled it from the stone without reading the inscription. He hurried back to Sir

また、アーサーがまだ幼いのをいいことに、諸国の王の多くが、未来のブリテンの統率者としてのアーサーの王座を奪おうとするさまも予見した。アーサーに危害を加える者も出てきて、戦争が起こることもわかった。そこでマーリンはひそかにアーサーの養育を高貴な騎士エクター卿に託したが、彼は自分がブリテンの次期国王を守っていることなど知るよしもなく、アーサーを自分の息子ケイと一緒にして育てた。

　まさにマーリンが予見したとおり、ウーゼル・ペンドラゴンが亡くなって何年かするうちに、諸国の王たちは戦争を始めた。ブリテン全土が敵対し合って、四分五裂の危機に見舞われていた。そこでマーリンは、イングランド最大の大聖堂のまえに大きな大理石を据えた。そして、その大理石に鋼鉄の鉄床（かなとこ）を埋めこむと、その大理石と鉄床の中に、きらきらと輝く魔法の剣を刺しこんだのである。その大きな石にはこういう言葉が刻まれていた——

　　　　この石塊と鉄床から 剣を抜き取る者こそは
　　　　　ブリテン全土を治める　由緒（ゆいしょ）正しき王

　マーリンはすべての王侯にたいして、全員が一堂に会する大宴を開き、そのあとで誰が石から剣を抜き取ることができるか見てみようではないかと呼びかけた。この難事をなしとげた者こそが王の中の王となり、ふたたび全土に平和をもたらすのである。それからまもなく、貴婦人や騎士たちを従えた王侯がこの祝典のために各地から集まってきた。その当時は、なにか祝典があれば、馬上槍試合と呼ばれる闘技や競技が行われて、騎士たちは武芸のわざを競ったのである。この祝典においても大がかりな槍試合が行われた。アーサーの継兄ケイ卿も、その試合に参加した騎士の１人であった。アーサーはまだ若く、ケイ卿に付きそう従者をつとめた。

　相手を目がけ地響きを立てて突進する馬には、ともに光り輝く鎧（よろい）に身を固めた騎士が乗っていた。騎士たちの鎧がガシャンとはげしくぶつかり合い、戦っているうちにケイ卿の剣が折れてしまった。彼は観戦席に走り、別の剣を持ってこいとアーサーに大声で命じた。急いで城に戻る途中、アーサーは教会の前を通りかかり、石に突き立つ剣に目をとめた。魔法の剣とは知るよしもなく、また命令をいちはやく果たすことだけを考えていたアーサーは、ここはその剣をひとまず拝借しようと考えて、石に刻まれた文言（もんごん）を読まずに、剣を石からすっと引き抜いてしまった。アーサーが急いで槍試合に

Kay, who recognized the sword at once and took it to his father.

"Look, Father," Sir Kay said, "I have pulled the magic sword from the stone. I will be king of all Britain." His father was amazed and doubtful, because Merlin had told him it would be otherwise. He told Sir Kay to put the sword back into the stone, and then draw it out again, to prove his claim. But no matter how hard he tried, Sir Kay couldn't thrust the sword into the stone. Finally, Sir Kay admitted that it was Arthur who had pulled the sword from the stone.

Arthur easily put the sword back into the stone, and easily pulled it out again. Sir Ector and Sir Kay both fell down on their knees before him.

"Why do you kneel down before me?" cried Arthur. He felt a little frightened.

"My lord," Sir Ector said, "only one man can draw the sword from the stone, and he is the king of Britain." He told Arthur the secret of his birth. "I am not your real father," Sir Ector explained. "When you were very young, Merlin gave you to me to raise. I can see now that you are the true son of Uther Pendragon, and heir to the realm." And he kissed Arthur's hand. But Arthur was sad and began to weep.

"Why are you crying?" Sir Ector asked. "You've just gained a kingdom."

"I've gained a kingdom," Arthur said, "but I've lost a father." He put the sword back into the stone. "I'd give the kingdom back if I could have you for my father again."

"That is not your destiny," said the magician Merlin, who suddenly appeared before them. "You are our king."

The next day all the kings tried to pull the sword from the stone, but none could. Only young Arthur, barely a man, could pull the sword from the stone. The kings were reluctant to accept him because of his age,

もどると、ひと目見て魔法の剣であることに気づいたケイ卿は、それを父のところに持っていった。
「ごらんください、父上」とケイは言った。「わたしが魔法の剣を石から抜き取ったのです。ブリテン全土を治めるのは、このわたしです」父は驚くとともにいぶかしく思った。マーリンの予言ではそういうことではなかったからだ。父は、もしそれがまことなら剣をもう1度石に刺してから抜き取ってみよ、とケイ卿に命じた。しかし、あらんかぎりの力をふりしぼってみたものの、ケイ卿は剣を石に突き刺すことはできなかった。とうとうケイ卿は、石から剣を抜いたのはアーサーであることを白状した。

アーサーがいとも簡単に剣を石に突き刺し、やすやすと抜いてみせると、エクター卿とケイ卿は彼の前に膝をついてひれ伏した。
「なぜわたしに向かってひざまずくのですか」とアーサーは叫んだ。彼は恐れすら感じた。
「王様」とエクター卿が言った。「あの石から剣を抜くことができるのはただ1人、そしてその方がブリテンの王なのです」。彼はアーサーに出生の秘密を明らかにした。「わたしはあなたの本当の父親ではございません」とエクター卿は語り始めた。「あなたがまだ幼いころにマーリンから預かって育てることになりました。今になってわかったのは、あなたがウーゼル・ペンドラゴンの実の息子であり、領土の継承者であるということです」。そう言って、エクター卿はアーサーの手にキスをした。しかし、アーサーは悲しみのあまり泣き出した。
「なぜお泣きになる」とエクター卿は言った。「1つの王国をわが手に収めたのですぞ」
「わたしは王国を1つ手中にした」とアーサーは答えた。「しかし、父を1人失ってしまったのです」。彼は剣をふたたび石に突き刺した。「もう1度あなたが父になってくれるのであれば、王国など返上いたします」
「あなたの運命はそうなってはおりませぬ」と魔法使いのマーリンが言った。彼は突然その場に姿を現したのだった。「あなたはわたしたちの王なのです」

その明くる日、諸国の王は競って石から剣を抜き取ろうとしたが、いずれも失敗に終わった。それを成し遂げたのは、まだ少年の面影が残る若きアーサーだけであった。諸国の王は若すぎるアーサーを王に迎えるのをしぶったが、民衆は若き英雄に喝采を惜しまなかっ

but the people cheered for their young hero. And so Arthur became king of all Britain. He made Sir Kay his right-hand man and began his reign, destined to be one of the most famous kings in all the world.

The Sword Excalibur and the Lady of the Lake

The Sword in the Stone was famous, but Arthur was to have a sword called Excalibur that was more famous still. One day in a terrible battle, the sword Arthur had pulled from the stone was broken. Arthur was rescued by Merlin, who then took him to find another sword. Merlin led him to a lake in a forest. In the center of the lake, an arm, clothed in white silk, jutted up from the surface. The hand held a gleaming sword in a jeweled scabbard.

"That is the magic sword Excalibur," Merlin said. "The Lady of the Lake will give it to you. Look! She's coming from her castle, which is carved in the rock. You must be respectful to her, and do what she tells you."

The Lady of the Lake appeared to them. "You may have the sword," she said softly, "if you give me a gift when I ask for it."

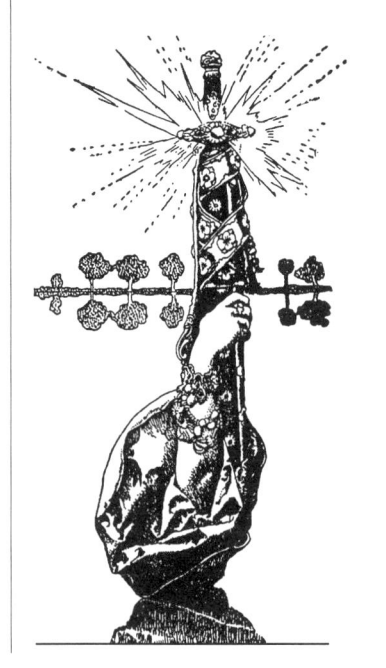

"That I shall do," said Arthur. Then he and Merlin rowed out into the lake. Arthur lifted the sword by its handle, and the arm and the hand sank under the water. Then Arthur and Merlin bid the Lady of the Lake good-bye.

"Tell me," said Merlin as they rode along, "which do you prefer, the sword or the scabbard?"

"The sword," said Arthur, who was greatly pleased with it.

"You are a fool," said Merlin, "for the scabbard is magic too, and whoever wears it cannot lose blood, no matter how badly he is injured."

た。かくしてアーサーはブリテン全土の王になった。ケイ卿を頼みの右腕としたアーサー王の時代が始まったのである。世界でもっとも名高い王の1人としての未来が彼を待っていた。

宝剣エクスカリバーと湖の姫

「石に刺さった剣」は世に名高いが、アーサーはそれよりもさらに有名な宝剣エクスカリバーを手にすることになる。ある日、はげしい戦いのさなかに、アーサーが石から抜き取った剣が折れてしまった。アーサーを救ったのはマーリンで、彼はアーサーを連れて新たな剣を探しに出かけた。マーリンの行く先は森の中の湖であった。その湖の中ほどに腕が見えた。白い絹布をまとって、水面からすっと突き出されている。その手は、鞘に宝飾をほどこした剣を握っていた。

「あれが魔剣エクスカリバーですぞ」とマーリンが言った。「湖の姫からあなたさまへの贈り物です。ほら、あそこに！ 姫が城から出ておいでになる。岩山を削って造った城です。姫には鄭重に接して、言われるとおりにしなければなりませぬ」

湖の姫は2人のまえに姿を現すと、「あの剣はそなたに与えよう」とも静かに言った。「ただし、わたくしが望んだときに贈り物をいただけるならば、というのが条件です」

「約束しよう」とアーサーは答えると、マーリンとともに湖へと舟を漕ぎ出した。アーサーが剣の柄を握って持ち上げると、突き出ていた腕と手は水面下に消えた。それからアーサーとマーリンは湖の姫に別れを告げて去った。

「1つお訊きしたい」と、帰り道で馬を走らせながらマーリンがたずねた。「剣と鞘、選ぶとすればどちらをお取りになる？」

「剣だ」とアーサーは答えた。彼はその剣がすっかり気に入っていたのだ。

「愚かな方じゃ」とマーリンが言った。「あの鞘にも魔力があって、身につけていれば、どんなに深い傷を負っても血が流れ出ることはないのです」

Guinevere

One day Arthur heard that a friend, King Leodegrance, was going to be attacked by an enemy, the Duke of North Umber. The Duke wanted to take King Leodegrance's lands and his daughter, the beautiful princess Guinevere. So Arthur and Merlin set off to Leodegrance's castle to help him.

Arthur had met Guinevere once before and was so struck by her that he felt foolish and could barely speak. He longed to see her again, but in such a way that she wouldn't notice him. So Merlin made a magical cap for him. When he wore it, Arthur looked like an ordinary gardener's boy, not a great king that everyone stared at. Arthur was hired to work in Guinevere's garden as a gardener's boy. And in this way he saw Guinevere every day without feeling bashful.

But one morning, when she looked out the window, Guinevere saw a golden knight bathing in the fountain. It was Arthur, who had taken off his cap to wash. When she hurried out to meet him, she found only the gardener's boy, for Arthur had put his cap back on. Guinevere asked where the handsome young knight had gone.

"Lady, there has been no one else here," replied Arthur, "only me."

"Really?" said Guinevere, with fire in her eyes. "And what of this?" She picked up the golden knight's collar, which Arthur had left beside the fountain, and flung it at him. "Take this and tell your knight that it is very rude to bathe in a lady's private garden."

All day Guinevere tried to figure out how the knight had suddenly vanished, leaving only the gardener's boy. So she summoned the boy to her, asking him to bring her roses. When he came into the palace, he wouldn't take his cap off. "How now," Guinevere said, "haven't they told you it's rude to leave your hat on in the presence of a lady?"

グィネビア

　ある日のこと、アーサーは盟友レオデグランス王が、敵対しているノース・アンバー公爵の攻撃を受けるという知らせを聞いた。公爵は、レオデグランス王の領土とその娘、美しきグィネビア姫を奪おうとしていた。そこでアーサーとマーリンは、加勢するためにレオデグランスの城へと向かった。

　アーサーは以前に１度だけグィネビアに会ったことがあるが、その美貌を前にたじろぐばかりで、ほとんど口をきけなかった。もう１度会いたいという気持ちは強かったが、姫に自分であると気づかれぬように、と思っていた。そこでマーリンはアーサーのために魔法の帽子を作った。その帽子をかぶると、アーサーはふつうの庭師の徒弟に変身した。どう見ても人の目を釘づけにする偉大な王には見えなかった。アーサーは庭師の徒弟として、グィネビアの庭園で働くことになった。こうして彼は恥じらいにとまどうこともなく、毎日グィネビアの姿を見ることができるようになった。

　だが、ある朝のこと、窓辺に立っていたグィネビアは、黄金の鎧の騎士が庭の泉水で水を浴びているのを見た。それはアーサーであった。顔を洗おうとして帽子を脱いでいたのだ。グィネビアは急いで庭に駆け出したが、そこには庭師の徒弟しかいない。アーサーが帽子をまたかぶってしまったからだ。グィネビアはハンサムな若い騎士はどこへ行ったのかと尋ねた。

　「姫君さま、ここには他に誰もおりませんでした」とアーサーは答えた。「わたくし１人でございます」

　「そう？」と言うグィネビアの目には、怒りの炎があった。「では、これは何なの？」姫は黄金の鎧の騎士が首につけていた首飾りを拾って言った。それはアーサーが泉水のそばに置き忘れたもので、姫はそれをアーサーに向かって投げつけた。「それを持っていって、おまえの知っている騎士に、貴婦人の内庭で体を洗うのは無礼千万であると伝えなさい」

　その日ずっとグィネビアは、騎士が忽然と姿をくらまし、後に庭師の徒弟が１人残ったのはどういうことかと考えてみた。そして徒弟を呼ぶと、庭のバラを摘んでくるよう命じた。館の中に入ってきた徒弟は、帽子をかぶったままだった。「なんとまあ」とグィネビアは尋ねた。「そなたは、貴婦人のまえでかぶりものを取らぬのは無礼であると教わらなかったのですか」

"My lady," said the gardener's boy, "I can't take my cap off—I have an ugly spot on my head."

"Then bring the roses here to me," Guinevere said. And as he handed her the roses, she snatched off his cap. Instantly he was transformed into a shining knight. All of Guinevere's maids shrieked and laughed, but Guinevere recognized the knight as the great King Arthur himself. She was awed, but she wanted to get even for the trick he had played on her. "Here," she said, and flung the cap at him laughing, "take your cap and go to your work, you gardener's boy with the ugly spot on your head!" And Arthur put on his cap, and went his way.

That very day, the Duke of Umber arrived with his army to make war on the king and take Guinevere captive. Arthur quickly borrowed some armor and rode out on his great white horse to meet him. The two horses, carrying Arthur and the duke in their shining armor, thundered toward each other. The two warriors met with a tremendous crash, and the duke's lance broke. He was hurled to the ground, and lay bleeding, but just then his army charged forward and saved him.

Arthur retreated back into the castle. He could tell that the duke would be back to fight again, so he sent for other knights to help in the fight for Princess Guinevere. When they arrived, they asked Guinevere who would lead them. She told them they must follow the gardener's boy, the one with the ugly spot on his head! They were furious until Arthur took off his cap, and showed himself in all his kingly splendor. Then the knights rejoiced and rode out with their king and conquered the Duke of Umber and all his knights.

When Guinevere saw this, she was embarrassed at how she had treated so great a king as Arthur. But Arthur declared his love for her, and asked her to become his queen. So King Arthur and Guinevere were married.

For Guinevere's dowry, King Leodegrance gave Arthur a great Round Table with fifty seats where noble knights could sit. Each time a worthy knight appeared, his name would be magically inscribed on one of the seats, and each time a knight died his name would vanish. Arthur took Guinevere and the Round Table to his home, Camelot, and so began the adventures of King Arthur and the Knights of the Round Table.

「姫君さま」と庭師の徒弟は言った。「帽子を取ることができないのです。つまりその、わたくしの頭には醜いところがありまして」
「では、そのバラをここに持ってきなさい」とグィネビアは言った。そして徒弟がバラを渡そうとすると、帽子をさっとつかみ取ってしまった。すると一瞬のうちに徒弟は光り輝く騎士に変身した。その場にいたグィネビアの侍女たちは驚きの声をあげて笑ったが、グィネビアは、その騎士こそが偉大なアーサー王その人であることをさとった。姫は、王を畏れ敬いながらも、王が奇策でだましたことになんとか仕返しをしてやりたいという気持ちを抑えられなかった。
「さあ」と姫は言って、笑いながらその帽子を彼に投げつけた。「帽子を持って仕事にもどるがよい。おまえは頭に醜いところがある庭師の徒弟なのですものね」。アーサーは帽子をかぶるとその場を去った。

折も折、その日に、レオデグランス王に戦をしかけてグィネビア姫を奪おうと、アンバー公爵が軍を率いてやってきたのである。アーサーはすぐに甲冑を借りて白い愛馬にまたがると、敵将をむかえ討った。光りきらめく甲冑を身につけたアーサー王と公爵が乗る2頭の馬は、相手目がけて稲妻のごとき速さで突進した。2人の戦士が激しい音を立ててぶつかり合うと、公爵の槍が折れてしまった。地面に投げ出された公爵が血を流して動けずにいると、ちょうどそこに公爵の軍勢が突撃をしてきて彼を救いだした。

アーサーはひとまず城に退却した。公爵がふたたび攻撃してくることはわかっていたので、アーサーは、グィネビア姫を守る戦いに駆けつけるようにと、他の騎士たちのもとへ使いを送った。やってきた騎士たちはグィネビア姫に、誰の指揮をあおげばよいのでしょうかと尋ねた。姫は、頭に醜いところがある庭師の徒弟の命に従うのですよ、と答えた。騎士たちは憤然としたが、それもアーサーが帽子を取り、王としての威光に輝く姿に変身するまでのことだった。すぐに騎士たちは喜び勇んで彼らの王とともに馬を駆り、アンバー公爵とその臣下の騎士たちを打ち負かしてしまったのだった。

これを見たグィネビアは、偉大なるアーサー王になんという振る舞いをしたことかと深く恥じ入った。しかし、アーサーは姫に寄せる想いをみずから告白し、どうかわたしの妃になってくださいと願い出たのである。かくしてアーサー王とグィネビア姫は結婚することとなった。

グィネビアが持参する結婚の贈り物として、レオデグランス王は、

Sir Launcelot

As the fame of King Arthur's Knights of the Round Table spread, knights from near and far wanted to share in their glory. One day, there appeared at Camelot a young man who would later become the greatest knight of all. He was called Sir Launcelot of the Lake, because he had been raised by the Lady of the Lake.

When Launcelot arrived at Camelot, all were struck by his strong and graceful appearance —and none more so than Queen Guinevere, who felt as though her heart had been captured by the bold young knight. The charms of Guinevere made an equally strong impression on Launcelot. After a single glance, he fell deeply in love, and vowed to do many great deeds for her sake.

Launcelot served King Arthur well. He loved him like a father, and was loved by Arthur in return. But the love between Launcelot and Guinevere would eventually bring great sadness to Arthur and ruin upon Camelot. Before that happened, though, Launcelot would perform many brave feats, win many tournaments, and have many adventures.

One day, Launcelot said to his nephew, Sir Lionel, "Let us go out and seek adventures." They put on their armor, which gleamed so brightly in the sun that it would dazzle your eyes to see it. They hefted their shields, swords, and spears. Then they mounted their impatient steeds and rode forth. The sun beat down upon them and made Launcelot sleepy, so they stopped under the shade of an apple tree. Launcelot removed his helmet, lay down, and fell fast asleep.

Sir Lionel, who stayed awake, soon heard a sound like distant thunder, getting louder and louder. Then he saw three knights riding as fast as the wind. Close behind them came a knight riding even faster, a knight more powerful than any Sir Lionel had seen before. This knight overtook the other three, knocked them from their horses, and tied them

50人の高貴な騎士たちが座る巨大な円卓をアーサー王に献上した。それは、不思議なことに、誉れ高い騎士が出現すると椅子の座板の1つにその名が刻みこまれ、騎士の1人が死ねばその名が消えるという円卓であった。アーサーはグィネビアを伴い、円卓とともに居城キャメロットに帰還した。こうしてアーサー王と円卓の騎士団の物語は始まったのである。

ランスロット卿

アーサー王と円卓の騎士団の名声が広まるにつれて、近隣からも遠方からもその栄誉にあずかろうと騎士たちがやってきた。ある日のこと、のちに騎士の中の騎士と謳われることになる若者がキャメロットに姿を現した。その名を〈湖のランスロット卿〉といったが、それは〈湖の姫〉に育てられたからであった。

ランスロットがキャメロットに着くと、見るからに強そうでなおかつ優雅なその姿に誰もが衝撃をうけた。とりわけグィネビア王妃は、若く勇敢な騎士に心をすっかり奪われてしまったかのように感じていた。同じように、グィネビアの魅力もランスロットの心に深く刻み込まれた。ただひと目見ただけで彼は深い恋に落ち、王妃のために多くの華々しい武勲を立てることを誓った。

ランスロットはアーサー王の臣下としてよく仕えた。アーサー王を父のように愛し、王も愛情をもってこれにこたえた。しかし、結局ランスロットとグィネビア王妃の恋愛はアーサー王を悲嘆にくれさせ、キャメロットを破滅させることになるのである。だが、それは結末であって、そのまえにランスロットは、幾度も輝かしい武勲をおさめ、数多くの馬上槍試合で勝ち名乗りをあげ、度重なる冒険で活躍したのであった。

ある日のこと、ランスロットは甥のライオネル卿に、「冒険を探しに城外に行ってみようではないか」ともちかけた。2人が鎧をつけると、陽の光りをあびて、まぶしいほどの輝きを放った。彼らは盾、剣、槍を手に取ると、いかにも待ちきれぬようすの馬にまたがり、城の外へ出た。暑い日ざしに照りつけられたランスロットは眠気におそわれ、リンゴの樹の木陰で休むことにした。ランスロットは兜を脱ぎ、身を横たえるとたちまちぐっすり眠りこんでしまった。

ほどなくして、眠らずにいたライオネル卿の耳に遠くからの雷鳴のような地響きが聞こえてきて、その音はしだいに大きくなってき

> **NOTE**
> **キャメロット**
> キャメロットはアーサー王の居城ですぐれた治世の象徴。実在は確認されていない。現代ではケネディ大統領の在職した時代(1961–63)を「キャメロット」と呼ぶ。輝かしい未来を予感させながら凶弾にたおれた大統領をいにしえの王国の崩壊に重ね見ているのだ。

up. Sir Lionel, taking care not to wake Launcelot, quietly prepared himself and then rode after the strong knight. He challenged him to fight.

The strong knight charged Sir Lionel and struck him so hard that both Sir Lionel and his horse fell to the ground. Then he tied up Sir Lionel, and took him with the other three knights to his castle, where he threw them in a deep dungeon, already crowded with many other knights he had defeated.

When Launcelot awoke, he went in search of Sir Lionel. On the road he met a damsel riding a white horse. "Fair damsel," said Sir Launcelot, "what do you know of this region?" "Sir Knight," replied the damsel, "near here lives a knight more powerful than any other. His name is Sir Turquine, and he is a sworn enemy of King Arthur. Within a mile is his castle. Near it is a tree. From that tree hang the shields of many good knights that are his prisoners. And from that tree hangs a copper basin. Strike it, and await whom you seek."

Launcelot thanked the damsel and departed. He soon found the tree and struck the basin many times. Soon he saw a huge knight approaching, with a captured knight draped across his horse. Launcelot recognized the captured knight, who appeared to be injured, as Sir Gaheris of the Round Table.

"Fair knight," Launcelot called out, "remove that wounded man from your horse. You have shamed the Knights of the Round Table. Now, prepare to defend yourself."

た。そのとき3人の騎士が疾風のように馬を駆っているのが見えてきた。そのすぐ後ろには、さらに速く走る騎士の馬がせまっていたが、ライオネルが知る誰よりも強そうな騎士であった。前をゆく3人に追いつくや、この騎士は彼らを馬から打ち落として縛りあげてしまった。これを見てライオネル卿は、眠っているランスロットを起こさないように静かに武具を整えると、その勇猛なる騎士の後を追い、戦いをいどんだ。

その勇猛なる騎士は、ライオネル卿めがけて突進してくると、はげしく剣でうちすえて、馬もろともにライオネル卿を地面にたたきつけてしまった。それからライオネル卿を縛りあげると、他の3人の騎士とともに城に連れ帰り、深い地下牢にほうりこんだ。そこには、この騎士に打ち負かされた騎士たちがひしめいていた。

目をさましたランスロットは、ライオネル卿がいないのに気づいて探しはじめた。道を走っていると、彼は白馬に乗った若い貴婦人に出会った。「お嬢さま、この土地をご存じでしょうか」とランスロットはたずねた。「これは貴きおかた」と貴婦人は答えた。「この近くには誰よりも強い騎士が住んでおりまして、その名はタークィン卿。アーサー王を不倶戴天の敵と見ております。ここから1マイルほどのところに城があり、すぐそばに樹が立っております。樹の枝には盾がいくつもかけてありますが、それは敗れて囚われの身となった雄々しき騎士たちのものにございます。その樹には銅の鍋が吊るしてありますので、叩き鳴らしてお探しの方をお待ちになればよろしいかと」

ランスロットは貴婦人に礼を言って城に向かった。すぐに樹は見つかり、その銅鍋を何度も叩き鳴らした。待つまでもなくすぐに巨漢の騎士がやってきて、見ると馬の背に横がけにして捕まえた騎士を乗せていた。ランスロットは、傷を負って捕らえられたその騎士が円卓の騎士ガヘリス卿であることに気づいた。

「貴公」と、ランスロットが呼ばわった。「その負傷した騎士を馬から降ろすのだ。これまで貴公は円卓の騎士団を笑いものにしてきたが、さあ、戦いの用意はいいか」

「おぬしが円卓の騎士団の仲間なら」とタークィン卿は答えた。「わしはおぬしとその仲間すべてに戦いを挑もう」。そう言うと槍を突き出してランスロットに向かって突進してきた。ランスロットもすばやく打ってかかり、双方が激しくぶつかりあったので、ともに馬から落ちてしまった。両者が剣を抜いたかと思うと、たちま

"If you are of the Round Table," said Sir Turquine, "I defy you and all your fellow knights." Then he held forth his spear and rushed at Launcelot. Launcelot rushed at him, and they clashed so hard that both were knocked from their horses. They drew their swords and at once the clang of their blows shook the land. Back and forth they battled until, exhausted, they paused, and Sir Turquine said, "Truly, you are the strongest man I have ever met. For your sake I will release all the prisoners that I hold, unless you should be Launcelot, the knight I hate most of all, for he slew my brother."

"I am Sir Launcelot of the Lake."

"Then," said Sir Turquine with renewed fury, "let us fight on until only one of us shall live."

For two hours they battled, exchanging blow after blow, wounding each other sorely until the ground ran red. At last, after one fierce stroke of Launcelot's sword, Sir Turquine fell lifeless to the dirt.

Sir Launcelot sent Sir Gaheris to free the knights from Sir Turquine's dungeon. Then Launcelot mounted his horse and went in search of other adventures.

As the years passed, no knight proved stronger than Launcelot, who sent many a defeated knight to Camelot, commanding each to bow down before the feet of Queen Guinevere.

Alas, the love between Launcelot and Guinevere eventually tore Camelot apart. Launcelot and Arthur fought many battles against each other though they had once been the best of friends. Their battles left the kingdom vulnerable to plunder by the evil prince Mordred and his followers.

Though the great age of Camelot ended unhappily, it stands in our minds even today as a time of peace and nobility when chivalry shone as bright as polished armor and adventure was always waiting beyond the next turn in the road.

ちガシャン、ガシャンと打ち合う剣の音が大地を揺るがした。押しつ押されつの戦いを続けた２人がやがて疲れきって動きを止めたとき、タークィン卿がこう言った。「確かに、おぬしはわしがこれまで戦った中で最強の男だ。おぬしに免じて、わしが捕らえたものどもをすべて返してやってもよい。だが、まさかおぬし、わしが誰よりも憎むあの男、わしの弟を殺した騎士ランスロットではあるまいな」
「わたしが湖の騎士ランスロットだ」
「ならば」と、ふたたび燃え上がった怒りをこめてタークィン卿が言い放った。「おぬしかわしのどちらか１人になるまで、戦い続けるだけのことよ」
　２時間もの間２人は死闘を続け、一撃の応酬を繰り返し、ともに負った深手から流れた血で地面は赤く染まった。そしてついに、ランスロットの振り下ろした必殺の一撃をくらうと、タークィン卿は息絶えて倒れ、地に伏した。
　ランスロット卿は、ガヘリス卿を遣わして、タークィン卿の地下牢から騎士たちを出してやった。それからランスロットはふたたび馬上の人となり、あらたな冒険を求めて旅に出た。
　それから長い歳月が流れたが、どの騎士もランスロットを打ち負かすことはできなかった。ランスロットは倒した騎士たちを次々とキャメロットに送り、グィネビア王妃の足元にひれ伏して仕えるよう命じた。
　だが、なんと悲しいことか。ランスロットとグィネビアの恋愛が、ついにはキャメロットを崩壊させてしまったのだ。かつては最高の友情で結ばれていたランスロットとアーサー王の２人が、たがいを敵として幾度も戦うことになった。長引く戦いに王国は弱体化し、邪悪なモルドレッド王子とその一派が略奪をほしいままにするまでになってしまった。
　キャメロットの偉大な時代は不幸な終わりを迎えたが、こんにちでもわたしたちの精神の中にしっかりと生き続けている。それは平和で高貴な時代であり、騎士道精神が磨きぬかれた甲冑のように光り輝き、道を曲がったその先にいつも冒険が待ちかまえている時代であった。

LANGUAGE ARTS ● 国語

Sayings and Phrases　ことわざと熟語

Beauty is only skin deep
「美しいのは皮膚1枚分だけ」

People use this saying to mean that you can't judge a person's character by how he or she looks.

このことわざは、人間の人格は容貌のよしあしで判断することはできないといっている。

Birds of a feather flock together
「鳥は同じ種類で群れをつくる」

People say this to mean that similar types of people, or people who have similar interests, like to be with each other.

似たようなタイプの人々、あるいは同じようなことに関心を持っている人々は互いに好んで集まるものだ、と言おうとするときにこの格言を使う。

Don't count your chickens before they hatch
「卵から孵(かえ)らないうちは雛(ひな)として数えるな」

Because not every egg in a nest hatches into a baby chicken, people use this saying to mean that you may be disappointed if you count on having something before it is really yours.

巣にある卵のすべてが雛になるわけではないことから、このことわざは、何かが本当に自分のものにならないうちから当てにするとあとで失望を味わうこともある、という意味で使う。

Haste makes waste
「急ぐほどに無駄をする」

This saying means that when you rush you don't do as good a job as you do when you are careful and take your time.

このことわざは、ばたばた急ぐと、時間をかけて丹念にしたときほどいい仕事はできないという意味だ。

4th GRADE

Don't put all your eggs in one basket
「持っている卵全部を1つの籠(かご)に入れてはいけない」

What would happen if you dropped a basket full of eggs? When people use this saying, they mean that you shouldn't count on one single thing and ignore other possibilities. If you do, you could lose out.

卵をいっぱいに入れた籠を、もし落としてしまったら？ このことわざを使うのは、1つのことに賭けて他の可能性に目をつぶってしまうのはよくないということを言うときだ。そんなことをすれば、すべてダメになってしまうこともありうる。

Once in a blue moon
「青いお月さまのときに1度（ごくまれに）」

A blue moon isn't really blue. It's the second full moon in a calendar month. They're pretty rare: there have only been two in the last five years. So people use this phrase to describe something that happens only once in a while.

青い月といっても実際に青いわけではない。ひと月のうちに2度目に現われた満月を青い月という。きわめて稀なことで、過去5年間に2度あっただけである。だからこの慣用句は、めったにないことが起きたときなどに使う。

Laugh, and the world laughs with you; weep, and you weep alone
「君が笑えば世の中も笑うが、泣くときはひとりぼっちだ」

This saying means that when you are happy, people want to join in with your cheerful mood but when you are sad, people don't want to be with you.

このことわざは、楽しくしていると他の人もその陽気なムードに誘われてやってくるが、悲しみに沈んでいると人は離れていく、ということを言っている。

Lightning never strikes in the same place twice
「雷は同じ場所には2度と落ちない」

People use this saying to mean that if something unfortunate happens, it usually won't happen again in exactly the same way.

何か不幸なことが起こったとしても、全く同じことがもう1度起こることはまずない、ということを言うときにこのことわざを使う。

Make hay while the sun shines
「陽の高いうちに干草を作れ」

Why do farmers harvest hay and grains like corn or wheat when the weather is fair? Because once it starts to rain, the crops can be spoiled. So people use this saying to mean that you should take advantage of your good fortune when things are working out in your favor.

農家の人が天気のいいときに干草を作り、トウモロコシや小麦のような穀物を収穫するのはなぜなのだろうか。雨が降りはじめたら、せっかくの作物が台なしになってしまうからだ。これでわかるように、このことわざは、ものごとが思い通りに運んでいるうちにその好運を生かすべきだ、という意味で使われる。

Seeing is believing
「目で見れば信じる（百聞は一見にしかず）」

This saying means that you can't necessarily believe that something exists or is true unless you see the evidence for yourself.

このことわざは、何かが実在するとか本当だとかいうことは、自分の目で確かめるまではなかなか信じられないものだ、という意味である。

Two wrongs don't make a right
「悪いこと2つしても正しいこと1つにはならない」

People use this saying to mean that you can't correct one wrong thing by doing something else that's wrong.

このことわざは、過ちに過ちを重ねても帳消しにはならない、ということを言うときに使う。

When it rains it pours
「降ればどしゃぶり」

When people say this, they mean that something that starts out as a little bit of bad luck can turn into a disaster.

このことわざは、ちょっとした不運で始まったことが大きな惨事になったりすることがある、という意味で使う。

You can lead a horse to water, but you can't make it drink
「馬を水辺に連れて行くことはできても、無理に水を飲ませることはできない」

This saying means that you can show people what you want them to do, but you cannot force them to do it.

このことわざは、人に何をしてもらいたいかを伝えることはできるが、それをするよう強制することはできない、という意味である。

Break the ice
「氷を砕く」

This phrase means doing something to make people who are uncomfortable more comfortable. You can also "break the ice" if you are the first person to begin speaking with someone who has not yet spoken to you.

この慣用句は、気詰まりな思いをしている人の気持ちをほぐすようなことをする、という意味だ。また、1度も話したことのない人に向かって初めて声をかけるようなときも、「氷を砕く」と言ったりする。

Bull in a china shop
「せともの屋の大牛」

People use this phrase to describe someone who is clumsy in a place where things can be upset or broken, or someone who handles a delicate situation badly.

ものがひっくり返ったり壊れたりしやすい場所で粗忽な振舞いをしてしまう人とか、細かい気配りができずにメチャメチャにしてしまう人を指してこの表現を使う。

Bury the hatchet
「斧を埋める」

People use this saying to mean stop holding a grudge. This saying is very similar to the sayings "let bygones be bygones" and "forgive and forget."

このことわざは、恨みつらみを捨てる、という意味で使う。「過去は過ぎ去るにまかせよ」や「許せよ忘れよ」のようなことわざとほとんど同じことを言っている。

4th GRADE

LANGUAGE ARTS • 国 語

Haiku

Poetry is a form of writing that pays particular attention to sounds and to the associations between words. Many forms of poetry use patterns of verses and rhyme at the end of each line, but haiku is different. For one thing, haiku are short, usually only three lines. For another, they express a single feeling or impression. For another, they are usually unrhymed.

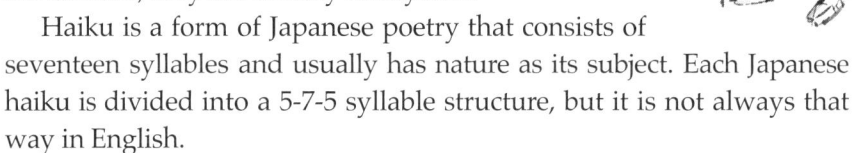

Haiku is a form of Japanese poetry that consists of seventeen syllables and usually has nature as its subject. Each Japanese haiku is divided into a 5-7-5 syllable structure, but it is not always that way in English.

One of the greatest composers of haiku once said, "Haiku is simply what is happening in this place, at this moment." In other words, haiku is about what is around us in our daily life—if we just take time to look, listen and notice the world around us. The themes are not complicated but are easy for other people to understand and appreciate, because they can recognize the daily situation that is being written about. Although it isn't always easy to write a good haiku, it is an easy form to use and they are fun to write.

Usually broken into three lines of 5-7-5 syllables, a haiku usually has several characteristics. First, it has a seasonal theme. Each haiku uses a kigo, a season word, which indicates in which season the haiku is set. A Japanese haiku might use snow to indicate a winter setting and cherry blossoms to indicate spring, but sometimes the season word is not so obvious. With haiku, the key is to "show, not tell." Use your imagination to come up with a way of expressing when the event of the poem takes place, without actually telling it.

Second, haiku each have a "cutting word" which divides the poem

俳句

　詩は言葉の音や言葉の組み合わせに特別な工夫をこらした文芸の一種である。詩の形式の多くは、特定の詩形を用いて各行の終わりで韻を踏んだりするが、俳句はそうではない。まず俳句は短く、たいていは3行で書く。また、俳句はある1つの情感や印象を表現する。そして俳句はふつう韻を踏まない。

　俳句は日本の詩の一形式で、17音節からなり、多くの場合自然を主題とする。日本の俳句は5-7-5音という構造になっているが、英語の俳句はかならずしもそうはならない。

　ある偉大な俳人はこう言っている。「俳句とは、まさにこの場所でこの瞬間に起こっていることなのだ」と。言葉を変えれば、俳句は日常生活においてわたしたちの身辺で起きていることをとらえる。身近な世界を眺めてみて、耳を澄まし、何かに気づくところから始まるのである。テーマは複雑なものではなく、誰でも容易に理解し味わうことができる。書かれている出来事が日常的でわかりやすいからだ。すぐれた俳句を作るのはなかなか難しいが、俳句という形式は入りやすく、実際に作ってみると面白い。

　俳句はふつう5音、7音、5音と3行に分けて書くが、いくつか特徴がある。まず俳句には季題がある。どの俳句も季語と呼ばれる季節を表す言葉を用いて、どの季節に詠まれた句であるかを示す。日本の俳句では雪ならば時節は冬であり、桜の花ならば春だが、ときには季語が明確でない場合もある。俳句において大事なことは、「はっきり言うのではなく、それとなく示す」ことだ。句がとらえる出来事がいつの時季のことであるかをそのまま言うのではなく、時季がわかるようによく考えて表現を工夫せよということだ。

　2番目の特徴は、俳句には句を2つに分ける「切れ字」というものがあって、たいていは1行目か2行目の終わりにコロンや長いダッシュ、省略符号などを使うことが多い。2つの部分はそれぞれ別のこと、関連のないことがらを扱っているかもしれないが、詩人はそ

NOTE
俳句
俳句は20世紀初めころから英米の現代詩に影響を与えてきた。英詩の伝統である韻にこだわらずに日常を詠むことのできる俳句は、アメリカの小中等教育の現場で盛んだ。小学校の文集などにも多くのhaikuが載る。

into two sections, usually at the end of the first or second line, where there is a colon, a long dash or an ellipsis. The two parts may be about different and unrelated things, but the poet shows us that they are somehow related to each other.

Third, a haiku should be about a specific event, not a general idea. Fourth, it should be in the present and not in the past. And finally, it should be clear enough that other people can share its emotion.

The best-known haiku poet was Matsuo Basho (1644–94), who spent many years traveling around Japan writing haiku along his route. Perhaps his best-known poem is the following:

> *The ancient pond—*
> *A frog jumps in,*
> *The sound of the water.*

As you can see, a haiku may be about an insect, a flower, or even a frog, but the important thing is that it should give other people a fresh new experience of a well-known situation. The poet Issa (1763-1827), in fact, is known for his poems that show affection for small creatures that most people don't like.

> *Hey! Don't swat him!*
> *The fly rubs his hands, rubs his feet*
> *Begging for mercy.*

You can write about something you see or hear right now, something in your classroom or outside the window. You can write about something that you have experienced, such as what you did on the weekend. Or you can create something and make it sound as if it is real.

Part of the enjoyment of writing haiku is sharing the poems with others. Each person who hears or reads the haiku may have different associations. One person may take a haiku in a completely different way from the person who wrote it, and that is okay. So when you write haiku, don't be afraid to be creative and don't be afraid to share your poems with others.

の間になんらかのつながりがあるように表現する。
　３番目の特徴は、俳句は概念的なことではなく、具体的なことがらを詠むということ。４番目の特徴は、過去ではなく現在を詠むということだ。そして最後に、他の人もその句が表現する情感を共有できるような明快さが俳句には必要だ。
　最高の俳句の詩人といわれたのは松尾芭蕉(1644–1694)で、芭蕉は日本国内を何年も旅をして回り、各地で俳句を作った。芭蕉の句の中でいちばんよく知られているのは次の句であろう。

古池や 蛙 飛びこむ水の音

　このように俳句の題材は虫でも花でもいいし、カエルであってもちっともかまわない。大事なことは、俳句が、日常見慣れたものをまったく新鮮な出来事のように経験させる力を持っているということだ。たとえば俳人小林一茶(1763–1827)はたいていの人が敬遠するような小さな生き物への愛情を表現した詩で知られている。

やれ打つな蝿が手をすり足をする

　俳句は、今この瞬間に教室の中あるいは窓の外で見えたり聞こえたりするものを使って作れる。先週の週末にしたことなど、自分の経験をもとに作ることもできる。また、空想で何かをこしらえて、それを本当のことのように表現することもできるだろう。
　俳句の楽しみの１つは、作った作品を他の人と共有できるということだ。俳句を読む人、聞く人、それぞれが違った連想をするかもしれない。作者の意図とは全然違う読み方をする人もいるだろうが、それでかまわないのである。だから、俳句を作るときには、遠慮せずに斬新な発想を楽しんで、恐れずに自分の作品を他の人にも読んでもらうことだ。

NATURAL SCIENCE ● 科 学
Pangaea: Continental Drift

It is thought that the earth's seven continents were once attached to one another, forming one large continent. Scientists call this super-continent Pangaea. Over a very long period of time, the pressures inside the earth that caused earthquakes and volcanoes cracked the crust of Pangaea, dividing it into several plates. Continued pressure forced the plates to move apart, and Pangaea broke into smaller pieces. These smaller pieces became the continents we know today. We call this the theory of continental drift, because the continents drifted apart.

There are several clues that have led scientists to the theory of continental drift. One is the fossils that are found in the rocks of different continents. The fossils of certain prehistoric animals that could not swim far are found both in South America and in Africa. Geologists think that, since these animals couldn't cross the Atlantic Ocean, the two continents were joined at one time.

Another clue is the shape of the continents. Let's look back at the map of the world to see why this is so. Can you see how South America fits next to Africa like a puzzle piece?

When they separated, the continents divided the large body of water that covered three quarters of the earth's surface into sections. We call these sections oceans. The four major oceans of the world are the Atlantic, the Pacific, the Indian, and the Arctic.

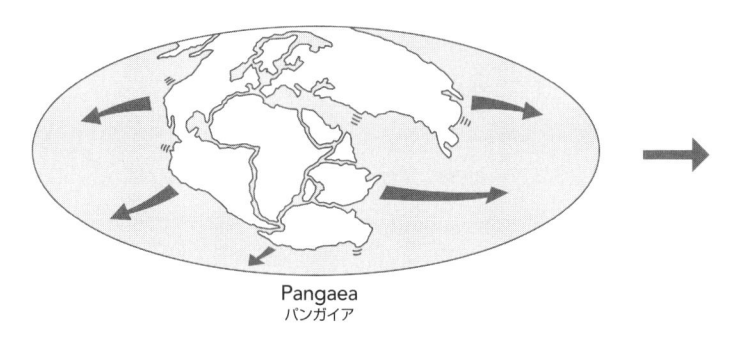

Pangaea
パンガイア

4th GRADE

パンガイア：移動する大陸

　かつて地球の7つの大陸はすべてつながっていて、1つの大きな大陸だったと考えられている。この超大陸を科学者たちはパンガイアと呼ぶ。きわめて長い歳月の間に、地震や噴火を起こしたりする地球内部の圧力がパンガイアの地殻を割り、いくつかのプレートに分けてしまったのである。地球内部の圧力はその後もプレートを動かし続け、パンガイアはさらに細かく分割された。こうして分かれた地殻がこんにちの大陸となったのである。大陸が切り離されて漂流したと考えるこの理論は、大陸移動説と呼ばれている。

　いくつかの事実が手がかりとなって科学者たちは大陸移動説を考えるようになった。その1つは化石で、異なる大陸の岩石に同じような化石が見つかっている。それほど遠くまで泳げるはずのない有史以前の同じ動物たちの化石が、南アメリカとアフリカで発見されている。こうした動物たちが大西洋を渡れるはずはないので、この2つの大陸はかつて陸続きであった、というのが地質学者の説である。

　もう1つの手がかりは大陸の形だ。もう1度地図を見て、どうしてこの説が成り立つのか考えてみよう。そう、まるでジグソーパズルのピースのように、南アメリカにアフリカがぴたりとはまってしまうのがわかる。

　大陸が切り離されたときに、地球表面の4分の3を覆っていた大きな海はいくつかに分かれることになった。この分割された海を大洋という。世界の4大洋といえば、大西洋、太平洋、インド洋、北極海である。

> **NOTE**
>
> **パンガイア**
> pangaeaのpanはギリシャ語で「すべて」、gaeaは「大地」の意味。ドイツの気象学者の造語で、「汎大陸」と訳されている。

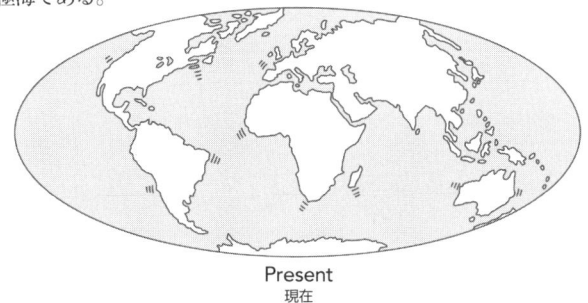

Present
現在

MATHEMATICS • 算数

Roman Numerals ローマ数字

The numerals we use most often—the digits 0, 1, 2, 3, 4, 5, 6, 7, 8, 9—are called Arabic numerals. But you may also come across Roman numerals on clocks and in books.

Here are the Roman numerals from 1 to 10. Look at them carefully, especially the numerals for 4 and 9.

私たちがもっともよく使う数字—0, 1, 2, 3, 4, 5, 6, 7, 8, 9—はアラビア数字という。しかし、時計の文字盤や本などでローマ数字を見かけたりすることもある。

下に並んでいるのは1から10までのローマ数字である。特に4と9に注意しながらよく見てみよう。

I II III IV V VI VII VIII IX X

Here are the Roman numerals from 10 to 100, counting by tens:

今度は10から100までのローマ数字を10ごとに並べたものである。

X XX XXX XL L LX LXX LXXX XC C

If you learn the values of the following Roman numerals, you can use these symbols to write numbers into the thousands.

次のようなローマ数字の値がわかるようになれば、この記号を使って4桁の数字を書き表すことができる。

I is 1.　　X is 10.　　C is 100.　　M is 1000.
V is 5.　　L is 50.　　D is 500.

Here are two rules:
1) When a Roman numeral that is the same size or smaller comes after another Roman numeral, you add their values together.

規則は2つある。

あるローマ数字のあとにくる数字が、前の数字と同じかそれよりも小さい場合は、その値を合計する。

4th GRADE

XV is (10+5), or 15
XV は (10+5)、すなわち 15

XXX is (10+10+10), or 30
XXX は (10+10+10)、すなわち 30

2) When a Roman numeral that is smaller comes right before one that is larger, you *subtract* the smaller one from the larger one.

あるローマ数字の前にそれより小さな数字がくる場合は、大きい方の数から小さい方の数を引く。

IV is (5−1), or 4
IV は (5−1)、すなわち 4

IX is (10−1), or 9
IX は (10−1)、すなわち 9

XL is (50−10), or 40
XL は (50−10)、すなわち 40

XC is (100−10), or 90
XC は (100−10)、すなわち 90

Often you need to use both of these rules to write numbers in Roman numerals. These examples show you how grouping numbers within a long Roman numeral helps you read it:

ローマ数字を使って数を書くときには、たいていこのルールをどちらも使うことになる。次に掲げる例を見ると、長いローマ数字を読むにはその中にある数のグルーピングが役立つことがわかる。

CDXLVIII is 448
CDXLVIII は 448

$$\begin{array}{ccc} CD & XL & VIII \\ (500-100)+ & (50-10)+ & 8 \\ 400 \quad + & 40 \quad + & 8 \end{array}$$

MCMLXXXVII is 1987
MCMLXXXVII は 1987

$$\begin{array}{cccc} M & CM & LXXX & VII \\ 1000 \;+ & (1000-100) \;+ & 80 \;+ & 7 \end{array}$$

We often write a year number like 1987 in Roman numerals. Practice turning numbers that are in Roman numerals, like MCMLXXXVII, into Arabic numerals.

1987年のような、年号をローマ数字で書くことは珍しくない。MCMLXXXVIIのようなローマ数字で書かれた数をアラビア数字に変換する練習をしてみよう。

NOTE 文房具の英語

ball-point pen（ボールペン）
mechanical pencil（シャープペンシル）＊シャープペンシルの芯は lead。
pencil sharpener（鉛筆削り）
eraser（消しゴム）
highlighter（蛍光ペン）＊highlight とは目立たせること。
marker（マーカー）
glue / paste（のり）
Scotch tape（セロテープ）
stapler（ホッチキス）
＊ホッチキスとはいわない。針は staple、針はずしは staple remover。
thumbtack（画鋲）＊画板は drawing board。
ruler（定規）
compass（コンパス）
＊「コンパスで円をかく」は draw a circle with a compass。
protractor（分度器）
＊「分度器で角度をはかる」は measure (the numbers of degrees in) the angle with a protractor。

5th What American GRADERS Learn in Textbooks

LANGUAGE ARTS • 国語

The Iliad and the Odyssey

According to tradition, the greatest storyteller of ancient Greece was Homer. He was a blind poet who lived about 3,000 years ago. He told stories about heroes in war, gods and goddesses, and incredible monsters. He told two of the greatest stories of all time, the Iliad and the Odyssey, long poems about great heroes and famous deeds.

The Iliad

The Iliad is the story of a long war between the Greeks and the people of the Troy called the Trojan War. It was a war caused by the gods and goddesses and a handsome prince named Paris.

Paris was one of the sons of the king and queen of the walled city of Troy. Due to a dream that his son Paris would bring destruction on Troy, the king had the baby taken to a mountain and left to die. But a shepherd found Paris, raised him and took him as a son. Paris became a strong, handsome young man who did not know that he was really a prince. In the meantime, the king and queen did not know that Paris was still alive.

At a wedding feast, a quarrel began between three goddesses as to which was the most beautiful. Hera, queen of the gods; Athena, goddess of wisdom; and Aphrodite, goddess of love and beauty, each claimed to be the most beautiful of all. They demanded that Zeus, king of the gods, make the selection. Zeus knew that whoever he chose, two of the goddesses would be angry. So he left the choice to the handsome young shepherd Paris.

Paris selected Aphrodite, after she promised him the fairest woman in the world as his reward. Aphrodite kept her promise. First she helped restore Paris to his position as prince of the royal family. Then

イリアスとオデュッセイア

古代ギリシャの最高の物語作者といえばホメロスであった。盲目の詩人ホメロスが生きていたのは、今からおよそ3000年も昔のことになる。彼は戦争の英雄や神々、女神たち、驚くべき怪物たちの物語を語った。文学史上の最高傑作とされる物語『イリアス』と『オデュッセイア』を作ったのはそのホメロスだが、2作とも偉大なる英雄たちや名高い偉業を詠みこんだ長篇詩である。

イリアス

『イリアス』は、トロヤ戦争と呼ばれるギリシャ人とトロヤ人の長期にわたる戦いの物語である。この戦争を起こしたのは、神々と女神たち、そして美しい王子パリスであった。

パリスは、城壁に囲まれた都市トロヤの王と王妃の間にできた子の1人であった。息子パリスはトロヤを破滅に導くであろうという夢のお告げを聞いた王は、部下を使って生まれたばかりのパリスを山に置き去りにした。しかし羊飼いがパリスを見つけ、自分の息子として育て上げた。パリスは武勇にすぐれた美貌の若者に成長したが、自分が王子であることは知らなかった。一方、王と王妃もパリスがまだ生きているとは知らずにいた。

あるとき、結婚の宴で、3人の女神の中で誰がいちばん美しいかをめぐって争いが起きた。神々の女王ヘラ、叡智の女神アテナ、愛と美の女神アフロディテのそれぞれが、自分が最高の美女であると言い張った。3人の女神たちは神々の王ゼウスに審判をあおいだが、誰を選んでも残った2人が憤ることは明らかだったので、ゼウスは若く美しい羊飼いパリスに判断をゆだねた。

パリスが選んだのはアフロディテで、それはアフロディテが褒美としてパリスに人間の世界の絶世の美女をめとらせることを約束したからであった。アフロディテは約束を守った。彼女はまずパリスを王子として王家の一員にもどしてやった。それから大艦隊ととも

NOTE
ホメロス
紀元前700年頃の人とされるが詳細は不明。吟誦詩人で、暗記した叙事詩を聴衆の前で朗誦した。『イリアス』(約16,000行)、『オデュッセイア』(約12,000行)の作者とされるが、複数の詩人が作ったという説もあり、いまだに論争には決着がついていない。

NOTE
トロヤ戦争
ドイツの考古学者シュリーマンは、少年時代にホメロスの叙事詩を読んで感動し、トロヤ遺跡を探し続け、ついに1870年代に遺跡を発掘し、ホメロスの叙事詩が史実に基づくことを立証した。トロヤ戦争の年代は紀元前13世紀頃と推測されている。

Paris set off for Greece with a great fleet of ships, to find Helen, the most beautiful woman in the world, lived.

Paris was welcomed by the Greeks and especially by King Menelaus, who was Helen's husband. But while Menelaus was on a hunting trip, Aphrodite made Helen fall in love with Paris. Paris carried Helen off to Troy, along with gold and many treasures belonging to Menelaus. It was this carrying off of Helen that is the cause of the Trojan Wars, and it was said of her beauty that hers was "the face that launched a thousand ships."

Menelaus and the other Greek kings were not about to allow this to go unpunished. All of the Greek kings joined forces against Troy, both to take back Helen and to gain glory and riches for themselves. Among these Greek heroes was the swift-footed warrior Achilles.

The Quarrel Between Agamemnon and Achilles

When the Greeks reached Troy, they found the Trojans ready for battle. The greatest of the heroes defending Troy was Hector. The Trojans, headed by Hector, came out from the city through the great gate in the high walls. They met the Greeks on the open plains between the walls of Troy and the beaches where the Greek ships had landed. They fought with swords, axes, bows and arrows, and sharp javelins. The ground ran red with the blood of many a hero whose groaning soul fled unwillingly to the realms of the dead.

The most feared of all the Greek warriors was Achilles. Clad in the shining armor that was a gift of Zeus, and hurtling forth in his chariot drawn by immortal horses, he struck terror into the hearts of Trojans, who, seeing him, would run back to their walled city.

Though the Trojans fought bravely, they were unable to keep up a steady fight in the open fields against the vast numbers of Greeks.

にギリシャに向かったパリスは、ついに人間界最高の美女ヘレネに出会った。

ギリシャ人たち、特にヘレネの夫であるメネラオス王はパリスを喜んで迎えた。しかし、そのメネラオスが狩猟の旅に出ている間に、アフロディテはヘレネに魔法をかけてパリスに恋するようにしてしまった。パリスはヘレネをトロヤへと連れ去り、ついでにメネラオス王の金銀財宝をも持ち帰ってしまった。トロヤ戦争を引き起こしたのはこのヘレネの拉致である。ヘレネの美しさはといえば、「その美貌が1000の軍船を動かした」という言葉があるほどだ。

メネラオスも他のギリシャの王たちもこの略奪を黙って見逃すつもりはなかった。全ギリシャの王たちはトロヤと戦うために結束し、ヘレネを奪い返すとともに栄誉と富をも手中におさめようとした。このときのギリシャの英雄の中に、俊足の戦士アキレスがいた。

アガメムノンとアキレスのいさかい

ギリシャ軍がトロヤに着いてみると、すでにトロヤ軍は戦闘態勢を整えていた。トロヤを守る勇士たちの中で最強の者はヘクトルである。そのヘクトルの率いるトロヤ軍が、高い城壁に囲まれた都市から大門を通って出てきた。トロヤ軍とギリシャ軍がぶつかったのは、トロヤの城壁とギリシャの船団が上陸した浜辺の間にある平原地帯だった。両軍はそこで剣、斧、弓矢、投げ槍を武器に戦った。勇士たちのおびただしい血が大地に流れ、彼らの魂はうめき声を上げながら、無念の思いで死者の地へと旅立っていくのであった。

ギリシャの戦士たちの中でももっとも恐れられていたのはアキレスである。ゼウスからの贈り物である光り輝く鎧に身を固め、アキレスは不死身の軍馬に引かせた戦闘馬車を駆って敵を次々と蹴散らし、トロヤ軍兵士たちを恐怖で金縛りにした。アキレスの姿を見るや、トロヤ軍は城壁に囲まれた都市へと退却してしまった。

トロヤ軍の戦いぶりは勇敢であったが、逃げ場のない平原でギリシャの大軍勢と休みなく戦うほどの力はなかった。敗北をまぬがれるには都市の高い城壁にたよるほかないことを悟ったトロヤ軍は、城壁の中に立てこもった。

ギリシャ軍は9年間にわたって都市トロヤを包囲し、攻撃し続けた。しかし、1度も高い城壁を崩すことはできなかった。何年も戦いが続くうちに、ギリシャ軍は食料、衣料、軍需物資の補給が必要

Seeing that they must depend for safety on the high walls of their city, they withdrew inside those walls.

For nine years the Greeks besieged the city of Troy. Never could they break through the high walls. As years passed, the Greeks came to need food and clothes and supplies. So they left part of the army to watch over Troy, and sent part to attack other cities to get supplies and to take captives. After the raids, the spoils were divided among the chiefs, as was customary. For the Greek kings, honor and glory in battle were measured in part by the riches and captives they won.

In these raids, two maidens, named Chryseis and Briseis, were taken captive. They would soon become the cause of a bitter quarrel between Agamemnon and Achilles.

Chryseis was given to Agamemnon, while Briseis went to Achilles, who became very fond of the lovely maiden. The father of Chryseis, a priest named Chryses, came to beg Agamemnon to return his daughter. He wore his priestly garments, and brought many valuable gifts as ransom for his daughter. But Agamemnon scornfully refused his plea. "Away with you, old man," he barked. "As for your daughter, I will carry her back with me when I have taken Troy."

Now Chryses prayed to Apollo, the sun god, asking him to make Agamemnon return his daughter. Apollo answered these prayers. For nine days, from his fiery chariot in the sky he shot arrows that carried death, first to the dogs and mules, then to the men. Finally, when the funeral pyres of the dead were burning day and night, Achilles called the Greek chiefs together to consider what to do.

At the meeting, the Greeks' soothsayer—a wise man who could understand the ways of the gods—revealed the cause of the plague: "Apollo is angry because his priest has been dishonored by Agamemnon. Chryseis must be restored to her father, and we must offer a great sacrifice to the Archer God, if we are to appease him."

Furious, Agamemnon jumped up and growled, "You prophet from hell! Never have you spoken anything good for me. Now you say I must give up the maiden. Then so be it—I would save our army, not destroy it. But hear me! Some other prize must be given to me, at once, for Agamemnon shall not be slighted!"

Achilles responded: "What prize is there to give? All the spoils have

になってきた。そこで彼らは、トロヤの監視に残る部隊と、他の都市を襲って軍需物資を確保し捕虜をつかまえる部隊とに分かれた。都市をいくつも襲撃してもどると、大将たちはいつものように戦利品の中から自分の分け前を取った。ギリシャの王族にとっては、自分の取り分となる財宝や捕虜の数の多い少ないが、ほぼそのまま彼らの手柄と栄誉の評価となった。

こうして行われた襲撃で、クリューセイスとブリーセイスという若い娘2人が囚われの身となった。この2人のことが原因で、やがてアガメムノンとアキレスが激しく争うことになるのである。

クリューセイスはアガメムノンに与えられ、ブリーセイスはアキレスのもとへ行ったが、アキレスはこの愛らしい娘をとても好ましく思った。クリューセイスの父はクリューセスという名の神官である。彼は、アガメムノンのもとへ駆けつけると、娘を返してくれるよう哀願した。神官職の衣をまとった父は、わが娘の身代金として高価な贈り物を数多く持参していた。しかし、アガメムノンは彼の懇願をさげすむように退けた。「親父さん、とっとと帰るんだ」と彼はどなり声をあげた。「おまえの娘は、我々がトロヤを陥落させたら、国へ連れて帰るつもりだ」

そこでクリューセスは太陽神アポロンに祈りを捧げ、アガメムノンが娘を返してくれるよう力をお貸しくださいと頼んだ。アポロンはこの祈りを聞き入れた。9日間にわたり、アポロンは天空を舞う炎の戦車から死の矢を放ちつづけ、その矢はまず犬やラバを、それから人間を射た。ついに死者を火葬にする薪の山が昼も夜も燃え続けるようになると、アキレスはギリシャ軍の隊長たちを招集して対応策を協議した。

その会議でギリシャ軍の預言者は――この男は神々のやり方を心得た賢者であった――この災厄の原因を明らかにしてこう言った。「アポロンが怒っているのは、彼の神官がアガメムノンに侮辱されたからです。クリューセイスは父のもとへ返さなければなりませぬ。そして射手の神アポロンの怒りをなだめるには、多大な生贄を差し出さなければなりません」

怒り狂ったアガメムノンは、立ち上がって大きな声を張り上げた。「地獄の預言者め！　わしが喜ぶような預言を1度だって言ったことがあるか。今度はわたしにあの娘を手放せという。ならば、好きにしろ。そうすればわが軍は救われる。壊滅させるわけにはいかぬからな。だが、よく聞け！　なにかほかの褒美はもらうぞ。今すぐ

been divided. We cannot ask our men to return what has been given to them. So, be satisfied and let the girl go for now. When we have taken the strong city of Troy, we will make it up to you, three and four times over."

"Is that your game, then, Achilles?" snapped Agamemnon. "You are to keep your prize, and I am to lose mine? No! This council must award a suitable prize to me, or else I will seize yours, or that of Ajax or Odysseus."

At this, the wrath of Achilles flared. "You greedy dog!" he shouted at Agamemnon. "How can the Greeks be expected to fight bravely under you? I have no quarrel with the Trojans; they have done me no wrong. I have been fighting against them for your sake and your brother's. But you—you sit in your tent at ease, and then, when the spoils are divided, you take the lion's share. And now you would take the little that was given to me. I have no desire to stay here and be dishonored by you. I will take my men and go."

"Go, then," said Agamemnon. "Take your ships and your Myrmidons. But hear this: to make clear to all who is the stronger man, I will come to your tent, and take the fair-cheeked Briseis, your prize, for my own."

Achilles's hand gripped the hilt of his sword. Slowly he slid the sharp blade from its scabbard. "Now I will slay this villain where he sits," he thought. But then he stopped—for at that instant the goddess Athena seized him by his long yellow hair. When he turned, he saw the goddess, who was visible only to his eyes.

"Put back your sword, swift-footed Achilles," said Athena. "Hera,

にだ。このアガメムノンを軽んじるのは許さん!」
　アキレスがこれに答えた。「褒美といっても何がある？　戦利品はすべて配分された。まさか部下たちにやってしまったものを、いまさら返せとは言えまい。だから、取り分に文句をいわず、あの娘を今すぐ返してやるがよい。堅固な都市トロヤを攻め落としたら、3倍にも4倍にもしてこの埋め合わせはしよう」
「アキレスよ、それがおまえの魂胆か？」とアガメムノンはくってかかるように言った。「おまえは自分の取り分を抱えこんで、わしには手放せというのか？　そうはいかん！　この会議で話し合って、わしにふさわしい褒美を用意するんだ。でなければ、おまえの取り分はわしがもらう。それがいやなら、アイアスの分でも、オデュッセウスの分でも持ってこい」
　これを聞いて、アキレスの怒りが炸裂した。「この業つくばり犬め！」とアガメムノンに向かって怒鳴った。「おまえのような指揮官のもとで、ギリシャ軍は命がけの戦いができると思うか？　わたしはトロヤ人と喧嘩をしているわけではない。彼らもわたしに何も悪いことはしていない。すべておまえとおまえの兄弟のためだけに彼らと戦っているのだぞ。それなのに、おまえはなんだ──宿営のテントに陣取って、さあ戦利品の山分けだというときになると、だれよりもいい分け前を欲しがる。その上、今度はわたしがもらったわずかな褒美をも横取りしようというのか。もうわたしはここに残っておまえに愚弄されるのはまっぴらだ。部下を連れて出てゆく」
「いいとも、行くがよい」とアガメムノンは言った。「おまえの船団とミュルミドン軍団を連れて帰れ。だがようく聞け──全軍にどちらが強者であるかをはっきりさせるために、おれはおまえの宿営テントへ行って、おまえの分捕った、頬の美しい娘ブリーセイスをおれのものにするぞ」
　アキレスの手は剣の柄を握った。そしてゆっくりと鋭い刀身を鞘から抜こうとした。「この悪党をいまここで切り捨ててやる」と心の中でつぶやいた。が、そのとき手を止めた──その瞬間女神アテナが、アキレスの長い金髪をつかんだのだ。アキレスがふりかえると、そこに女神がいた。女神は彼にしか見えない。
「俊足のアキレスよ、剣を鞘に収めなさい」とアテナが言った。「神々の女王ヘラもわたくしも、おまえとアガメムノンを、ともに愛している。さあ、おまえの怒りをぶつけるがよい。だが、武器は剣ではなく、言葉ですよ」。そういうとアテナの姿は消えた。

queen of the gods, and I love you and Agamemnon both. Now, show your anger, though not with a blade, but with words." So saying, she disappeared.

"When an immortal speaks," thought Achilles, "a man must obey." Then turning to Agamemnon, he lashed out with angry words: "Hear this solemn oath, you drunkard with the eyes of a dog and the heart of a deer! There will come a day when every Greek soldier will beg to have Achilles back. But on that day, though a thousand perish at the hands of Hector alone, Achilles will not come to help. You will regret the dishonor you have heaped upon the bravest man in your army!"

So saying, Achilles, with his dear friend Patroclus, returned to his tent, where they were soon visited by messengers of Agamemnon, who led away the fair-cheeked Briseis. Now the Greeks would have to face the Trojans without their greatest warrior, who sat by the wine-dark sea, firm in his implacable wrath.

The Arming of Achilles

As the fighting raged on, the tide began to turn against the Greeks. Their greatest heroes were all sorely wounded. Without Achilles, there was no one who could oppose the furious strength of Hector.

One night, Hector called his troops together and spoke: "Men of Troy, take your rest. Loose your horses from their chariots and give them food. Go, some of you, to the city, and fetch cattle, sheep, wine, and bread, that we may have plenty to eat and drink. For tomorrow we arm ourselves and drive these Greeks back to their ships! If the gods are willing, we will burn those ships with fire. We shall surely bring ruin upon these Greeks!" So Hector spoke, and the Trojans shouted with joy to hear such words.

While the Trojans made merry, the Greeks sat in worry and fear. And no one was more worried than Agamemnon. He called his chiefs together and spoke: "I acted as a fool the day that I sent my messengers to take the fair Briseis from Achilles. See how, when Achilles stands aside from battle, we Greeks are put to flight! As I did him wrong, so now will I make amends, and give him many, many times more than what I took from him. Now, three of you go and take my message to Achilles."

「不死の神の言葉とあらば」アキレスは思った。「従わねばなるまい」。そして、アガメムノンの方を振り向きざま、怒りを一気にぶちまけた。「酔いどれよ、おまえにあるのは貪欲な犬の眼に臆病な鹿の心臓だ。いいか、この神聖なる誓いを聞け！ やがてギリシャ軍の全兵士がもどってくださいとアキレスにすがりつく日がくるであろう。しかしその日がやってきて、敵のヘクトルただ1人に一千のギリシャ兵が倒れたとしても、アキレスは助けにはこぬ。おまえは、自軍のもっとも勇敢な男に与えた侮辱の数々を悔いることになるのだ！」

そう言うとアキレスは盟友パトロクロスとともに自分のテントに戻った。まもなくそこにアガメムノンの使いがやってきて、頬の美しい娘ブリーセイスを連れ去った。これからギリシャ軍は、最強の戦士を欠いたままトロヤ軍と対決することになるのだ。その戦士アキレスは、なだめようのない怒りをこらえて、暮れなずむワイン色の海のそばでじっと座っていた。

アキレスの武装

戦いが激しさを増すにつれ、形勢はギリシャ軍にとって不利になっていった。ギリシャ軍の偉大な勇士たちはみなひどい傷を負っていた。アキレスがいなければ、ヘクトルのすさまじい力に対抗できる者はいなかった。

ある夜、ヘクトルは兵士たちを集めてこう言った。「トロヤの兵士たちよ、休息をとるのだ。馬を戦闘馬車から放し、餌をやれ。誰か、街に行って、牛、羊、ワインとパンを持って来い。たっぷり飲み食いできるようにな。明日ともなれば、われわれは武器を手に、ギリシャ軍を彼らの船まで撃退するのだ！ もし神々が望むのであれば、その船に火を放つのだ。われわれはかならずやギリシャ軍を壊滅させてみせよう！」こうヘクトルが言い放つと、トロヤ軍の兵士たちは大歓声をもって応えた。

そのトロヤ軍が宴を楽しんでいるとき、ギリシャ軍は不安と恐怖をいだいてうずくまっていた。そして誰よりも深く悩んでいたのはアガメムノンであった。彼は上官たちを呼び寄せて言った。「我ながら愚かなことをしたものだ、美しいブリーセイスを奪わんとしてアキレスに使者を送るとは。アキレスが戦いから退いてからというもの、われわれギリシャ軍は敗走に甘んじている。彼に対して罪を

The messengers were graciously received by Achilles, who listened to their moving appeals. Then he made his answer. "Long ago," he said, "my mother, Thetis of the sea, said to me 'My son, you have two destinies, and you may choose only one. If you stay in this land and fight against Troy, then you may never go back to your own land, but will die in your youth. Only your name will live forever. But, if you will leave this land and go back to your home, then you shall live long, even to old age, but your name will be forgotten.' Once I thought that fame was a far better thing than life; but now that Agamemnon has shamed me before my people, and taken my fame from me, my mind is changed. So, find some other way to keep Hector and the Trojans from the Greek ships, for I will depart soon."

When the battle resumed the next day, Achilles remained in his tent. At first the Greeks did well, but then the Trojans came on more fiercely than before. Many a Greek hero fell, and the Trojans pressed closer to the ships.

Achilles was approached by that man he held dear above all others, his friend from childhood days, Patroclus. "Patroclus," asked Achilles, "why do you weep?"

犯したのだから、つぐないをしなければなるまい。わたしが彼から奪ったものを何倍にも、何十倍にもして返すのだ。よいか、おまえたちのうちの3人がアキレスのもとへ行き、わたしの申し出を伝えるのだ」

　アキレスは3人の使者を丁重に出迎え、彼らの切々たる訴えに耳を傾けた。そしてこう答えた。「ずっと昔のことだが」と彼は言った。「わたしの母、海の精テティスに言われたことがある。『息子よ、おまえには2つの運命があり、選べるのはどちらか1つです。もしこの地にとどまってトロヤと戦えば、おまえは2度と故郷に帰ることなく、若くして死ぬことになるでしょう。永遠に永らえるのは、おまえの名だけです。しかし、もしこの地を離れて故郷に戻るのなら、おまえは長く生きて老いを迎えることができましょうが、おまえの名は忘れられてしまうでしょう』。これを聞いて、わたしは命よりも名誉のほうがずっと大切だと思った。しかし、アガメムノンにわが民の前で辱めを受け、名誉を奪われた今、わたしの考えは変わった。ギリシャの船団をヘクトルとトロヤ軍の攻撃から守りたければ、何か別の策を講じてほしい。わたしはすぐにここを発つつもりだ」

　翌日、ふたたび戦いが始まったが、アキレスは自分のテントにとどまっていた。はじめのうちギリシャ軍は善戦したものの、トロヤ軍の攻撃はこれまでにも増して激しくなった。多くのギリシャ軍の勇士が倒れ、トロヤ軍はギリシャ軍の船の近くまで攻め寄ってきた。

　アキレスのもとに、彼がもっとも大切に思っている、幼いころからの友人パトロクロスが会見を求めてやって来た。「パトロクロス」とアキレスは尋ねた。「どうして泣いているのだ」

「怒るな、勇将アキレスよ」とパトロクロスは言った。「ギリシャ軍は窮地に立たされている。勇敢な隊長たちはみな傷を負っているのに、あなたの怒りはおさまらず、助けてくれようとはしない。ならば、頼みがある。あなたが戦闘にはせ参じるつもりがないならば、わたしを行かせてくれ。あなたの手兵ミュルミドン軍団を連れて行かせてくれないか。それから、あなたの鎧をお借りしたい。そうすれば、トロヤ軍はあなたが戦いに戻ってきたと思いこむにちがいない」

　パトロクロスはそう言ったが、こうしてみずからの死を引き寄せているとは知るはずもない。はじめアキレスは同意しなかったが、ギリシャ船団の最初の1隻が炎に包まれるのを見て、急いで行くようパトロクロスに言った。そこで、ゼウスからの贈り物であるアキ

"Do not be angry with me, great Achilles," said Patroclus. "The Greeks are in trouble, for all the bravest chiefs are wounded, and yet you sustain your wrath and will not help them. Now, listen: if you will not go forth to the battle, then let me go, and let your Myrmidons go with me. And let me put on your armor, for then the Trojans will think that you have come back to the battle."

So Patroclus spoke, not knowing that he asked for his own death. At first Achilles resisted, but when he saw the first of the Greek ships set afire, he bid Patroclus make haste. And so, clad in the shining armor of Achilles, gift of Zeus, Patroclus went forth, leading the Myrmidons. The Trojans saw the armor and, thinking that Achilles had returned to battle, they turned to flee. Over and over again Patroclus charged into the ranks of the Trojans, slaying many. Then Hector, aided by Apollo, realized, "This man is not Achilles, though he wears his armor."

Suddenly, Apollo struck Patroclus from behind, and he fell stunned to the ground. A Trojan soldier wounded him in the back with a spear. Then Hector arrived and thrust the mortal blow, driving his spear point in just above the hip. "Did you think, Patroclus," shouted Hector, "that you would take our city, and carry away our wives and daughters with your ships? This you will not do, for now the fowls of the air will eat your flesh."

"Mark you, Hector," gasped Patroclus with his dying breath, "death is very near to you, at the hands of the great Achilles."

When Achilles heard the news of the death of his dear friend, he threw himself upon the ground. "Cursed be the anger that sets men to strive with one another, as it made me strive with Agamemnon," he cried out. "As for my fate—what does it matter? Let it come when it may, as long as I may first have vengeance on Hector."

Then Zeus sent a messenger to Achilles, saying, "Rouse yourself, or surely Patroclus will be food for the dogs of Troy. You must hurry if you wish to save his body and give it proper funeral rites."

So Achilles, unarmed, went forth. Athena set about him a radiance that shone like a circle of fire. He shouted aloud, and his voice, trumpet-like, was terrible to hear, striking fear in the hearts of the Trojans, even frightening their horses, which were startled and clashed chariots together. The awed Trojans retreated, and the Greeks took up the body of Patroclus, with Achilles, weeping, walking by its side.

レスの輝く鎧を身にまとい、パトロクロスはミュルミドン軍団を率いて戦場に向かった。トロヤ軍は鎧を見ると、アキレスが戦いに戻ってきたと思い、逃げ出した。パトロクロスは何度も何度もトロヤ軍の隊列に突入し、多くの敵兵を殺した。そのときヘクトルは、アポロンの助けにより、はたと気づいた。「その男はアキレスではない。彼の鎧をまとっているだけだ」
　突然、パトロクロスは背後からアポロンの一撃を受け、気を失って地面に倒れた。トロヤの兵士が槍でパトロクロスの背中に傷を負わせた。そしてヘクトルがやって来ると、腰のすぐ上を槍先でぐいと突き刺して、致命傷を負わせた。「パトロクロスよ」とヘクトルは叫んだ。「われわれの街を征服し、われわれの妻や娘たちを船で連れ去るつもりであったろう。そんなことはできまい。ほれ、おまえの体は、空飛ぶ鳥どもの餌食となるのだ」
「よく聞け、ヘクトル」とパトロクロスは虫の息であえぎながら言った。「死がおまえに迫っている。おまえは勇将アキレスの手にかかって死ぬのだ」
　大切な友の死の知らせを聞くと、アキレスは地面に身を投げて嘆いた。「呪うべきは、人々を戦いに駆り立てる怒りだ、わたしとアガメムノンをあい争わせた怒りだ」と彼は叫んだ。「わたしの運命？　それがなんだというのだ。運命がどうでも、逃げはせぬ。とにかくヘクトルに復讐せずにはおくものか」
　ゼウスはアキレスに使者を送ってこう伝えた。「立ち上がるのだ。ぐずぐずしていると、パトロクロスはトロヤの犬どもの餌食になってしまう。彼の遺体を守り、正式の葬礼をしてやりたいなら、急がなくてはならない」
　アキレスは武器を持たずに出発した。女神アテナの与えた炎のように燃える光の輪が彼を包んでいた。アキレスは大声で叫び、そのトランペットのような声の恐ろしさにトロヤ軍はおののいた。彼らの軍馬さえおびえ、おどろきのあまり馬車同士がぶつかり合った。おそれをなしたトロヤ軍は退却し、ギリシャ軍はパトロクロスの遺体を回収したが、アキレスは涙を流しながら遺体の横について歩くのだった。
　アキレスの鎧はトロヤ軍に奪われてしまっていたので、アキレスの母親である海の女神テティスは、金、銀、鉄をつかさどる神ヘーパイストスの鍛冶場へ急いで赴いた。テティスに頼まれ、ヘーパイストスは光り輝く頑丈な鎧とみごとな盾を作りあげた。その盾には、

Since the armor of Achilles had been captured by the Trojans, Achilles's mother, the sea goddess named Thetis, traveled swiftly to the forge of Hephaestus, the god who worked in gold and silver and iron. At her request, Hephaestus crafted strong and splendid armor, including a great shield upon which he inscribed images of war and peace, life and death, love and hate, work and play. It was as though the wide world were embraced within the rim of the huge, heavy shield.

When next the rosy-fingered Dawn arose, Thetis placed the great armor at the feet of her son. It dazzled the eyes of the Myrmidons, who dared not look directly at it. Only Achilles looked at it, and as he looked the wrath within him burned, and his eyes flared like the sun.

When he was fully armed, Achilles went to Agamemnon, and said, "Let our foolish quarrel end. Here I make an end of my anger. Make haste, and call the Greeks to battle!"

The Death of Hector

When he returned to battle, Achilles was like a wildfire that burns everything in its path, until the trees of the forest fall in flames, and the sides of the mountains are scorched black. In terror the Trojans ran like fawns to take refuge behind the high walls of the city—all except Hector, who waited to meet Achilles in mortal combat.

Hector's father and mother, old King Priam and Queen Hecuba, called out from atop the city walls, begging their son not to fight Achilles. But Hector refused, saying, "It is far better to meet in arms and see whether Zeus will give the victory to him or me."

Then Achilles approached, his armor blazing, and shaking over his shoulder a huge spear. Even brave Hector trembled at the sight, and he turned and ran. As when a hawk in the mountains swoops down upon a trembling dove, so Achilles in fury flew after Hector. Three times around the walls of Troy they ran. Then Athena appeared by the side of Hector, though in the form of one of his brothers. "My brother," she said to Hector, "we two will stand against Achilles." Encouraged by these words, Hector turned and faced Achilles, calling out: "Three times you have pursued me round these walls, but now I will stand and face you. Only let us agree: if Zeus gives me the victory today, I

戦争と平和、生と死、愛と憎しみ、仕事と遊戯を表す絵柄が刻み込まれていた。あたかもその大きくずっしりとした盾の縁どりの中に、全世界が封じこめられているかのようであった。

翌日、ばら色の光の差す夜明けが訪れると、テティスは大きな鎧を息子の足元に置いた。ミュルミドン軍団は目が眩んでしまい、その鎧をよく見ようとはしなかった。しかしアキレスはじっと鎧に目を向けた。そうすると、心中の怒りは熱く燃えたち、彼の目は太陽のように輝いた。

武具をすっかり身につけると、アキレスはアガメムノンのもとへ行き、こう言った。「愚かないさかいは終わりにしようではないか。わたしは怒りを捨てることにした。急いでギリシャ軍に戦闘の号令を！」

ヘクトルの死

戦場に帰ってきたアキレスは、さながら野火のようであった。行く手を阻むものすべてを焼き、燃えさかる炎で森の樹々を倒し、山腹を黒々と焼き焦がす野火のようにアキレスは戦った。おびえたトロヤ兵たちは、都市の高い城壁の向こうへと子鹿のように逃れ去った。しかし、ひとりヘクトルだけは残り、アキレスと生死をかけた戦いにのぞんだ。

ヘクトルの父である年老いたプリアモス王と母であるヘカベ女王は、城壁の上に立って、戦うのはやめておくれと息子に大きな声で頼むのであった。しかしヘクトルはこれを拒み、「武器を持って戦い、ゼウスの神が勝利を授けるのはわたしなのか彼なのか決着をつけます。わたしにとってはそのほうがずっとましなのです」と答えた。

そのときアキレスが近づいてきた。鎧はまぶしいほどに輝き、頭上に大きな槍をふりかざしている。これを見て勇士ヘクトルも恐れおののき、さっと向きを変えて走り出した。怒ったアキレスは、山中の鷹がおびえる鳩を急襲するように、ヘクトルのあとを追いかけた。走り続けた2人は、トロヤの城壁の周囲を3度回った。そのとき不意にアテナがヘクトルのかたわらに姿を現した。アテナはヘクトルの兄弟のひとりに変身していた。「兄上」とアテナはヘクトルに声をかけた。「2人でアキレスに1歩も譲らず立ち向かいましょう」。これを聞いて勇気を取りもどしたヘクトルは、ふり向いてアキレスにこう呼ばわった。「この城壁を回ること3度、おまえは逃

will give back your body to the Greeks; if you should be the victor, promise to do the same with me."

Achilles scowled. "Hector," he said, "lions do not make agreements with men, nor wolves with lambs." Then he threw his great spear, which Hector barely avoided. "You have missed!" cried Hector. "Now see whether my aim is true." And with all his strength he hurled his spear at Achilles. It struck full force upon the great shield, and bounced off. "Give me your spear, brother!" cried Hector—only to turn and find no one there. Then he knew his fate: "The gods have decreed my doom. But let me not die without a struggle. Let me do some great thing that men will remember in years to come."

So Hector drew his sword and charged at Achilles. Achilles ran at Hector, seeking the most vulnerable spot, not protected by strong armor. He found it where the neck meets the collarbone, and there he drove his spear deep through the soft part of the neck.

Dying, Hector gasped, "O Achilles, I entreat you, do not make my body food for dogs, but give it to my father and mother that they may duly bury it. They will reward you with silver and gold."

"No amount of gold will buy you back," said Achilles. "Now, cur, die!" To shame the dead Hector, Achilles stripped him of his armor, then bent down and cut holes in the space between the ankles and heels. Through these holes he drew cords of ox-hide, then fastened the cords to his chariot, and so dragged Hector's dead body back to the

げるわたしを追いかけてきたが、もう逃げずに対決してやる。ただ、1つだけ取り決めをしたい。もしゼウスが今日の戦いの勝利をわたしに授けてくれたら、おまえの亡骸はギリシャ軍に返してやろう。もし勝者がおまえなら、同じようにわたしをトロヤへ返すと約束してくれ」

　アキレスは睨みすえた。「聞けヘクトル、ライオンは人間と取引などせぬものだ。狼と子羊とても同じことよ」。こう言うとアキレスは大きな槍を投げたが、ヘクトルはかろうじてこの槍をかわした。「しくじったな！」とヘクトルは叫んだ。「今度はこの必殺の一撃を受けてみよ」。そう言うと、ヘクトルはあらん限りの力でアキレスめがけて槍を投げた。槍はもののみごとに無双の盾に当たったものの、はねかえされた。「弟よ、おまえの槍をよこせ！」とヘクトルは叫んだ――だが、ふりかえって見ると、そこにはだれの姿もなかった。彼はおのれの運命を悟った。「神々はわたしをお見捨てになったか。だが、戦わずに死ぬようなことはさせないでほしい。この先長く人人の記憶に残るような、立派な戦いをわたしにさせてくれ」

　こう言うとヘクトルは、剣を抜き取ってアキレスめがけて突進した。アキレスはヘクトルに向かって走りながら、頑丈な鎧に被われていない、いちばん弱いところを探していた。見つけたのは首と鎖骨の間のところで、そこを突いたアキレスの槍は、やわらかな首筋を、深く刺し貫いた。

　息を引きとる前に、ヘクトルは虫の息でこう懇願した。「アキレスよ、お願いがある。どうかわたしの亡骸を犬の餌食にはしないでくれ。きちんとした埋葬ができるよう、父と母のもとに返してくれないか。彼らは金銀を持ってお礼にうかがうだろう」

「どんなに金を積んでも、おまえを買いもどすことはできぬのだ」とアキレウスははねつけた。「さあ、野良犬よ、死ね！」死んだヘクトルを辱めるために、アキレスは死者の鎧をはぎとると、かがみこんで足首と踵の間のところに穴をあけた。この穴に雄牛の皮で作った紐を通し、その紐を自分の戦闘馬車に結びつけると、ヘクトルの死体をギリシャ軍の船団のあるところまで引きずってもどった。怒りのおさまらぬアキレスは、さらに数日もの間、戦死した盟友パトロクロスの墓の周りをヘクトルの死体を引いてぐるぐる回らせた。だが、ヘクトルを憐れと思った神々は、死体が傷まぬようにずっと守っていた。

　それだけではなかった。ヘクトルの亡骸をトロヤへ返すという

Greek ships. For the next few days, in his fury, Achilles caused the dead body to be dragged about the tomb of his fallen friend, Patroclus. Yet the gods took pity on Hector, and kept his dead body from harm.

It was, furthermore, the will of the gods that Hector's body should be returned to Troy. So the gods helped old Priam make his way safely to Achilles. When he entered Achilles tent, Priam, great King Priam, threw himself at Achilles's feet and kissed his hands, saying, "Achilles, take pity; I kiss the hands of the man who has killed my children."

Achilles was moved, remembering his own father and his fallen friend, Patroclus. He called upon two servants to wash and anoint the body of Hector. This done, he went out to the wagon full of treasures brought by Priam. He accepted the treasures but left one cloak to cover Hector's body, which he now lifted into the wagon.

When Achilles returned to his tent, Priam asked, "Let there be a truce for nine days between the Greeks and Trojans, that we may bury Hector with all due ceremony."

"It shall be as you ask," replied Achilles. Then he took the aged king by the hand, and led him to a place of rest. The next day Priam returned to Troy, and so began the splendid funeral for Hector, fallen son of the city whose high walls would soon fall.

Epilogue to the Iliad

Homer's Iliad ends with the funeral of Hector. Other accounts tell us of the fate of Achilles, and the end of the Trojan War.

The Fate of Achilles: After the funeral of Hector, fighting resumed. Achilles killed many Trojans, but he was himself slain by Paris. Paris was no match for Achilles in single combat, but he was a skilled archer. He shot Achilles in the one place he could be hurt, his heel. Except for his heel, Achilles was invulnerable. When Achilles was a baby, his mother had dipped him into the river Styx, the magical waters of which protected his body from injury. But in dipping him, Thetis had held the infant by his heel, so his heel was unprotected. Even today, we speak of a person's "Achilles' heel," meaning a person's one great weakness.

The Trojan Horse: Troy fell because of a clever plan on the part of the Greeks, devised by the wily Odysseus. The Greeks built an enor-

が神々の意志であった。こうして老いたプリアモスは、神々の助けを得て無事にアキレスのもとへ行くことができた。アキレスのテントに入ると、プリアモスが、あの偉大な王プリアモスが、アキレスの足もとに身を投げ出し、彼の手に口づけをしてこう言った。「アキレスよ、憐れと思し召せ。わが子たちを殺した男の手に唇をつけるのだ」

　アキレスは心を動かされた。自分の父親や亡くなった友パトロクロスのことを思い出したのだ。彼は召使を2人呼んで、ヘクトルの死体を洗い、香油を体に塗った。これがすむと、外に出たアキレスは、プリアモスが持参した宝物を山と積んだ馬車のところへ行った。彼は宝物を受け取ったが、マントを1枚残し、それをヘクトルの死体にかけてやった。それから死体を抱き上げ、馬車に乗せた。

　アキレスがテントに戻ると、プリアモスがこう願い出た。「ギリシャ軍とトロヤ軍の間で9日間の休戦協定を結ばせていただきたい。そうすれば死者にふさわしい葬儀をとり行って、ヘクトルを葬ることもできよう」

「その申し出どおりにさせよう」とアキレスは約束した。それから彼は年老いた王の手を取ると、休息できる部屋へと招き入れた。翌日、プリアモスはトロヤに帰り、戦いに倒れたトロヤの息子ヘクトルの壮麗な葬儀がとり行われた。トロヤの高い城壁が崩れ落ちたのは、それから間もなくのことであった。

『イリアス』の結末

　ホメロスの『イリアス』はヘクトルの葬礼で幕を閉じる。また、アキレスの運命とトロヤ戦争の終結について物語る箇所もある。

アキレスの運命

　ヘクトルの葬礼が終わると、戦いはふたたび始まった。アキレスは多くのトロヤ兵を殺したが、彼自身はパリスによって命を奪われた。1対1の戦いではアキレスにとても敵わなかったパリスだが、彼は弓の名手だった。パリスはアキレスの体に傷を負わせることのできる唯一の箇所であるかかとを弓で射った。かかとを除けば、アキレスには弱点はなかった。赤ん坊のとき、アキレスの母親は彼をスティクス川に浸し、特別な力を持った水が彼のからだを守って傷つくことのないようにしたのだ。ところが、水に浸すとき、母親のテティスは赤ん坊のかかとを手で握っていたので、そこだけは無

mous, hollow horse out of wood. They left it outside the walls of the city, and then pretended to sail away, though they went no farther than a nearby island. Inside, however, were hidden some of the bravest Greek warriors.

When the Trojans saw the huge wooden horse, some were suspicious, but most thought it was an offering to the gods, so they hauled it within the walls of the city. That night, the Greek warriors crept out of the horse and opened the gates of the city to the other soldiers, who had returned under cover of darkness. The Greeks set fire to Troy, and conquered the great city at last.

The story of the fall of Troy is told in moving detail in an epic poem called The Aeneid, written by Virgil, a great Roman poet who lived in the first century B.C.

防備だった。こんにちでもわたしたちはだれそれの「アキレス腱」と言ったりするが、それはその人の大きな弱点という意味で言っているのである。

トロヤの木馬

　ギリシャ軍側の巧みな戦術によってトロヤは陥落したが、その戦術は策略に長けたオデュッセウスの考えたものだった。ギリシャ軍は中が空洞になっている巨大な木製の馬を作った。彼らはその木馬を街の防壁の外側に置いたまま、船でトロヤから去っていくふりをして、近くの島までしか行かなかった。木馬の内側には、ギリシャ軍の中でもとりわけ勇敢な戦士たちが隠れていたのだ。

　トロヤ人は大きな木馬を発見して、怪訝に思う者もいたが、たいていの者は神々への捧げものだと思い、防壁の内側へと引き入れた。その夜、ギリシャの戦士たちは木馬からそっと出て、街の門を開き、夜の闇にまぎれて戻ってきていたほかの兵士たちが入れるようにした。ギリシャ軍はトロヤに火を放ち、ついに大都を征服したのだった。

　トロヤの陥落については、紀元前1世紀に生きたローマの詩人ウェルギリウスが、『アエネイス』という叙事詩の中で詳しく感動的に描いている。

> **NOTE**
> **トロヤの木馬**
> トロヤは現在のトルコの小アジア半島にある。1998年に世界文化遺産として登録された。現在でも毎年世界から集まった数百人の研究者が発掘を続けている。この遺跡が実際にトロヤ戦争の舞台であったのか、あるいはホメロスがトロヤを戦争の舞台に見立てただけなのかという議論には決着がついていない。

The Odyssey

Homer's Odyssey is an epic poem about the adventures of a Greek hero, Odysseus, as he made his difficult journey home after the Trojan War. You might also hear Odysseus sometimes referred to as Ulysses, which is the name given to him by the Romans, who were great admirers of Homer and the rest of Greek culture.

After the ten long years of the Trojan War, Odysseus looked forward to a speedy voyage home. But it was not to be: it took Odysseus another ten years before he reached his native island, Ithaca. Through the will of the gods, and sometimes through mistakes of his own or his crew, Odysseus wandered far and wide before returning home.

His wanderings took him to the island of Circe, a beautiful sorceress who turned men into swine; to Hades, the realm of the dead, where he spoke with the sad shade of Achilles; between Scylla, a six-headed monster, and Charybdis, a devouring whirlpool; and, past the Sirens, maidens who sang alluring songs that drew sailors to their deaths.

As Homer tells it, the Odyssey is not only the story of the wanderings of Odysseus, but also of the voyages of his son, Telemachus, who goes in search of Odysseus, and during his travels hears many tales of the adventures of his famous father.

Odysseus and the Cyclops

Sing in me, Muse, the story of the man resourceful beyond all others, the wanderer, who met with woes unnumbered, after raiding the ramparts of the strong city of Troy.

This was Odysseus, king of Ithaca, one of the Greek chieftains who fought at Troy. They fought for ten years until, after the fair Helen had been retrieved, the great city was at last destroyed, and Greek ships, filled with plunder, set sail for home.

When Troy had been taken, Odysseus set sail for the island of Ithaca in twelve ships with fifty good crewmen in each. Little did these mariners think that it would be ten years before any saw their home. Nor did they know that by their own recklessness, and despite the

オデュッセイア

　ホメロスの『オデュッセイア』は、ギリシャの勇士オデュッセウスの冒険をめぐる叙事詩で、彼は、トロヤ戦争に勝ったものの、故郷に帰るまでに数々の苦難を強いられたのだった。ときにはオデュッセウスをユリシーズと言うこともあるが、これは古代ローマ人の呼び方で、彼らはホメロスをはじめとするギリシャ文化に心酔していたのである。

　10年もの間続いたトロヤ戦争が終わると、オデュッセウスは海を渡って一刻も早く故郷に帰りつく日を心待ちにしていた。だが、そうはならなかった。生まれ故郷のイタカに着いたのは、それからさらに10年後のことである。神々が許さぬこともあったし、自分自身の過ちや部下の過ちなどに阻まれたこともあったが、オデュッセウスは、帰郷を果たすまでに、遠くの地を延々とさまよったのである。

　さすらいの旅をするオデュッセウスは、キルケーの島へとたどり着く。キルケーは美しい魔女で、人間を豚に変えてしまう。オデュッセウスは死者の国ハデスへも行く。そこで彼は、死者アキレスの悲しげな影と言葉をかわすのだ。さらにオデュッセウスは、一方に6つの頭を持つ怪物スキュラが、もう一方に渦潮の怪物カリュブディスが立ちはだかる場所を脱し、セイレーンたちからも逃れる。若い女の姿をしたセイレーンは、船乗りたちを美しい歌声で魅了し、最後は命を奪ってしまう。

　詩人ホメロスの語りを追っていくと、『オデュッセイア』にはオデュッセウスの放浪の物語だけではなく、その息子テレマコスの航海の物語もある。父を探しに船出したテレマコスは、勇名とどろく父オデュッセウスの苦難の物語を、旅の先々で幾度も聞くことになるのである。

オデュッセウスとキュクロプス

　ミューズよ、わたしに宿りて歌え、誰よりも智略にまさる放浪者、堅固な都市トロヤの防壁を襲撃したのち、数知れない苦難に襲われた者の物語を。

　その者とはオデュッセウス。イタカの王であり、トロヤと戦ったギリシャの隊長の1人だ。彼らは10年ものあいだ戦い、美しいヘレネを取りもどし、ついに大都を破壊した。そして、戦利品を満載したギリシャの船団は故郷に向かって出帆したのだった。

　トロヤを征服すると、オデュッセウスは12隻の船それぞれに50人の

NOTE
セイレーン
火事のときなどに鳴らす「サイレン」の語源。

NOTE
ミューズ
ギリシャ神話の女神たち。ホメロスの時代、詩人はミューズから与えられた霊感（inspiration）によって詩を作ることができると信じられていた。

brave efforts of their king to save them, only one—Odysseus himself—would return.

Not long into their journey, a great storm fell upon the ships and carried them far to the south, past their island home. Late one evening, in a dense fog, the ships' keels grazed the shore of an island. Odysseus and his crew beached the ships, then slept through the night. When the rosy fingers of Dawn touched the sky, they woke and found fresh water, as well as numbers of wild goats, which made a fine feast for the hungry sailors.

Nearby was another island. Odysseus and his men could see wisps of smoke rising from it, and heard the bleating of flocks. "Friends and shipmates," announced Odysseus, "in my own ship, with my own crew, I will make the crossing to that island, and find out who lives there, and whether they be good people or lawless savages."

Odysseus thought to bring some food, as well as a big goatskin full of strong, sweet wine, a gift from a priest of Apollo. There never was a more precious wine: one measure of it could be mixed with twenty measures of water, and still it would remain wonderfully sweet and potent.

Upon reaching the island, Odysseus picked twelve of his bravest men. They set off and soon found a huge cave, apparently the home of some shepherd, since many rams and goats were walking about. The men looked inside and saw pens full of young sheep and goats, baskets full of cheeses, and milk pans stacked against the walls. "Let us take these cheeses," cried the men, "and open the pens and drive the goats and lambs aboard our ships, then head back out to sea."

Odysseus knew this was good advice. But he wanted to see what kind of man this shepherd might be. So the men built a fire, helped themselves to some cheese, and sat down to wait.

As evening neared, they were startled by a loud crash! It was the sound of a huge bundle of logs dropped into the cave from the shoulder of a great giant, one of those creatures called Cyclops. He was a brutish man, with only one large eye in the middle of his forehead, and one shaggy eyebrow above it.

Odysseus and his frightened men scrambled to the back of the cave. The Cyclops drove his flocks into the cave, then closed the entrance

優れた水夫を乗せ、イタカ島に帆を向けた。自分たちの誰かが故郷を目にするまでにまさか10年もかかろうとは、水夫たちの誰も考えもしなかった。また、自分たちの軽率な行動がもとで、主君が勇敢にも自分たちを救おうとしたのも空しく、たった1人――オデュッセウスただ1人――しか故郷にたどり着けないことになろうとは知るよしもなかった。

　航海を始めてまもなく、船団はひどい嵐に襲われ、故郷の島を通りこし、はるか南方へと流されてしまった。ある晩遅く、深い霧を進むうちに、ある島で船の底が浅瀬に乗り上げてしまった。オデュッセウスと船員たちは船を浜に引き上げると、朝まで眠った。夜が明けて空にばら色の光が差すと、彼らは目を覚まし、真水と野生の山羊の群れを見つけた。腹を空かせた船乗りたちにとっては格好のごちそうとなった。

　その島のそばには、もう1つ別の島があった。オデュッセウスと兵士たちには立ち上っている煙が見え、山羊の群れの鳴き声も聞こえた。「航海をともにする仲間たちよ」とオデュッセウスは言った。「わが船に乗り、わが仲間を率いて、あの島に渡るぞ。どのような者が住んでいるのか、善良な人々なのか、手に負えぬ野蛮人なのか、確かめてこよう」

　オデュッセウスは食料のほかに、アポロン神殿の神官に贈られた強い甘口のワインを、大きな山羊の皮袋にたっぷり入れて持っていこうと考えた。それはこのうえなく貴重なワインで、20倍の水で薄めても、不思議なことに甘さも強さも変わることがなかった。

　島に到着すると、オデュッセウスはとりわけ勇敢な男を12人選び出した。探索を始めてまもなく、彼らは大きな洞窟を見つけた。どうやら羊飼いの住処(すみか)のようだった。というのは、たくさんの羊や山羊があたりを歩き回っていたからだ。男たちが中をのぞき込むと、子羊や子山羊でいっぱいの家畜囲いがあり、チーズを山盛りに入れた籠(かご)があり、ミルク鍋が壁にずらりと並んでいた。「チーズをいただこう」と男たちは叫んだ。「家畜囲いを開き、山羊や子羊をわれわれの船に追い込んで、船を出そう」

　そうしたほうがいいとオデュッセウスは思ったが、ここに住んでいる羊飼いがどんな男なのか見てみたかった。そこで彼らは火をおこし、チーズを食べ、腰を下ろして時間をつぶした。

　夕方が近づいてくるころ、彼らをびっくりさせるようなドシンという大きな音が鳴り響いた。それはキュクロプスと呼ばれるとてつもない巨人の怪物が、肩にかついでいた大きな丸太の束を洞窟に投げ入れた音だった。キュクロプスは残忍な男で、ひたいのまん中に大きな目が1つだけあり、目の上にはもじゃもじゃの眉毛が生えていた。

with a boulder so big that twenty wagons could not carry it. He milked the ewes and she-goats, setting aside half the milk to curdle for cheese, and half for his own supper. He threw some logs on the fire and stirred up a great flame, the glare from which revealed Odysseus and his men.

"Who are you?" said the giant, his voice a deep rumble. "Are you men of the sea-traders or pirates?"

Odysseus replied, "We are Greeks, sailing home from Troy, where we have been fighting for King Agamemnon, whose fame is known far and wide. We are homeward bound, but great gales have blown us off course. Now, as the gods love those who show hospitality to strangers, we ask you to be hospitable to us."

"The gods!" roared the Cyclops. "We Cyclops care not for the gods. We are greater and stronger than your Zeus with all his thunder. Now, tell me, puny one, where have you left your ship?"

Odysseus knew that, if he revealed the location of the ship, the Cyclops would crush it to splinters and leave them no hope of escaping. So with his quick and ready mind, he answered, "We have no ship, for our ship was driven upon the rocks and broken. My men and I are the only survivors."

The giant said nothing, but quickly grabbed two of the men, as a man might pick up two squirming puppies. He dashed them on the ground, then tore them limb from limb. Like a mountain lion gnawing and crunching a fresh kill, he devoured them entirely—flesh, bones, organs, everything—and washed it all down with great swallows of milk. And when he had filled himself with this awful food, he lay down among his sheep and slept.

Odysseus drew his sharp sword and rushed to the giant's side, preparing to stab him to the heart, when he stopped: "If I kill him," he thought, "then I condemn myself and my men as well, for we could never move that great boulder from the doorway." So, sad at heart, he waited, thinking.

When morning came, the giant awoke, milked his flocks, then seized two of the men and devoured them as before. He opened the cave and went forth with his flocks to the pastures, though before leaving he placed the great boulder over the entrance.

All day Odysseus thought of how he might save himself and his

オデュッセウスとおびえた兵士たちはあわてて洞窟の奥に逃げこんだ。キュクロプスは家畜を洞窟に追いこみ、20台の荷車でも運べないくらいの大きな岩で洞窟の入口をふさいでしまった。彼は羊と山羊の乳をしぼり、そのうちの半分をチーズにするために残し、残りの半分を自分の夕食用に取り分けた。キュクロプスが丸太を何本か火にくべると、大きな炎が舞い上がり、その光でオデュッセウスと兵士たちの姿が照らし出された。

「おまえらは何者だ」と巨人は低くとどろく声で言った。「海のものどもか――商人か、それとも海賊か？」

　オデュッセウスは言った。「われわれはトロヤから故郷に向かって航海をしているギリシャ人だ。トロヤでは、広く遠く名の知れわたるアガメムノン王のために戦ってきたのだ。われわれは故郷を目指していたのだが、強風のために航路を逸れてしまった。神々はよそ者を親切にもてなす者を愛するという。われわれにももてなしをお願いしたい」

「神々だって！」キュクロプスはうなり声をあげた。「俺たちキュクロプスは、神々などなんとも思っていない。おまえたちのゼウスがありったけの雷を集めても、俺たちのほうがもっと偉大で力強いのだ。さて、教えてもらおうか、ちっぽけな人間よ。どこに船を停めてきたのだ？」

　もし船の位置を教えてしまったら、キュクロプスは船を粉々に壊してしまい、島から脱出する望みはなくなることがオデュッセウスには分かっていた。そこで彼はすばやく機転を利かせて、こう答えた。「船はない。岩場に乗り上げて壊れてしまったのだ。助かったのはわたしと兵士たちだけだ」

　巨人は何も言わず、兵士のうちの２人をさっとつかんだ。まるで人間がじゃれ動く２匹の仔犬をつかむかのようだった。キュクロプスはつかんだ兵士たちを地面に叩きつけ、手足を引き裂いた。豹がしとめたばかりの獲物を噛みちぎってムシャムシャ食べるように、キュクロプスは兵士たちをまるごと――肉も、骨も、内臓も、なにもかも――むさぼるように食い、それをがぶりがぶりとミルクで流し込んだ。そしてこの恐ろしい食事で腹いっぱいになると、羊の群れの中で横になって眠った。

　オデュッセウスはするどい剣を抜いて巨人の脇に駆けより、心臓を貫こうとしたが、そこで彼は手を止めた。「もしこいつを殺してしまったら」とオデュッセウスは考えた。「自分と兵士たちはもうおしまいだ。われわれにはあの巨大な岩を入口から動かすことなど絶対にできまい」かくしてオデュッセウスは、悲嘆を胸に、じっと考えこんだ。

　夜が明けると巨人は目を覚まし、家畜の乳をしぼり、兵士のうちの２

companions. He noticed a great pole in the cave, the trunk of an olive tree, which the giant planned to use as a walking staff. Odysseus cut off a six-foot section and sharpened one end, then turned the pointed end in the fire to harden it.

In the evening, the Cyclops returned, and once again seized two prisoners and feasted on them. Then Odysseus stepped forth, holding in his hands a bowl filled with wine from the wineskin he had brought, full of the powerful and tempting drink. "Drink, Cyclops," said Odysseus. "Wash down your scraps of flesh. I had meant to offer this to you as a gift if you would help us home."

The Cyclops greedily swallowed all that was in the bowl. "Give me more," he commanded, "and tell me your name. Then I will make you a gift as a proper host should."

Then wily Odysseus said, "My name is No-Man. Now, give me your gift."

"My gift," laughed the giant, "is that you shall be eaten last." Saying this, he toppled over in a drunken sleep. Drops of wine and bits of human flesh dribbled out of his mouth.

"Come, my brave friends," said Odysseus. They grabbed the sharpened stake and heated the point in the fire till it glowed red. Then, running at top speed, they thrust it into the giant's single eye, and leaned with full force, twisting and turning the stake as a man turns a drill. The burning wood hissed in the eye as a red-hot iron hisses when dipped in water.

The Cyclops roared and thrashed out. Odysseus and his men fell back in fear. Blood spurted as the Cyclops tore the hot stake from his eye. He roared so loudly that other Cyclops came running from their nearby caves to see what had happened. From outside they called out, "Polyphemos!" —for that was this giant's name—"Polyphemos, what's wrong? Why do you cry out? Is someone stealing your sheep or hurting you?"

The giant bellowed, "No-Man! No-Man has hurt me! No-Man!"

"Well," replied the other Cyclops, "if no man is hurting you, then it must be yourself or the gods, and we can do nothing about that." And they returned to their caves.

Groaning, the Cyclops groped till he grabbed the boulder blocking

人をつかんで、昨日と同じように食べてしまった。彼は洞窟の入口を開き、家畜といっしょに牧草の生えているところへ行ったが、その場を離れる前に入口に巨大な岩を置いていった。
　オデュッセウスは1日中、どうすれば自分と仲間たちが助かるだろうかと考えた。彼は洞窟の中に大きな杭があることに気づいた。それはオリーブの木の幹で、巨人が杖に使おうと思っていたものだった。オデュッセウスはその幹から6フィート（およそ180センチメートル）の長さを切りだし、一方の端を鋭くとがらせ、焼いて硬くした。
　夕方になって戻ってきたキュクロプスは、またもや囚われた兵士2人をうまそうにたいらげた。オデュッセウスは、ワインをなみなみとついだ杯を持って進み出た。それは、彼が持参した皮袋に入れてあった、強くてうっとりするような味の酒だ。「これを飲め、キュクロプス」とオデュッセウスは言った。「人肉の食べ残しを流し込むといい。もしわれわれが帰るのを手助けしてくれるなら、このワインを贈りものにしようと思っていたのだ」
　キュクロプスは杯のワインをうまそうにすべて飲み干した。「もっとくれ」とキュクロプスは言った。「それから、おまえの名前を教えるんだ。そうしたら、客をもてなす主人らしく、おまえに贈りものを進呈してやろう」
　策略に長けたオデュッセウスは言った。「わたしの名前は〈誰でもない〉だ。さあ、贈りものをいただこう」
「俺の贈りものはな」とキュクロプスは笑って言った。「おまえを食べるのを最後に回してやることだ」。そう言うと彼はよろよろ倒れこみ、酔っ払ったまま眠ってしまった。口もとからは、ワインのしたたりと人肉の断片が垂れ落ちていた。
「来てくれ、勇敢な同志たちよ」とオデュッセウスは言った。彼らは先を尖らせた杭を抱え、先端が真っ赤になるまで火にかざして熱した。そして、全力で走って杭を巨人の1つ目に突き刺すと、全身の力を杭に傾けてドリルのようにグイグイねじって回した。燃える棒杭は、赤く焼けた鉄を水につけたときのように、シューシューと音をたてた。
　キュクロプスはうめき声をあげてのたうち回った。オデュッセウスと兵士たちは恐ろしさのあまり後ずさりした。キュクロプスが熱い杭を眼から引き抜くと、血がほとばしった。彼の大きななうなり声を聞いて、ほかのキュクロプスたちが、いったい何があったのかと近くの洞窟から走ってやってきた。洞窟の外で彼らは叫んだ。「ポリュペーモス！」──というのが巨人の名前だったのだ──「ポリュペーモス、何があったんだ？

the entrance to the cave. He removed the boulder then sat down in the entrance, feeling around him to grab any of his prisoners that should try to escape. Odysseus could see that there was still no easy way out. So, he called upon all his wits to devise yet another plan.

He took strips of willow from the giant's bed. With these he tied together three rams, side by side, then bound a man under the belly of the middle ram. He did this for all six of his remaining men. Then he found the largest, woolliest ram and pulled himself tight under his belly, gripping the fleece as tightly as he could.

When morning came, the Cyclops, as was his habit, let his flocks out to graze. He stroked each ram but did not feel the men hiding beneath. When he felt the biggest ram, however, he stopped it and spoke: "What is this, my sweet creature? You never lag behind, but are always first out of the cave in the morning. What now keeps you back?" Odysseus remained as silent and still as possible. "Could it be," continued Cyclops, his huge fingers rubbing the ram's fleece, "that you are sad for your poor master's eye, which that villain No-Man has destroyed? I swear he will not get out alive! If only you could speak and tell me where he is, I would splatter his brains upon the ground!" Then, with a sigh, he let the ram proceed.

どうしてわめいているんだ？ 羊を盗むやつがいるのか、それともひどい目にあっているのか？」

巨人は大声でわめいた。「〈誰でもない〉！ 俺を傷つけたのは〈誰でもない〉！〈誰でもない〉！」

「そうか」とほかのキュクロプスたちは言った。「誰もおまえを傷つけていないなら、自分でやったか、神々の仕業に違いないな。それじゃ俺たちにはどうしようもない」。こういうと、彼らは自分たちの洞窟に戻っていった。

苦痛にあえぎながらキュクロプスは手探りで歩き、洞窟の入口をふさいでいる岩をつかんだ。彼は岩をどかして入口に座り、身の回りを手でさわって、逃げようとする囚人を捕まえられるようにした。オデュッセウスの見るところ、まだ簡単に脱出できそうにはなかった。そこで彼は新たな策を考えようと知恵のかぎりをつくした。

オデュッセウスは巨人のベッドから柳の細長い枝を抜き出した。その枝でオデュッセウスは3匹の牡羊をくっつけて1つに結びつけ、まん中にいる牡羊の腹の下に兵士をくくりつけた。彼は生き残った6人の兵士すべてにこれと同じことをした。それからオデュッセウスは、いちばん大きく、毛のふさふさした牡羊を選び、毛をしっかりとつかんでその腹の下にしがみついた。

夜が明けると、キュクロプスはいつものように家畜を外に出して草を食ませた。彼は羊を1匹ずつ手でなでてみたが、下に男たちが隠れているのは分からなかった。ところが、いちばん大きな牡羊に触ったとき、キュクロプスはその羊を止めてこう言った。「どうしたんだ、おれのかわいい羊よ。おまえは決してぐずぐずしないで、朝になればいつも真っ先に洞窟から出ていくじゃないか。なんで遅れたんだ？」オデュッセウスはできるかぎり静かにじっとしていた。「ひょっとしたら」とキュクロプスは大きな指で羊毛をなでさすりながら言った。「あわれな主人の目のことで悲しんでいるのかい？ あの悪党の〈誰でもない〉にやられた目のことを。あいつをぜったいここから生きては帰さないぞ！ もしおまえが口をきけて、あいつの居場所を教えてさえくれりゃ、あいつの脳ミソを地面に叩きつけてやるんだが！」そう言うと、ため息をつき、彼は羊を外へ行かせた。

外に出てしまうと、オデュッセウスは羊をつかんでいた手を放して、仲間たちを羊からほどくために走っていった。彼らは巨人の羊をできるだけたくさんかき集め、急いで船に戻った。船で心配していた仲間はオデュッセウスたちを喜んで迎えたが、6人の男がいないことに気づい

Once outside, Odysseus released his grip and ran to untie his companions. They rounded up as many of the giant's sheep as they could, then hurried back to their ship. Their worried companions welcomed them, but were saddened to see that six men were missing. "Quiet yourselves," said Odysseus, "I will explain. For now, row with all your might!"

When they were far from shore, Odysseus could not resist shouting back, "O Cyclops! You beast who feeds on men! How do you like what No-Man has done to you? May the gods punish you even more!"

The Cyclops heard Odysseus and was angered. He broke off a hilltop and heaved it in the direction from which he had heard Odysseus's voice. It struck just in front of the ship and caused a great wave, pushing the ship all the way back to the shore! "Row, men, row or die!" urged Odysseus. So they rowed, and when they were twice as far out as before, Odysseus again stood up and cupped his hands to shout. His men exclaimed, "Captain, stop! For the love of Zeus, don't make the brute angry! He'll smash us to bits!"

But Odysseus, enraged, cried out again: "Listen, Cyclops! If any man asks you who put out your eye, then tell them truthfully that it was I, Odysseus of Ithaca!"

The giant took up another huge rock and threw it. This time it struck just behind the ship and propelled the craft farther away. The blind giant dropped heavily upon the ground and sobbed. "So, my fate has come," he groaned. "Long ago, a wizard on this island predicted that I would lose my eye at the hands of Odysseus. But I always thought Odysseus would be some giant, powerful and armed—not a puny, scrawny thing."

Then the Cyclops rose and, turning his blind eye to the heavens, prayed to his father, Poseidon, god of the sea: "Hear me, father! Grant this one request: may Odysseus of Ithaca never reach home! Let him lose all his companions, and taste bitterness in days to come."

Poseidon, who rules the seas, heard this request and granted it. He turned his rage upon Odysseus, sending storms, shipwrecks, and disaster at every turn, forcing Odysseus to wander for ten years before returning home.

て、喜びは悲しみに変わった。「落ち着くのだ」とオデュッセウスは言った。「あとで詳しく話をしよう。いまは死に物狂いで船を漕ぐんだ!」

海岸から遠く離れると、オデュッセウスは島に向かって叫びたい気持ちを抑えられなかった。「キュクロプスよ! 人食いのけだものめ! 〈誰でもない〉にやられた気分はどうだ? 神々にもっとひどい罰を受けるがいい!」

キュクロプスはその言葉を聞いて怒り狂った。彼は丘の頂上の岩をたたき割って、岩の塊をオデュッセウスの声のする方に放り投げた。岩はちょうど船の前方に落ち、大きな波が立って船はふたたび海岸まで押しもどされてしまった。「漕げ、みんな、漕がなければ死ぬぞ!」とオデュッセウスはせきたてた。兵士たちが船を漕ぎ、先ほどより倍も遠いところまで進んだとき、オデュッセウスはふたたび立ち上がり、手を口もとにあてて叫ぼうとした。兵士たちはたまらず言った。「船長、おやめください! どうかお願いですから、怪物を怒らせないでください! われわれは粉々に叩きつぶされてしまいます!」

しかし、怒りに駆られたオデュッセウスは、もう1度叫んだ。「聞け、キュクロプス! 誰に目をつぶされたのかと訊かれたら、それはわたしだと、イタカ島のオデュッセウスだと、正直に教えてやるんだ!」

巨人はまた大岩を持ち上げて投げた。こんどは船のちょうど後ろに着水し、船をずっと沖の方へと押しやった。盲目の巨人はばったりと地面に倒れふし、泣きじゃくった。「運命が現実のものとなってしまった」と彼はうめいた。「ずっと昔、この島の魔法使いが、オデュッセウスの手にかかって目を失うことになるだろうと予言したのだ。でもおれは、オデュッセウスとは力強い、武器を持った巨人か何かだと思っていた——痩せたちびの人間などではなく」

キュクロプスは立ち上がり、見えなくなった目を天に向けると、父親である海の神、ポセイドンに祈った。「聞いてください、父よ! わたしの願いを1つかなえてください。イタカ島のオデュッセウスが故郷にたどり着くのをけっして許さないでください! すべての仲間を失わせ、来たる日々に苦しい目に合わせてやってください」

海を支配するポセイドンはこの願いを聞きいれ、かなえてやった。オデュッセウスに向けられたポセイドンの憤怒は、ことあるごとに嵐を起こし、船を難破させ、惨事をもたらした。オデュッセウスは故郷に帰り着くまでに、10年間にわたる流浪の旅を強いられたのだった。

GEOGRAPHY • 地理

The Language of Geography

Hemispheres, parallels, and meridians are not actual features of the earth like mountains, rivers, deserts, or lakes. You cannot see them on a photograph of our earth taken from space; they are imaginary markings created by geographers to help them draw maps and make accurate globes. These markings, as well as others you will read about in this chapter, form grids, allowing geographers to divide the world into sections. Grids also make it easier to locate places on our earth.

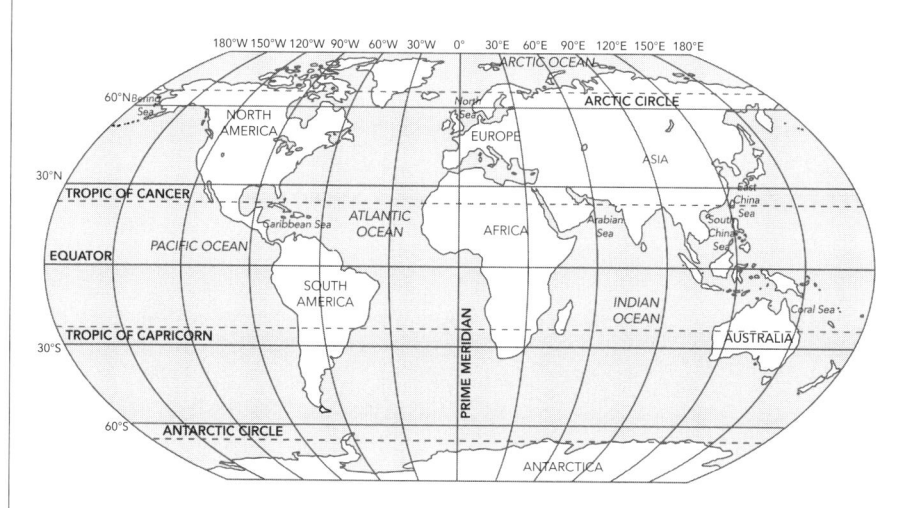

The Prime Meridian

You may remember that the prime meridian, which is 0° longitude, passes through Greenwich, England. Here, the word "prime" means first or most important. The prime meridian is the most important meridian because all distance east or west is measured from this line.

The location of the prime meridian was agreed upon by geographers from around the world who met in 1884 in Washington, D.C. They could just as easily have chosen another meridian, but this one

地理の用語

半球、緯線、子午線は、山、川、砂漠、湖のような地形とはちがって、地球の上に実際に線が引いてあるわけではない。どれも宇宙から撮影した地球の写真には写っていないが、こうしたものは、地図を書いたり正確な地球儀を作ったりするために地理学者が考えだした想像上の印だからだ。この章で扱うほかの印も含め、こうした印で格子線を作れば、地理学者が地球を区分できるようになるのである。格子線はまた、地球上のさまざまな場所を特定するのにも役立つ。

本初子午線

本初子午線、つまり0度の子午線はイギリスのグリニッジを通過するものだということを覚えているだろうか。この「本初」という言葉は、「最初の」とか「もっとも重要な」という意味である。本初子午線がもっとも重要なのは、東への距離も西への距離も、すべてこの線を基準にして測るからである。

本初子午線をどこに定めるかは、1884年にワシントンで開かれた世界各国の地理学者たちの会議で決定した。どの子午線を本初子午線に選んでもよかったわけだが、グリニッジを通る線上に有名な天文観測所があって、そこで何世紀にもわたって天文学者たちが星を観察し、航海士のために海図を作ったのだ。グリニッジがすべての子午線の基準点として選ばれたのは、多くの人々がその場所をよく知っていたからである。

基準点

もし仲間のみんなにある映画館への行き方を説明するとしたら、みんなが知っている場所、たとえばメイン・ストリートや学校からの道を教えるとうまくいくものだ。このようにすれば、映画館までの行き方を誰もが同じ道順で理解できるようになる。

passed through the location of a famous observatory, where for centuries astronomers had studied the stars and prepared charts for navigators. Because many people were familiar with the location of Greenwich, it was chosen as the reference point for all other meridians.

Reference Points

If you want to tell a group of your friends how to get to a particular movie theater, it helps to give them directions from a place all of you know, such as Main Street, or your school. That way, everyone can understand the same set of directions.

In the same way, agreement on reference points is very important to geographers. Let's play a game that will show you why. You and five of your friends each pick a different continent that you will call "home base." Then choose a location (Greenland, for example), and give the compass directions (N, S, E, W, NW, NE, SW, SE) and distance (near or far) to Greenland from each home base. What happens? No two sets of directions or distances agree, though you are all talking about the same place—Greenland. That is because you all have a different home base, or reference point. This can be a problem for geographers, too, so they use agreed-upon reference points such as the equator and the prime meridian.

As the prime, or 0°, meridian continues on the other side of the two poles, it becomes the 180° meridian. This meridian is 180° both east and west of the prime meridian, because it is exactly halfway around the world from the prime meridian. Just as the equator divides the globe in half horizontally—into the Northern and Southern Hemispheres—the prime meridian and the 180° meridian divide the world in half vertically, into the Eastern and Western Hemispheres.

European geographers who first developed maps and globes as we know them today frequently used major cities or continents as reference points. The terms Near East and Far East, for example, described regions that were near to or far from the cities of London and Paris and the continent of Europe. Similarly, the Eastern Hemisphere was described as the Old World, because it was familiar to European mapmakers and navigators, while the Western Hemisphere was described

これと同じように、地理学者にとって基準点について合意することはとても重要なことだ。なぜそうなのか、ゲームをしてみるとよく分かる。きみと5人の友だちがそれぞれ別々の大陸を選んで、自分の大陸を「ホームベース」と呼ぶことにする。それから、ある場所(たとえばグリーンランド)を決めて、それぞれのホームベースからグリーンランドへの方角(北、南、東、西、北西、北東、南西、南東)と距離(近い、または遠い)を言うとする。こうすると、どうなるか。みんなが同じ場所、グリーンランドについて話しているのに、方角と距離がともに一致する人はだれもいない。なぜかといえば、みんながそれぞれ異なるホームベース、すなわち基準点を持っているからだ。これでは地理学者たちも困ってしまうので、赤道や本初子午線といった、合意に基づいて定められた基準点を用いるのだ。

　本初子午線を0度の子午線ともいうが、この北極と南極を結ぶ線をさらに延長して反対側へ行くと、子午線180度になる。この子午線は、本初子午線から東にも180度、西にも180度ということになる。というのも、本初子午線からちょうど正確に地球を半分回ったところにあるからだ。赤道が地球を水平方向に——北半球と南半球に——2分するように、本初子午線と子午線180度は地球を垂直方向に、東半球と西半球に2分する。

　現在私たちが使っている地図や地球儀をはじめに考案したヨーロッパの地理学者たちは、大きな都市や大陸を基準点として用いることが多かった。たとえば近東、極東といった用語は、ロンドン、パリなどの都市やヨーロッパ大陸から見て近くにある地域、遠くにある地域を指すものだ。同様に、東半球を旧世界と称したのは、ヨーロッ

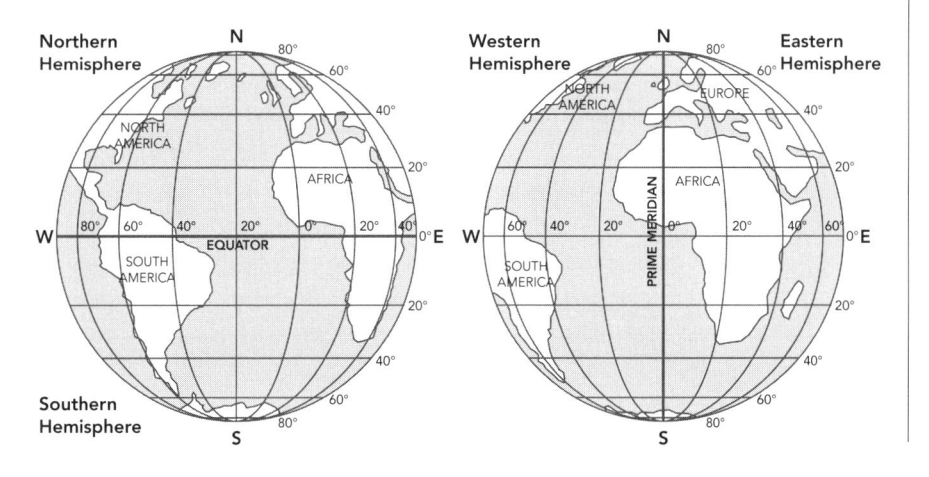

as the New World, because it was new and uncharted territory for them. Today, we still use some of the terms that describe distance and direction from European reference points.

Where on Earth Are You?

If you live in the United States, you live in the Western Hemisphere, which includes all parts of the world west of the prime meridian and east of the 180° meridian. Since a hemisphere is one half of the world, knowing which half you live in doesn't really pinpoint your exact location, does it? Let's take another step. You know that the world is also divided in half by the equator. The half above the equator is called the Northern Hemisphere, and the half below the equator is the Southern Hemisphere.

If the world were a grapefruit and you cut it in half both vertically and horizontally, you would have four quarters of it to consider. Geographers call these quarters "quadrants," from a Latin word meaning fourth part. Can you see that the United States is in the northwestern quadrant of the world?

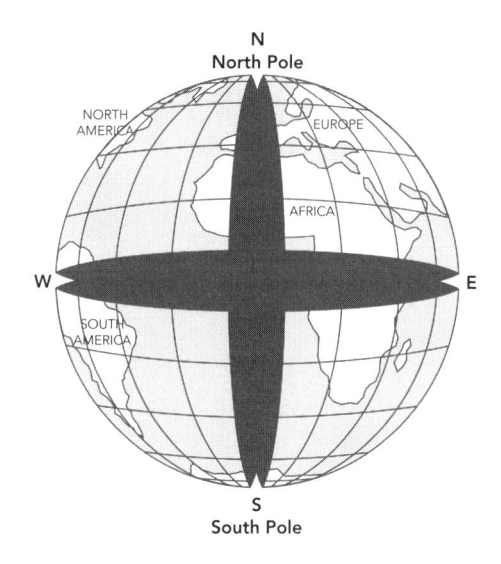

パの地図製作者や航海士のよく知る地域であったからだ。一方、西半球は新世界と呼ばれたが、それは海図のない新しい地域であったからだ。私たちは現在でもまだヨーロッパを基準点とした距離や方角の用語をいくつか使用している。

いったいきみは地球のどこにいるのさ？

アメリカに住んでいるならば西半球に住んでいるということになるが、本初子午線から西、そして子午線180度から東にあるすべての地域を含むのが西半球である。半球は地球の半分に相当するものだから、どちらの半球に住んでいるのかが分かっても、自分のいる正確な位置を特定することはできない。一歩、先に進んでみよう。地球が赤道を境に２つに分けられるということは学んだ。赤道から上の半分は北半球と呼ばれ、下の半分は南半球と呼ばれる。

地球をグレープフルーツに見立てて、垂直方向、水平方向にそれぞれ２分したら、地球は４分割されたものと考えることができる。地理学者はこの４分割された部分を、ラテン語で４分の１の部分を意味する quadrants「四象限」という言葉で呼んでいる。アメリカは北西の象限にあるのが分かるだろうか。

GEOGRAPHY • 地 理

Regions of the United States

Before the United States was formed there were thirteen original colonies and that when the United States was formed, these colonies became the first thirteen states. We think of the thirteen original states as belonging to three regions: the New England states, the Mid-Atlantic states, and the Southern states.

As our country began to grow, newly formed states were added to these three regions. But as the country expanded all the way to the Pacific coast, new regions came into being: the Midwest, the Great Plains, the Southwest, the West, and the Pacific Northwest states were added, as you can see from the map below. States are grouped into regions according to similarities in their location, climate, land forms, economy, traditions, and history.

These names for regions are just convenient labels for different parts of the country. Their boundaries and even their names are not agreed on by everyone, but people will understand what you mean when you speak of these eight regions: New England, Mid-Atlantic, South, Midwest, Great Plains, Southwest, West, and Pacific Northwest.

アメリカ合衆国の地域区分

アメリカ合衆国の建国の前にあったのは、最初に作られた13の植民地で、合衆国が誕生したときにはこの植民地が最初の13州となった。私たちは最初の13州を3つの地域に分けている。すなわち、ニューイングランド諸州、中部大西洋岸諸州、そして南部諸州である。

わが国が地理的に拡大し始めたころ、新しくできた州はこの3つの地域のどれかに加えられた。しかし、合衆国の領土が大陸を横断して太平洋岸まで広がると、地域も新しく生まれることとなった。左の地図を見るとわかるように、中西部、グレートプレーンズ、南西部、西部、そして太平洋岸北西部があらたに加わった。州を地域にグループ分けするときの根拠になるのは、地理的な位置関係や気候、地形、経済、伝統、歴史などである。

こうした地域の名称は、合衆国のさまざまな地域に貼りつけられた便宜的なラベルにすぎない。地域を分ける境界線も、そして名称でさえもすべての人が納得しているわけではない。だが、ニューイングランド、中部大西洋岸、南部、中西部、グレートプレーンズ、南西部、西部、太平洋岸北西部という8つの地域の名前をいえば、聞いている人はそれがどの地域かということは分かるはずだ。

NOTE アメリカの地域

アメリカの各州を地理、歴史、文化の違いなどに基づいて地域に分ける方法は他にもある。「South 南部」の中でも、サウス・カロライナ、ジョージア、アラバマ、ミシシッピ、ルイジアナの諸州は文化・歴史的な背景から「Deep South ディープ・サウス」と呼ぶことが多いが、フロリダ州は入らない。「Mountain States 山岳州」といえばモンタナ、アイダホ、ワイオミング、ユタ、コロラド、アリゾナ、ニューメキシコの諸州のことで、いずれも州内にロッキー山脈の一部を含んでいる。コロラド州とユタ州は、ニューメキシコ、アリゾナ、カリフォルニア、ネバダの諸州と一緒にして「Southwest 南西部」ということもある。

カリフォルニア、オレゴン、ワシントンの諸州には「Pacific States 太平洋岸州」という呼び方もある。カリフォルニアを例にとれば、他の南西部の州とはスペイン文化の伝統、乾燥した気候という共通点があるが、オレゴン州、ワシントン州と同様に太平洋に面してもいる。地域のまとめ方もいろいろあるのだ。

MATHEMATICS・算 数

Geometry 幾何学

Polygons

多角形

A closed figure that is formed by line segments is called a polygon. Triangles, rectangles, and squares are polygons; circles are not polygons.

複数の線分によってできあがる閉じた図形を多角形という。三角形、長方形、正方形などは多角形であるが、円は多角形ではない。

In a polygon, each side is a line segment. The point where two line segments meet is called a vertex. (The plural of vertex is vertices or vertexes.)

多角形の辺はすべて線分である。2つの線分が出会う点を頂点という。（頂点vertexの複数形は verticesもしくはvertexes）

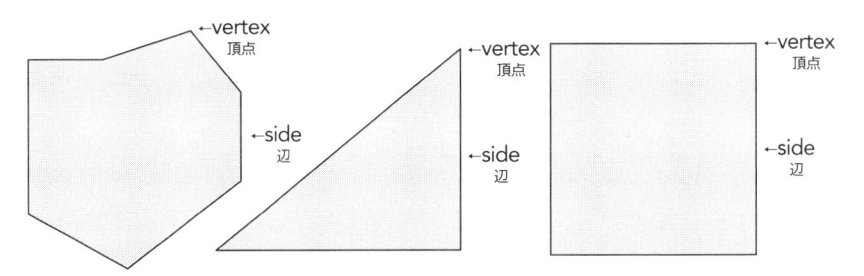

←vertex 頂点　←side 辺

Triangles

三角形

We classify triangles according to the length of their sides.

三角形は辺の長さで分類する。

equilateral triangle 正三角形

isosceles triangle 二等辺三角形

scalene triangle 不等辺三角形

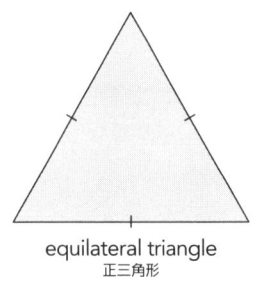

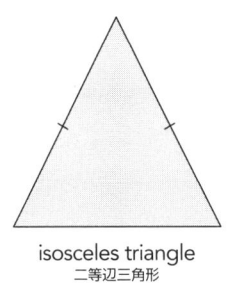

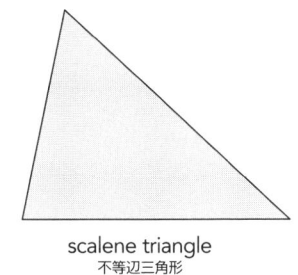

We also classify triangles according to their angles.

三角形はまた角度によっても分類できる。

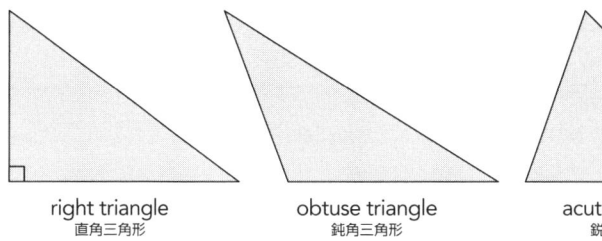

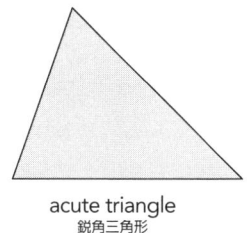

right triangle
直角三角形

obtuse triangle
鈍角三角形

acute triangle
鋭角三角形

Quadrilaterals

The prefix "quadri-" means "four" and "lateral" means "side", so quadrilaterals are polygons with four sides.

四角形

接頭辞 quadri- は4を、lateral は辺を意味する。ゆえに、quadrilateral は4つの辺をもつ多角形である。

Rectangles and Squares

Rectangles and squares are quadrilaterals.

長方形と正方形

長方形と正方形は四角形である。

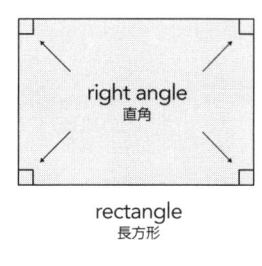

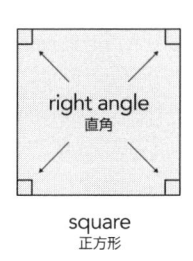

right angle
直角

right angle
直角

rectangle
長方形

square
正方形

The figures below are also quadrilaterals.

下の図形も四角形である。

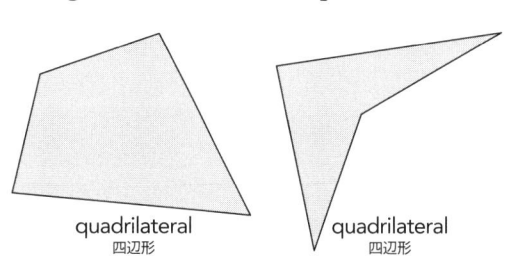

quadrilateral
四辺形

quadrilateral
四辺形

Trapezoid
A quadrilateral with only one pair of parallel sides is called a trapezoid.

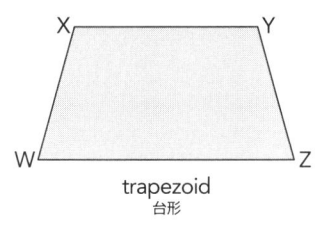

台形
1組の対辺だけが平行な四角形を台形という。

trapezoid
台形

Quadrilateral WXYZ is a trapezoid. XY and WZ are parallel.

四角形 WXYZ は台形である。XY と WZ は平行である。

Parallelogram
A quadrilateral with two pairs of parallel sides is a parallelogram.

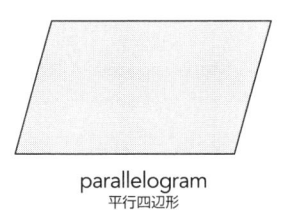

平行四辺形
2組の対辺が平行な四角形は平行四辺形である。

parallelogram
平行四辺形

Rhombus
A parallelogram with four sides of the same length is called a rhombus. The diagonals of a rhombus are perpendicular to one another, and divide each other in half where they intersect.

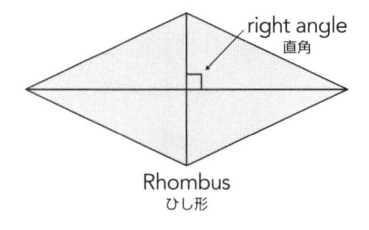

ひし形
4つの辺の長さが等しい平行四辺形をひし形という。ひし形の対角線は相互に垂直に交わり、また対角線はその交点で2等分される。

right angle
直角

Rhombus
ひし形

Other Polygons

Remember that a polygon is a closed figure formed by line segments.

その他の多角形

多角形とは線分によって閉じられた図形であることを覚えておこう。

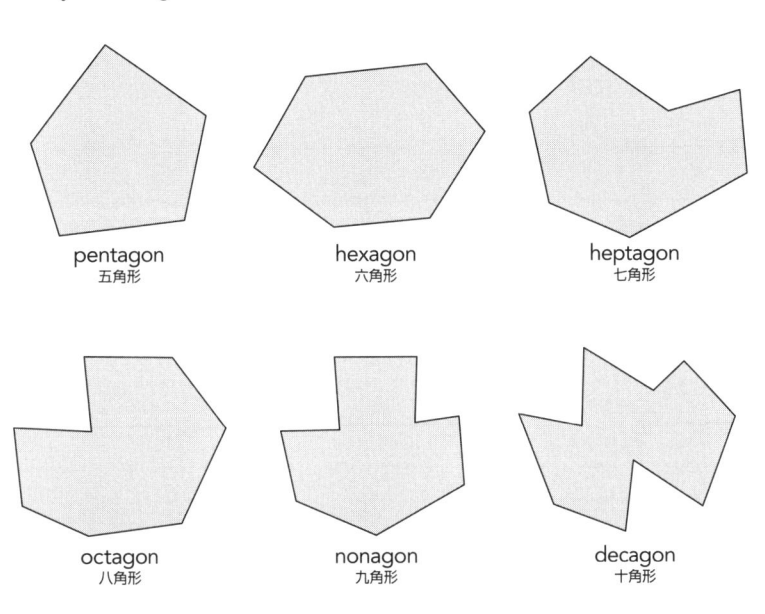

pentagon
五角形

hexagon
六角形

heptagon
七角形

octagon
八角形

nonagon
九角形

decagon
十角形

Regular Polygons

A regular polygon has sides of equal length and angles of equal measure.

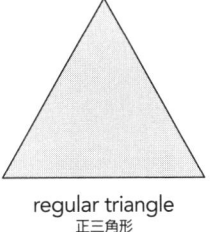

正多角形

正多角形はすべての辺の長さが等しく、すべての角が等しい。

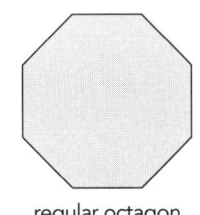

regular triangle
正三角形

regular quadrilateral
正四角形

regular octagon
正八角形

A regular triangle is also called an equilateral triangle and a regular quadrilateral is also called a square. A stop sign has the shape of a regular octagon.

正三角形は等辺三角形ともいい、正四角形は正方形ともいう。「止まれ」の交通標識は正八角形の形をしている。

Circles | 円

A circle is a closed figure, but not a polygon. (Polygons have sides.) All the points on a circle are the same distance from the center of the circle.

円は閉じた図形であるが多角形ではない。(多角形には辺がある)円周上の点はすべて円の中心から等しい距離にある。

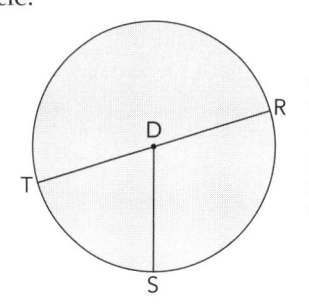

On this circle with center D you can see three segments of equal length: DR, DS, and DT.

中心Dをもつこの円において、3つの線分 DR、DS、DTはすべて長さが等しいことがわかる。

Radius | 半径

A line segment whose end points are the center of a circle and a point on the circle is called a radius of the circle. The plural of radius is radii. Segments DR, DS, and DT are radii of the circle above. Since all the radii of a circle have the same length, we also call the length of any radius of a circle its radius.

円の中心と円周の一点を結ぶ線分を円の半径という。radiusの複数形はradiiと書く。線分DR、DS、DTは上図の円の半径である。円の半径はすべて長さが等しいので、どの半径をとってもその円の半径といえる。

Diameter | 直径

A line segment whose end points are both on the circle and which passes through the center of a circle is called a diameter of the circle. Segment RT is a diameter of the circle above. All the diameters of a circle have the same length so we call the length of any diameter of a circle its diameter. The diameter of a circle is always twice as long as its radius.

円の中心を通る線分で両端が円周上にあるものを円の直径という。上の図で、線分RTは円の直径である。円の直径はすべて長さが等しいので、どの直径をとってもその円の直径といえる。円の直径はつねに半径の2倍である。

The Area of a Circle | 円の面積

The area of a circle is equal to π times the radius squared.

円の面積は円周率×半径の2乗に等しい。

Formula for the Area of a Circle
円の面積を求める公式

$$A = \pi r^2$$

The Circumference of a Circle

The circumference of a circle is equal to π times the diameter.

円周の長さ

円周の長さは直径×円周率に等しい。

Formula for the Circumference of a Circle
円周の長さを求める公式

$$C = \pi d \text{ or } C = 2\pi r$$

There are π diameters in the circumference of a circle: $C = \pi d$. You can also write this equation another way: $\pi = C/d$. So π equals the ratio of the circumference to the diameter of a circle. This ratio π is the same for all circles, but you cannot write it exactly as either a fraction or a decimal. From early times in history, the mathematicians among many peoples of the world have tried to write fractions that were close approximations of π, such as 256/81 (the Egyptians), 25/8 (the Babylonians), 22/7 (the Greeks), 355/113 (the Chinese). Today mathematicians have written a decimal approximation of π to thousands of decimal places.

$\pi = 3.14159265358979323846264383...$

For most calculations you can use the approximation $\pi \approx 3.14$ or $\pi \approx 22/7$. Remember, the symbol ≈ means "is approximately equal to."

円周の長さは円周率と直径をかけたものである。式にすればC=πd となる。この等式はπ=C/dと書くこともできる。つまり円周率は、円周の長さと直径の比に等しいということだ。この円周率πはすべての円において同じであるが、分数でも小数でも正確には書き表すことができない。歴史が始まって間もないころから今日にいたるまで、世界の多くの民族の数学者たちがπの近似値を分数にしようと試みてきた。近似値の例としては、256/81(エジプト人)、25/8(バビロニア人)、22/7(ギリシャ人)、355/113(中国人)などがある。こんにちの数学者たちはπの近似値を小数点以下数千桁までつきとめている。

計算をするときには近似値であるπ≈3.14やπ≈22/7を使うのがふつうである。≈という記号は「ほぼ等しい」という意味である。これは覚えておこう。

Solids

Three-dimensional figures are often called solids.

立体

三次元の図形は主に立体という。

cube
立方体

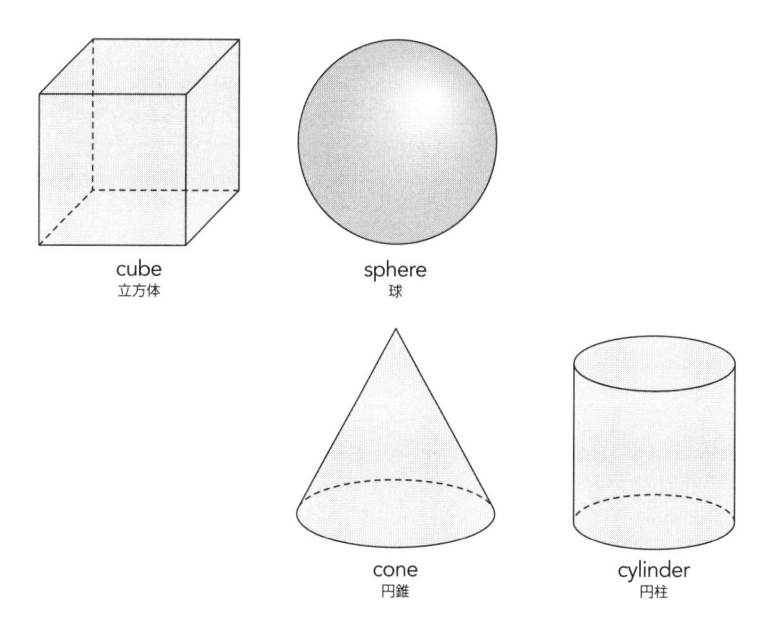

sphere
球

cone
円錐

cylinder
円柱

A flat surface on a solid is called a face. The line segment where two faces meet is called an edge. Edges come together at a vertex.

Learn this new solid: a rectangular prism. A rectangular prism has six sides that are rectangles.

立体のもつ平らな面を面という。2つの面が出会ってできる線分を辺という。辺と辺がぶつかるところが頂点である。

ここで新しく出てきた立体、直方体を覚えておこう。直方体は6つの長方形の面をもつ立体だ。

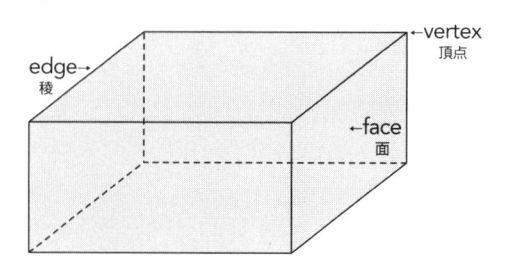

edge
稜

vertex
頂点

face
面

Polyhedrons

A polyhedron is a solid, each face of which is a polygon. Two kinds of polyhedrons are prisms and pyramids.

Prisms have two parallel congruent faces called bases. Prisms are named by the shapes of their bases. You can see that the shape of the base of a prism "runs through" the prism.

多面体

多面体は立体で、それぞれの面が多角形である。多面体には角柱や角錐がある。

角柱には平行して向かい合う2つの合同な面があり、それは底面と呼ばれている。角柱の呼び方は底面の形できまる。図を見ると、角柱の底面が同じ形のまま角柱を「貫いて」いるのがわかる。

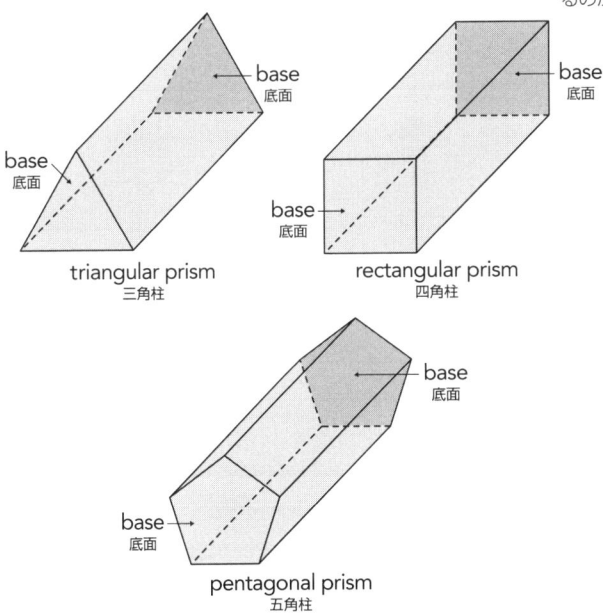

triangular prism
三角柱

rectangular prism
四角柱

pentagonal prism
五角柱

Pyramids are also named by the shapes of their bases.

角錐の場合も呼び方は底面の形からきている。

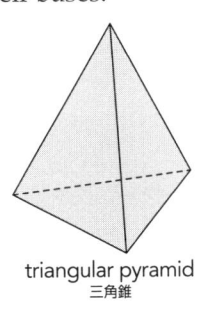

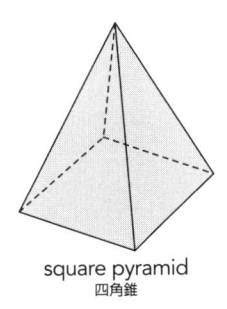

triangular pyramid
三角錐

square pyramid
四角錐

Graphs　　　　　　　　　　　　グラフ

Information, or data, is often given to us in numbers. You can make your own bar graphs, line graphs, or pictographs to show a set of data.

情報やデータは数字で与えられることが多い。集めたデータを使って棒グラフ、折れ線グラフ、絵グラフなどを自分で作ることができる。

Bar Graph　　　　　　　　　　棒グラフ

A bar graph is a good way to show the different sizes of amounts. Here is a table of data we will use to make a bar graph.

棒グラフは量の違いを示すのに適している。ここに棒グラフに使えるデータ表がある。

You can see right away from this graph that there was far more rain on Thursday than on any other day.

このグラフからは、他のどの曜日よりも木曜日の雨量がずっと多かったことがひと目でわかる。

Rainfall During One Week in Seattle
シアトルの1週間の降雨量

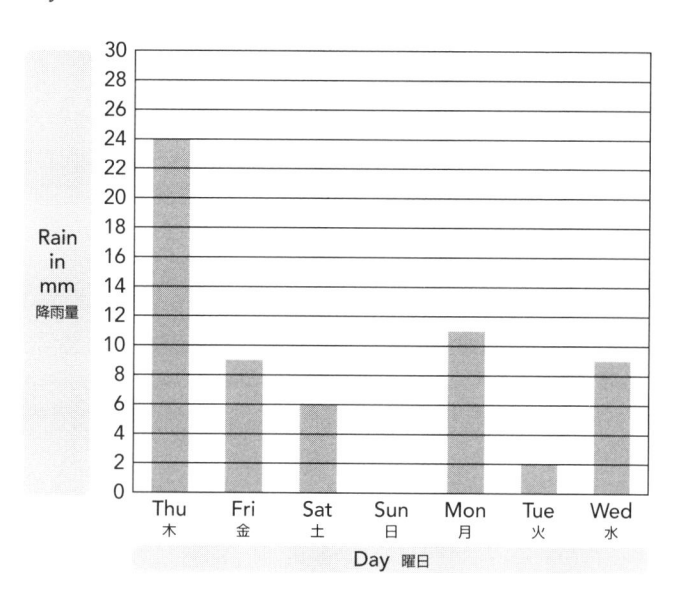

Rain in mm 降雨量

Day 曜日	Thu 木	Fri 金	Sat 土	Sun 日	Mon 月	Tue 火	Wed 水
Rain (mm)	24	9	6	—	11	2	9

Line Graph　　　　　　　　　折れ線グラフ

People often use line graphs to show how amounts or numbers change. At the end of each week for five weeks, Mrs. Sinclair found the average price per share of the stock she owned. Here is her table of data:

折れ線グラフをよく使うのは量や数がどう変化したかを示すときである。株を持っているシンクレア夫人は、5週間の間、週末に1株あたりの平均株価を調べた。データ表はこうなった。

204　MATHEMATICS • 算数

Mrs. Sinclair's Stock Prices
シンクレア夫人の株価

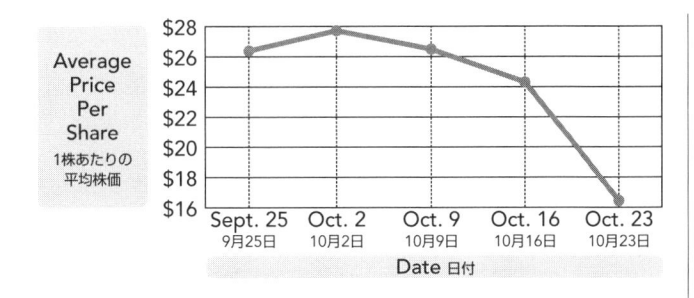

Average Price Per Share
1株あたりの平均株価

	Sept. 25	Oct. 2	Oct. 9	Oct. 16	Oct. 23
	9月25日	10月2日	10月9日	10月16日	10月23日

Date 日付

Pictograph
絵グラフ

A pictograph uses a symbol to show amounts. For example, a car dealership made a pictograph of the number of orange, white, or black cars it sold in one month.

絵グラフは量を示すのに物のイメージを使う。たとえば、ある自動車販売店は、1ヵ月間で売ったオレンジ色、白色、黒色の自動車の数を示す絵グラフを作った。

Number of Cars Sold at Car City in March
3月に「カーシティ」で売れた車の台数

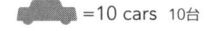

= 10 cars　10台

Color	Number Sold
Orange	🚗🚗🚗🚗
White	🚗🚗🚗🚗🚗
Black	🚗🚗🚗🚗

Circle Graph
円グラフ

A circle graph is used to show the relationship of different parts to a whole. It is usually divided by fractions or percentages.

You can see right away from the circle graph where the Brown family spent most of their money, and how much of their total income went to each area.

各部分と全体との関係を示すときには円グラフを使う。たいていは分数やパーセントの数字によって分割されている。

この円グラフを見ると、ブラウンさん一家が何にいちばんお金を使ったか、そして全収入のどれくらいがどの用途に当てられたかがすぐにわかる。

- Rent 26% 家賃
- Food 21% 食費
- Insurance 8% 保険料
- Clothing 17% 被服費
- Travel & Entertainments 14% 旅行娯楽費
- Savings 9% 貯金
- Other 5% その他

The Brown Family Income Last Year (After Taxes)
ブラウン一家の昨年の収入（税引後）

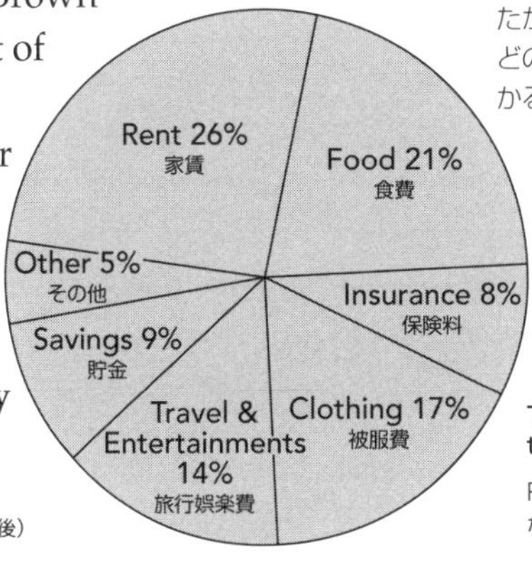

The percents add up to 100 in this circle graph.

円グラフの中のパーセントを足すと100になる。

NATURAL SCIENCE • 科 学

Reproduction

All living things are born, grow during their lifetime, and eventually die. Tadpoles are born, grow, change into frogs, and eventually die. Chicks are born, grow to be adult chickens, and eventually die. What would happen if no new chickens were born to replace those that died? There would be no more chickens in the world—they'd be extinct. In order to keep themselves from dying out, all living things reproduce themselves. "Reproduce" means to make again, or to make a copy. Reproduction is the process of making again.

The cells in your body reproduce themselves and increase in number, which is how you grow. Every day, for example, some of your skin cells reproduce themselves and some of them die. As you get older and bigger, your skin cells reproduce faster than they die, so you can keep fitting into your skin. As you grow taller, your bone cells make more bone cells. When you become an adult, the cells involved in growth reproduce more slowly, and as a result, dead cells are replaced more slowly—so slowly, in fact, that at about age twenty you stop growing. Then the birth and death of cells come into balance. For every new cell that reproduces and lives, another dies, so the number of cells stays about even.

Organisms reproduce in different ways. You already know some of these. Some plants make seeds. Mushrooms make spores. Frogs and chickens lay eggs. Dogs have litters of puppies. But what about protists and monerans? Let's read about two categories of reproduction: asexual and sexual.

Asexual Reproduction

One way that organisms copy themselves is through asexual reproduction. "Asexual" means nonsexual; that is, reproduction without using

生殖

　すべての生き物は、生まれると生命のあるかぎり成長変化し、最後には死んでゆく。オタマジャクシも、生まれると大きくなってカエルになり、最後は死ぬ。雛鳥(ひなどり)も生まれ、成長して親鶏(おやどり)となり、やがて死ぬ。もし鶏が死んで新しい雛(ひな)が生まれなかったらどうなるだろう？　世界には鶏がいなくなり──絶滅してしまう。生き物は自分の仲間が死滅しないように自分と同じものを生み出す。「生殖を行う」"reproduce"とは、再度作るあるいは同じものを生むということだ。生殖とは再度作る一連の過程をいう。

　人体の細胞は再生して数をふやす。それが成長するということだ。たとえば、毎日皮膚細胞は一部が再生し、一部が死ぬ。成長期に入った人間の皮膚細胞は、死ぬより速い速度で再生する。こうして体の成長と皮膚の成長がつりあうのだ。身長がのびるにつれて骨細胞の数が増える。成人して成長にかかわる細胞の再生する速さがゆっくりになると、死んだ細胞が取り替えられる速さもゆっくりになる──とてもゆっくりになって、事実20歳くらいで成長は止まってしまう。そこで細胞の誕生と死がつりあった状態になる。新しい細胞が1つ生命を持つと別の1つが死に、細胞の数はほぼ一定になるのだ。

　有機体の再生にはさまざまなタイプがある。そのうちいくつかは知っているだろう。植物には種を作るものがある。キノコは胞子を作る。カエルと鶏は卵を生む。犬は子犬を何匹も産む。では原生生物やモネラ界の生物はどうするのか？　無性生殖と有性生殖という2種類の生殖について読んでみよう。

無性生殖

　有機体が同種のものを作る方法の1つに無性生殖がある。「無性」とは有性ではないという意味だ。つまり、雌雄(しゆう)を必要としない生殖

males and females. The organism simply makes copies of itself through cell division.

Asexual reproduction can be very simple. Monerans (the simplest of all organisms) and many protists reproduce by fission, which means splitting. After duplicating their genetic material, monerans like bacteria simply split their single cell in half. This allows them to grow colonies very quickly. Under the right conditions, bacteria colonies can double their numbers every twenty minutes!

Mildews, molds, and mushrooms are fungi that reproduce by forming spores. Spores are single cells often protected by a hard covering. Spores drop off the parent, and become new organisms if there is enough water and food for them to live. Most yeasts, on the other hand, reproduce by budding. A "bud," or enlargement, forms on one side of the cell, and eventually breaks off to form a new yeast cell.

Asexual Reproduction in Larger Animals and Plants

Some plants and animals can reproduce themselves asexually in a process called regeneration, meaning to make or generate again. These organisms make new body parts to replace lost ones. In plants, the most familiar example of regeneration is called cloning, in which a piece of the plant—a leaf or stem cutting—is put into some moist material, and a whole new plant forms. Many garden plants like roses are reproduced by cloning, because you can be sure the new plant is exactly like the parent.

The amount of regeneration that can occur in asexual reproduction depends on the type of organism. You regenerate skin cells when you

A starfish regenerates amputated limbs.
ヒトデは切断された腕を再生する

である。有機体は細胞の分割だけで同じものを作っていく。

　無性生殖はきわめて簡単だ。モネラ類(有機体の中でもっとも単純な生物)や多くの原生生物は細胞の分裂、すなわち分割することで繁殖していく。バクテリアと同じようにモネラ類も、まず遺伝物質の複製が作られ、それから１つの細胞が２つに分割されるだけのことだ。こうするとごく短い時間にコロニー(群体)が作れるのである。環境条件がよければ、バクテリアのコロニーは20分で数が倍に増えるのだから驚く。

　カビや糸状菌、キノコなどは胞子によって繁殖する。胞子は１つの細胞で、たいていは固い覆いで保護されている。親細胞から落ちた胞子は、そこに生育に必要な水と栄養があれば新しい有機体になる。これと違ってイースト菌は菌芽によって繁殖する。「菌芽」とは拡張ということで、細胞の表面に芽が伸び、それが分離して新しいイーストの細胞となるのである。

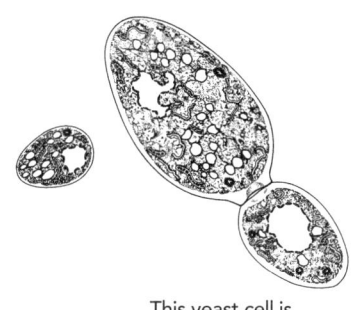

This yeast cell is reproducing by budding.
このイースト菌は菌芽によって繁殖している

より大きな動植物の無性生殖

　動植物の中には再発生とよばれる無性生殖の過程をへて再生するものもある。再発生とは再度作る、再度生むという意味だ。こうした有機体は、体の一部を失ったときに、同じものを新しく作り出す。植物の場合、いちばんなじみ深い再生の方法は、クローン技術である。植物の一部——葉や切った枝——を水分のある物の中に埋めておくと、同じ植物が新たに成長して出てくる。バラのような園芸植物をクローン技術で作ることが多いのは、もとの植物とまったく同じものがほしいからだ。

　無性生殖によってどの程度再生ができるかは有機体によってさまざまだ。人間の場合は指を傷つけると、皮膚細胞が再生して傷はなおる。しかし、人間の体の大部分はほとんど再生能力がない。

　ほかの動物は人間よりもはるかに再生能力がある。ヒトデは腕を切り落とされても、まったく新しく生えてくる。切られた腕も、ヒトデを作る細胞中枢を持っていれば、成長してまた新たなヒトデになることさえある。虫の中には、半分に切断されても、その半分それぞれが新しい虫になるものもいる。サンショウウオは足を失って

cut your finger and the wound heals. But for the most part, the human body has little ability to regenerate.

Other animals have a much greater ability to regenerate. A starfish can grow a whole new arm if one is cut off. The lost arm, if it still has a piece of the center of the starfish, can even grow into a new starfish. When certain worms are cut in half, each half grows into a new worm. Salamanders can regenerate a leg if they lose one. The leg can't regenerate a new salamander, though. More complex animals like salamanders and humans have a more limited ability to regenerate.

Sexual Reproduction in Mosses and Ferns

Sexual reproduction requires the joining of special male and female cells before reproduction occurs. These special cells are called gametes. In sexual reproduction, a male and female gamete come together to form a fertilized egg.

Mosses, which you may have seen in shady spots, reproduce by making spores. But, unlike fungi, which form spores without using male and female cells, moss spores are formed by bringing a male and

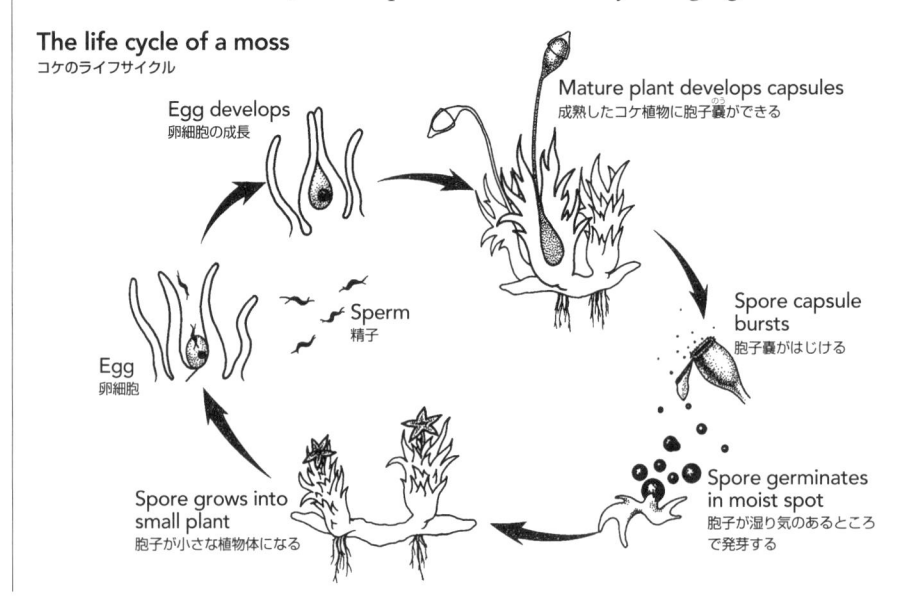

The life cycle of a moss
コケのライフサイクル

- Egg develops / 卵細胞の成長
- Mature plant develops capsules / 成熟したコケ植物に胞子嚢ができる
- Spore capsule bursts / 胞子嚢がはじける
- Sperm / 精子
- Egg / 卵細胞
- Spore grows into small plant / 胞子が小さな植物体になる
- Spore germinates in moist spot / 胞子が湿り気のあるところで発芽する

もまた再生することができる。しかし、切れた足が大きくなってサンショウウオになることはない。サンショウウオや人間のようにより複雑な動物は、再生能力がより限定されるのである。

コケ、シダ類の有性生殖

　有性生殖の場合は、生殖がおこるまえに特別な雌雄の細胞が合体しなければならない。このときの特別な細胞を配偶子という。雌雄の配偶子が1つになって受精卵を作るのが有性生殖である。

　日陰などでみかけるコケ類は胞子によって繁殖する。しかし、細胞が雌雄に分かれていなくても胞子ができる菌類とは異なり、コケ類の胞子は雌雄の細胞が合体してできる。コケ類のライフサイクルを示した絵を見てみよう。第一段階で胞子が養分の豊富な湿った場所に落ちると、そこで胞子は成長してある特殊な植物体になる。この植物体はふつう糸状で緑色をしている。しばらくすると、驚くべきことが起こる。糸状のものが芽を出し、それが小さな植物体になるのだが、その中に雄株と雌株とがあるのだ。その後、この糸状の植物体はほとんど死んでしまうが、雄の株から雄の配偶子ができ、雌の株からは雌の配偶子ができる。雌雄の株が近くにあってそこに

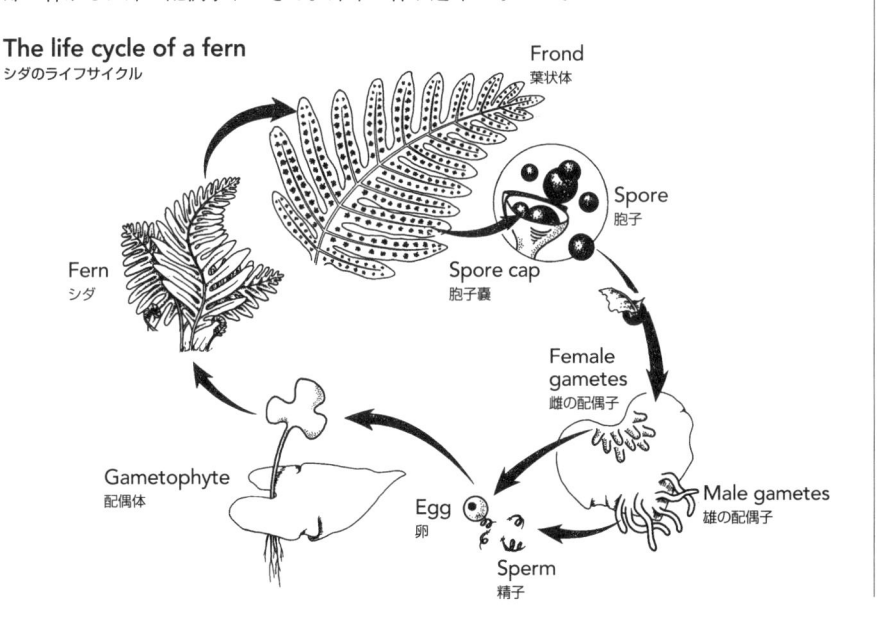

The life cycle of a fern
シダのライフサイクル

- Frond 葉状体
- Spore 胞子
- Spore cap 胞子嚢
- Female gametes 雌の配偶子
- Male gametes 雄の配偶子
- Sperm 精子
- Egg 卵
- Gametophyte 配偶体
- Fern シダ

female cell together. Look at the drawing of the moss's life cycle. In the first step, a spore has just landed in a moist, nutrient-rich spot where it grows into a special kind of moss plant. The plant usually looks like a green thread. After a time, something amazing happens. The thread develops buds that grow into small plants, some of which are male and others female. Afterward, the thread usually dies. The male moss plants make male gametes, the female plants make female gametes. When a male and female plant are close enough together, and there is some water present, a male gamete is able to swim to a female gamete and fertilize it. This fertilized egg makes a capsule in which new spores are formed; the mature spores fall on moist ground, and the process starts over again.

The life cycle of a fern is similar to that of a moss, but there are some differences. When the fern spore gets wet it germinates, turning into a tiny, heart-shaped plant that produces both male and female gametes. When these male and female gametes come together, the fertilized egg grows into a totally new and different plant that will become the large fern you can find in the woods. The mature fern produces spores under its leaves. You can usually see the spore caps if you look under the frond of a mature fern. In time, the spores burst from their caps and start the cycle over again.

The Human Reproductive System

The changes in a person's body during adolescence are in preparation for puberty, the time when male and female humans undergo physical changes which enable them to produce children. Human reproduction is very similar to reproduction in other mammals. In females, an egg cell is released each month from one of two ovaries. The egg then passes into one of the fallopian tubes, where it is either fertilized by sperm from a male, or not. If it is not fertilized, it passes into the uterus, and then out of the body along with the lining of the uterus. The uterus lining and egg pass through the vagina on their way out of the body. This monthly process of shedding the unfertilized egg and the lining of the uterus is called menstruation—from the Latin word *mensis*, meaning "month", because it typically occurs about once a month.

水分があれば、雄の配偶子は雌の配偶子のところまで泳いでいって受精が起こる。この受精卵から嚢(のう)がつくられ、その嚢の中に新しい胞子ができてくる。成熟した胞子が湿った土の上に落ちると、そこから繁殖の過程がまた始まるのである。
　シダのライフサイクルもコケに似ているが、いくつか違ったところもある。シダの胞子は水分を吸収すると発芽して小さなハート形の植物体になり、それが雌雄の配偶子を作り出す。この雌雄の配偶子が合体して受精卵ができ、それが成長すると、それまでとはまったく姿のちがう新たな植物体になる。やがてこれがよく森などで見かける大きなシダになっていくのである。成熟したシダは葉の裏に胞子をつくる。成長したシダ植物の葉状体の裏を観察してみると胞子嚢が見つかるはずだ。やがて胞子が嚢からはじけ出て、繁殖のサイクルがふたたびはじまるのである。

人間の生殖組織

　思春期のヒトの体の変化は成熟期への準備である。成熟期になると、男も女も子どもが作れるように体が変化していく。人間の生殖は、ほかの哺乳類動物ときわめてよく似ている。女性の体では、毎月、2つある卵巣のどちらかから卵子が1個生み出される。それから卵子は輸卵管に入り、そこで男性からの精子細胞によって受精することもあれば、受精しないこともある。受精しなかった場合、卵子は子宮に移動し、子宮粘膜とともに体外に出される。子宮粘膜と卵子は体の外に出るときに膣(ちつ)を通っていく。この毎月起こる、受精しなかった卵子と子宮粘膜の排泄を月経と呼んでいる。月経の語源は月を意味するラテン語のmensisであるが、それはたいていの場合月経が毎月1度起こるからである。
　精子はどのようにして輸卵管の中の卵子にたどり着いて受精するのだろうか？　その前にまず男性の生殖器官について学ぶ必要がある。精子は睾丸(こうがん)で作られるが、睾丸とは、卵形をした分泌器官で、陰嚢(いんのう)という袋状の皮膚の中にあるが、その陰嚢は男性器の根元にあって垂れている。精子は、精液と呼ばれる白っぽい液体にまじって睾丸の中の管を移動する。そして、尿道と呼ばれる男性器の中の管を通って体外に出てゆく。
　性交のあいだに、男性は女性の膣の中に男性器を挿入する。男性

How does the sperm reach the egg in the fallopian tube to fertilize it? First we need to learn about the male reproductive organs. Sperm are produced in the testes, oval-shaped glands that are contained in a pouch of skin, the scrotum, which hangs below the penis. The sperm travel through tubes in the testes in a whitish fluid called semen. The semen can exit the male's body through the urethra, a tube in his penis.

During sexual intercourse, the male places his penis inside the female's vagina. The semen shoots out of his penis and into her vagina, and the sperm swim toward her uterus. After reaching the uterus, they swim toward the fallopian tubes, where one sperm cell—and only one—is admitted through the egg's outer covering. When egg and sperm join, fertilization has occurred.

If the egg is fertilized, it develops into a zygote, which travels down the fallopian tube and implants itself in the wall of the uterus. Here it grows into an embryo and further develops into a fetus. The fetus grows inside its mother for nine months, until it is developed enough to live in the outside world. When it is born, a baby needs constant care and attention.

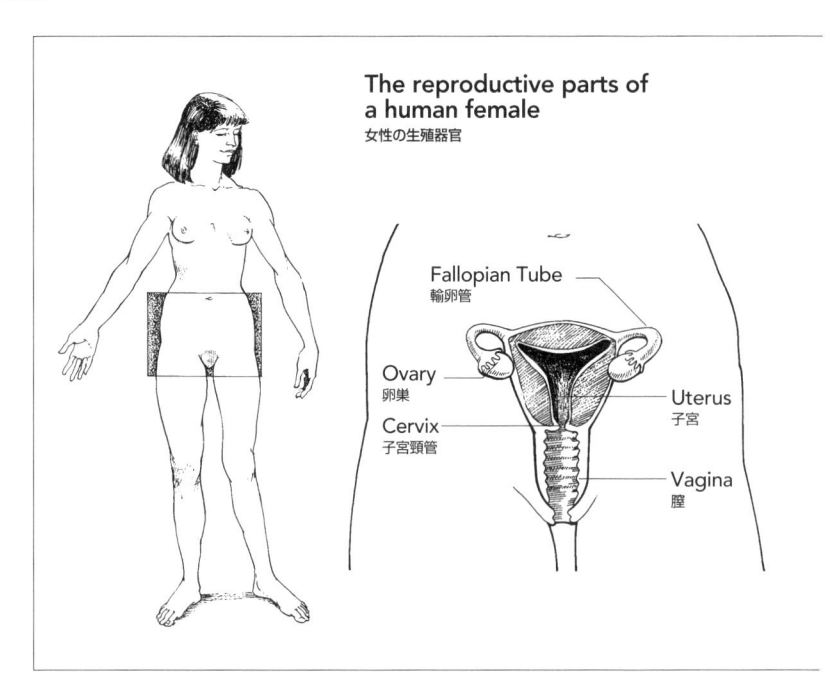

The reproductive parts of a human female
女性の生殖器官

- Fallopian Tube 輸卵管
- Ovary 卵巣
- Cervix 子宮頸管
- Uterus 子宮
- Vagina 膣

器から飛び出した精液は膣の中に入り、精子は子宮に向かって泳いでいく。子宮にたどり着くと、精子は輸卵管へと進み、そこで１つの精子細胞が──ただ１つだけである──卵子の外側を覆う膜を通って中へ入れてもらえる。受精が起こるのは、卵子と精子が合体して１つになったときである。

　卵子が受精すると受精卵になり、輸卵管の中を移動して子宮内の壁に入り込む。そこで受精卵は胎芽に成長し、それからさらに大きくなって胎児になる。胎児は、外の世界で生きる準備が整うまで、母親の体の中で９ヵ月間成長を続ける。赤ちゃんが生まれたら、たえず気をつけて世話をすることが必要である。

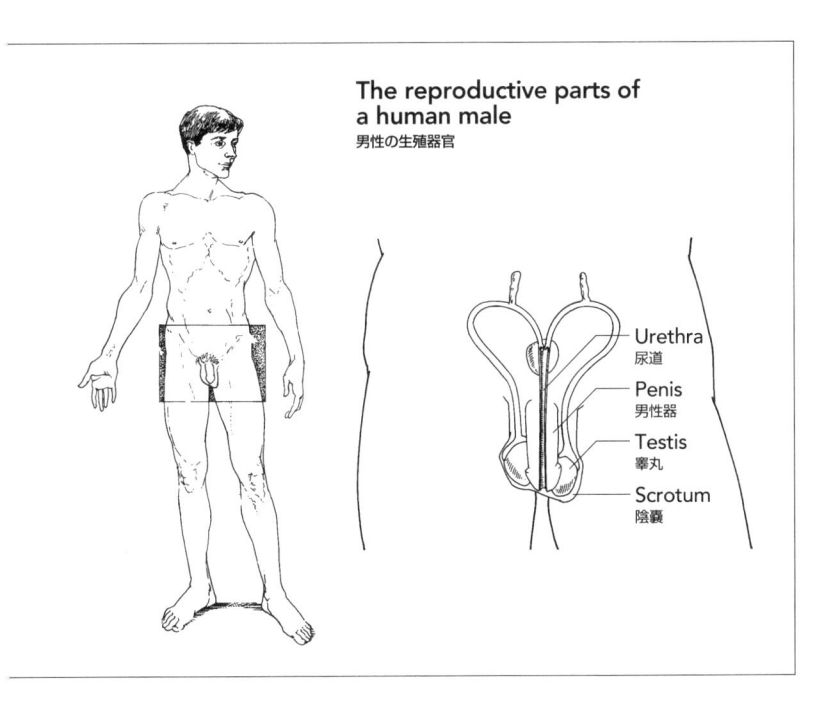

The reproductive parts of a human male
男性の生殖器官

- Urethra 尿道
- Penis 男性器
- Testis 睾丸
- Scrotum 陰嚢

LANGUAGE ARTS • 国 語

Learning About Literature

Kinds of Literature: Tragedy and Comedy

Look at the masks pictured here. How would you describe the emotions they express?

These masks are often used as a symbol of the theater, associated with two different kinds of literature, tragedy and comedy.

People today use the words "tragedy" and "comedy" in general ways that go beyond kinds of literature. For example, a terrible hurricane or plane crash in which many people die might be called a tragedy. Or, people might refer to a television show that makes them laugh as a comedy.

This basic real-life difference between tragedy—something terribly sad or disastrous—and comedy—something funny—also applies most of the time when we are talking about tragedy and comedy as specific kinds of literature.

Comedies tell stories in which everything works out well for the main characters. Sure, the characters may face problems and difficulties along the way, but when the comedy is over, things work out fine. Comedies tend to be funny, but in different ways. In some comedies, we might like the characters and laugh with them through their troubles. In other comedies, we might laugh at silly characters whose actions show just how foolish people can sometimes be.

In literature, a tragedy tells a serious story of a central character—usually an important, heroic person—who meets with disaster because of some personal fault or because of events that cannot be helped. The

文学を学ぶ

文学の種類：悲劇と喜劇

　この仮面の絵をじっと見てみよう。2つの仮面が表現している感情はどう言えばよいだろうか。

　これらの仮面は2つの相異なる文学、悲劇と喜劇を表す演劇のシンボルとして用いられている。

　「悲劇」と「喜劇」という言葉はこんにち文学のジャンルの枠をこえてごくふつうに使う。たとえば多くの死者を出した大きなハリケーンや飛行機事故などを悲劇と呼んだりするかと思えば、笑いながら見るようなテレビ番組を「喜劇」と言ったりする。

　大きな悲しみや惨事を悲劇といい、滑稽なものを喜劇というが、この基本的かつ現実的な分け方は、文学の特別なジャンルとして悲劇、喜劇について語る場合にもだいたい当てはまる。

　喜劇とは、主な登場人物たちにとってすべてがめでたしめでたしで終わるような物語である。もちろん劇の途中では登場人物たちも難問や苦しみに直面することもあるが、劇が終わるときにはものごとがうまく収まっているのである。喜劇といえば面白おかしいものであるが、そのおかしさはさまざまだ。登場人物が好きになって、数々の困難を切り抜けていくさまに私たちが拍手喝采を送るというような喜劇がある。そうかと思えば、人間の愚かしさを身をもって示すばかばかしい登場人物を私たちが笑うような喜劇もある。

　文学における悲劇は、ある主人公をめぐる深刻な物語である。主人公はたいてい力を持った英雄的な人物で、みずから犯した過ちのために、あるいは避けがたい運命のために悲惨な目に合う。イギリスの偉大な劇作家ウィリアム・シェイクスピアは古代ローマの支配者ジュリアス・シーザーの生と死を扱った悲劇を書いた。シーザーは強大な権力を手にしたが、友と信じていた者たちに殺されてしまう。シェイクスピアの偉大な悲劇には、この他に『ロミオとジュリエット』『リア王』『ハムレット』などがある。こうした悲劇はずっ

> **NOTE**
> **シェイクスピア**
> ウィリアム・シェイクスピア（1564–1616）は英語圏のみならず、世界文学史上最高の劇作家といわれる。有名な悲劇だけではなく、「夏の夜の夢」A Midsummer Night's Dream など喜劇にも傑作が多い。日常の英語に入り込んだせりふも数多い。All the world's a stage.（世界はすべて舞台のようなもの）、my salad days（世間を知らぬ青二才の頃）、All's well that ends well.（終わりよければすべてよし）、It was Greek to me.（ちんぷんかんぷん）などがよく知られている。

great English playwright William Shakespeare wrote a tragedy about the life and death of the Roman ruler Julius Caesar, who achieved great power but was murdered by men he thought were his friends. Other great tragedies by Shakespeare include *Romeo and Juliet*, *King Lear*, and *Hamlet*. These plays continue to be read, performed, and admired, even though in each play, after we get to know the main characters well, at the end we are made to feel very sad when we see them dead on the stage.

While it seems natural that people like comedy, since most comedies make us smile and laugh, why do people enjoy watching tragedies? Perhaps one reason people continue to be drawn to the painful stories of tragedies is that we all want to experience and understand tragic stories without having to live through one. A tragedy allows us to experience strong emotions vicariously, meaning through the experience of others ("vicarious" comes from the Latin word vicarius, which means "substitute").

In watching a tragic play, our emotions are strongly aroused: we can feel fear for the dangers that face the hero, or anger at his or her enemies, or frustration at not being able to change the course of events, or pity for the hero's sad fate. But when the play is over and we have lived through those strong emotions, we can go back to our own lives. We have a deeper understanding of what it means to be human, of the struggles and disappointments of life. But we also have a sense of relief that we can carry on, and perhaps a sense of determination to overcome the obstacles that defeated the tragic hero.

While many great tragedies end disastrously, they often provide glimpses of comedy along the way. Categories like "tragedy" and "comedy" can help you describe and understand literary works, but you'll find that literature, like life, often mixes joy and sorrow, laughter and tears.

Simile and Metaphor

When writers use imagery, they often put their images into special kinds of figurative language called simile and metaphor. In fact, if

と読み継がれ、舞台で上演され、高い評価を得てきたが、どの劇の場合も、他人とは思えないほど主人公たちを身近に感じたところで舞台上の彼らは死んでしまい、私たちは最後に大きな悲しみを味わうのである。
　喜劇は微笑や高笑いをさそうものだから人々が喜劇を好むのは当然のこととしても、悲劇の舞台を楽しむのはどういうわけだろう？　人々が悲劇特有の痛ましい物語に魅了され続けるのにはおそらく理由があって、私たちのだれもが、悲劇的な人生を送るのは避けたいが、その代わりに悲劇的な物語をわがことのように味わい理解したいという欲求を持っているのではないだろうか。悲劇は激しい情念を代理経験、すなわち他者の姿を通して経験させてくれる。("vicarious"は「代わりにさせる」という意味のラテン語"vicarius"から来ている)
　悲劇の舞台を見ていると私たちは強く感情をゆさぶられる。主人公が直面する危機に恐れおののき、その敵には怒りを覚え、避けがたいことの成り行きに落胆し、主人公の悲惨な運命には憐れみを覚える。しかし、芝居が終われば、こうした強烈な感情を経験した私たちもそれぞれの日常にもどっていく。そのとき私たちは人間であることの意味を、人生につきものの苦闘や挫折を、より深く理解している。しかしまた、自分は生き続けることができるとホッと胸をなでおろすことだろうし、おそらくは悲劇の主人公を打ち砕いたような苦難に負けまいとする気持ちも生まれていることだろう。
　偉大な悲劇の多くは悲惨な結末を迎えるが、劇の途中では人生の喜劇的な面もとらえて見せる。「悲劇」「喜劇」といった分類は文学作品を説明し理解する助けとはなるが、いずれ文学というものは、人生とよく似て、喜びと悲しみ、笑いと涙のいりまじったものであることがわかるのではないだろうか。

直喩と隠喩

　作家がイメージ形象を使うときには、自分の思い描くイメージを直喩、隠喩と呼ばれる特別な比喩的表現に置きかえることが多い。分かりやすくいえば、もしあなたが「あの子の速さはまるで稲妻だね」とか「彼って天使よ」というような言い方をしたことがあれば、直喩や隠喩を使ったことになるのだ。

you've ever said something like, "She's fast as lightning," or, "He's an angel," then you've used similes and metaphors yourself.

Similes and metaphors help us see things in unusual or imaginative ways by *comparing* one thing to another. Sometimes similes and metaphors bring together things you normally wouldn't think of comparing. For example, fog might not make you think of an animal, but see the surprising comparison Carl Sandburg makes in a poem called "Fog":

> The fog comes
> on little cat feet.
> It sits looking
> over harbor and city
> on silent haunches
> and then moves on.

A simile is a figure of speech that compares unlike things but makes the comparison obvious by including the word "like" or "as." (Simile comes from the Latin *similis*, meaning "like.") You've probably heard people use some common similes in everyday conversation: for example, "busy as a bee" or "sweet as honey" or "proud as a peacock." The great boxer Muhammad Ali described himself with some vivid similes: in the boxing ring, he said, he would "float like a butterfly, sting like a bee."

Like a simile, a metaphor is a figure of speech that brings together unlike things. But a metaphor doesn't use "like" or "as," so the comparison is not so obvious. For example, in talking about someone who's really stubborn, you might say:

simile: He's stubborn as a mule.
or
metaphor: He's a mule.

It's not important to dwell on the difference between metaphors and similes; they both make imaginative comparisons to help us understand and feel vividly.

直喩と隠喩を使ってあることを別のことに見立てれば、普通とは違った仕方で、あるいは想像力を使ってものを見ることができるようになる。ときには、直喩と隠喩は、ふつうならば比喩としては考えつかないようなものを結びつけてしまうこともある。たとえば、霧を見て動物を思い浮かべたりしないものだが、カール・サンドバーグが「霧」という詩で使った驚くべき比喩を見ていただこう。

> 霧は小さな
> 猫足でやってくる。
> 静かに背中を丸めて
> 港から街のあたりを
> ぼんやり座って眺め
> それからやおら動き出す。

　直喩は比喩的表現の１つで、似ていないものをたとえに使うが、「ような」「ように」といった言葉を用いて、比喩であることを明らかにする。あなたも日常の話の中で、なじみのある直喩を人が使うのを聞いたことがあるのではないだろうか。たとえば、「蜂のようにいそがしい」とか「蜜のように甘い」とか「孔雀のように高慢ちきな」といったものが直喩の例だ。偉大なボクシング選手だったモハメッド・アリは、自分の戦い方を生き生きとした直喩で語った。ボクシングのリング上で「蝶のように舞い、蜂のように刺す」と彼は表現した。

　直喩と同じように隠喩も、似ていないものを結びつける比喩的表現の一種である。しかし隠喩は「のような」「のように」といった言葉を使わないので、ただちに比喩だとはわからない。たとえば、とても頑固な人の話をしているときは、こんなふうに言うのではないだろうか。

　　直喩：あいつはラバのように頑固なんだ。
　　隠喩：あいつ、ラバだよ。

　隠喩と直喩の違いは、あれこれ考えるほどのことではない。どちらも想像力を使った比喩であり、私たちが物事を理解したり、生き生きと感じたりするのに役立つものだ。

NOTE
サンドバーグ
カール・サンドバーグ（1878–1967）はスウェーデン移民の子としてイリノイ州に生まれる。詩人、伝記作者、民衆音楽研究者。代表作に『シカゴ詩集』がある。『全詩集』と『リンカーン伝』でピュリッツァー賞を受賞。

White sheep, white sheep,
On a blue hill,
When the wind stops
You all stand still.

In the poem "Clouds," Christina Rossetti uses metaphors to describe the clouds and the sky. The poem compares clouds to white sheep and the sky to a blue hill. The metaphors help us see the clouds and sky in a way that we might not have seen them before. Perhaps the metaphor makes the sky seem more solid to us, and the clouds almost alive, as though you could reach out and touch them as you could a lamb's woolly coat.

Here is a poem you may know by Langston Hughes, called "Dreams." It has two metaphors. Can you find them?

Hold fast to dreams
For if dreams die
Life is a broken-winged bird
That cannot fly.

Hold fast to dreams
For when dreams go
Life is a barren field
Frozen with snow.

If you close your eyes and let your imagination see the metaphors in Hughes's poem—the "broken-winged bird" and the "barren field"—then you can appreciate how powerful metaphors can be. Think how unexciting and flat it would be to say something literal like, "If you let go of your dreams, life will be very disappointing."

Sometimes a metaphor may be almost hidden in the words. For example, there's a metaphor lurking in the following sentence:

The snow blanketed the town.

Can you find the comparison in that sentence? Do you see how the

白い白い、羊さん、羊さん
　みんな青い丘の上、
　風が止んだら、
　立ちどまったままね。

　この「雲」という詩で、クリスチーナ・ロセッティは雲と空を描写するのに隠喩を使っている。この詩は雲を白い羊にたとえ、空を青い丘にたとえている。この隠喩にうながされて、私たちにはこれまでとは違った雲や空が見えてくる。隠喩の働きで、空にはより物質的な手ごたえを感じ、雲には生き物のような感じをいだくのではなかろうか。子羊のふさふさした毛にさわるときのように、まるで手を伸ばせば雲にも触れることができるかのようだ。
　次に出てくるラングストン・ヒューズの詩「夢」は知っている人もいるだろう。この詩には隠喩が２つある。見つけられるだろうか。

　　夢は　しっかりとつかんでおけ
　　夢が　死んじまったら
　　人生も　翼の折れた鳥さ
　　飛べやしないのだ。

　　夢は　しっかりつかんでおけ
　　夢が　消えちまったら
　　人生も　不毛な荒地よ
　　雪に凍てつくばかりだ。

　目を閉じて、ヒューズの詩の隠喩「翼の折れた鳥」「不毛な荒地」を想像力の目で見てみると、隠喩がいかに強力かがわかってくる。「自分の夢をあきらめてしまったなら、人生はとてもつまらない」などと、考えをそのまま表現したら、めりはりに欠け、無味乾燥に聞こえることを考えてみればいい。
　ときには隠喩は言葉の中に隠れていることもある。例をあげよう。次の文には隠喩が潜んでいる。

　　雪が町を毛布でくるんだ。

　この文中にあるたとえが見つかっただろうか。雪が毛布に見立て

NOTE

ロセッティ
クリスティーナ・ロセッティ（1830–94）はイギリスの詩人。子ども向けの詩を数多く書いている。兄ダンテ・ゲイブリエル・ロセッティはラファエル前派の詩人・画家としてよく知られている。

NOTE

ヒューズ
ラングストン・ヒューズ（1902–67）はアメリカの詩人、小説家。ハーレム・ルネサンスと呼ばれる1920年代の黒人文学・美術運動の渦中にいた。ジャズとブルース音楽を黒人文化のエッセンスと考え、自分の詩のテンポやリズムの音楽性を高めようとした。代表作に『もの憂いブルース』（1926年）など。

snow is being compared to a blanket? Now find the metaphor in this sentence:

Darkness swallowed the explorers as they entered the cave.

Do you see how the figurative language creates an emotional effect different from a literal statement such as, "The explorers entered the dark cave"? When you use a metaphor to compare the darkness to a kind of hungry animal waiting to "swallow" the explorers, then you turn the cave into a place that most of us would rather not enter!

Keep your eyes and ears open for metaphors and similes. Use them when you talk and write and your words will spring to life.

Personification

Imagine you're trying to sharpen a pencil but the lead keeps coming out broken. Frustrated, you exclaim, "This pencil sharpener refuses to work!"

Did the pencil sharpener *actually* refuse? Did it say, "I'm tired and I won't sharpen your pencil"? Of course not. But when you said that the pencil sharpener refused to work, you expressed yourself in an imaginative way and used a kind of figurative language known as personification.

To personify is to give an inanimate object or an animal the qualities of a person, a human. In a poem called "Trees," the poet Joyce Kilmer personifies trees by giving them certain human qualities. Can you see the personification in the following lines?

A tree that looks at God all day,
And lifts her leafy arms to pray;

A tree that may in Summer wear
A nest of robins in her hair. . . .

られていることに気づいただろうか。それでは次の文中の隠喩を見つけてみよう。

　　　　探検家たちが洞窟の中に入ると、暗闇が彼らを呑みこんだ。

　事実をそのまま語る「探険家たちは暗い洞窟に入った」といった言い方とは違って、比喩的な表現は心理的な効果をもたらすことが分かるのではないだろうか。探険家たちを「呑みこ」もうとする腹を空かせた動物に暗闇を見立てると、その洞窟はほとんどの人が尻ごみするような場所に変わってしまう。
　隠喩や直喩に対して目を開き耳をすましてみよう。話をするときや文章を書くときに隠喩や直喩を使えば、たちまち言葉は生気あふれるものに変わるはずだ。

擬人法

　鉛筆を削ろうとするのだが、削っても削っても出てくる芯が折れている——こんな状態を想像してみよう。うまくいかないのでイライラしたあなたは、「この鉛筆削り、削るのいやがってる！」とつい叫んでしまう。
　鉛筆削り器は実際に「いやがった」のだろうか？「わたしはくたびれているので、きみの鉛筆なんか削らないよ」と言っただろうか？もちろん、言うはずがない。しかしともかく、鉛筆削りがいやがっているとあなたは言った。そのときあなたは、想像を働かせて自分の気持ちを表現し、擬人法という比喩的表現の一種を使ったのである。
　擬人化するというのは、無機物や動物などに人の特性や人間的な特質を与えることだ。「樹木」という詩で、詩人のジョイス・キルマーは樹木に人間の特徴を与えて擬人化している。次の詩行のどこに擬人法が使われているだろうか？

　　　　一日中じっと神を見ている木がある
　　　　そして、祈ろうと、葉の繁る腕を上げる

　　　　夏になると、木は髪に
　　　　駒鳥の巣を飾る

> **NOTE**
> **キルマー**
> ジョイス・キルマー（1886–1918）はアメリカの詩人・ジャーナリスト。第1次世界大戦に従軍し、フランスでの戦闘中に狙撃兵に撃たれて戦死した。

LANGUAGE ARTS • 国語

Sayings and Phrases ことわざと熟語

Birthday suit
「お誕生日服」

When you were born (on your "birthday"), you weren't wearing any clothes. When someone is said to be wearing his or her "birthday suit," it means that the person is naked.

人は生まれたときに（「誕生日」に）は、何も着ていない。だれそれは「お誕生日服」を着ていると言ったときには、裸のままでいるという意味だ。

Bite the hand that feeds you
「餌をくれる手を噛む」

An ill-tempered dog may bite his master, even though he depends on his master for food. When you do something to harm a person or thing that supports you, you are "biting the hand that feeds you."

怒りっぽい犬は、主人から餌をもらっていながら、その主人の手を噛むこともある。助けてくれる人やものに危害を加えたり、損害を与えたりすると、「餌をくれる手を噛んでいる」ということになる。

Chip on your shoulder
「肩に木っ端を乗せて（けんか腰で）」

When someone has a chip on his shoulder, it means that he is in a bad mood and would pick a fight eagerly.

「肩に木っ端を乗せている」というのは、怒りっぽくなっていてすぐにでもケンカをしそうだという意味である。

Count your blessings
「好運を数えてみよ」

People use this saying to mean, "Be thankful for what you have."

このことわざは、「自分が持っているものに感謝せよ」という意味で使う。

5th GRADE

Eureka!
「エウレカ！（わかったぞ！）」

Eureka is a Greek word that means, "I have found it!" It's well known as the expression of delight that the famous mathematician Archimedes used upon discovering how to find the volume of gold.

「エウレカ」とはギリシャ語で「発見したぞ！」という意味である。有名な数学者のアルキメデスが金の量を測る方法を見つけたときに発した喜びの表現としてよく知られている。

The grass is always greener on the other side of the hill
「向こうの丘の草はいつでもこっちより青い」

This saying is usually used to console someone who feels that what others have is better than what he has—no matter what it is!

なにかにつけ自分が持っている物よりも他の人の物のほうがいいと思って落ちこむ人がいるが、そういう人を慰めるときなどによく使う。

Well begun is half done
「始まりがよければ半ば終わったも同然」

This saying means that if you start something off well, it will be easier to finish.

このことわざは、ものごとの滑り出しが順調であれば、終わりがずっと楽になる、という意味だ。

What will be, will be
「成るように成る」

This saying means that some things are beyond our control.

このことわざは、どうやってもわれわれの思い通りにはならないこともある、という意味である。

It's never too late to mend
「改めるに遅すぎることはない」

This saying means that there is always time to improve yourself, or to change your ways.

このことわざは、自分を向上させる、あるいは自分の生き方を変える機会は常にあるという意味だ。

A watched pot never boils
「じっと見ていると鍋の湯はいつまでも沸かない」

This saying means that when you are anxiously waiting for something to happen, it always seems to take longer.

このことわざは、何かが起きるのを気をもんで待っていると、いつでも余計に時間がかかるように思われる、という意味である。

Out of the frying pan and into the fire
「フライパンから出て火の中へ」

People use this expression to describe what happens when you go from a bad situation to an even worse one.

困っているときにさらに悪い事態を迎えるとどういうことになるか。そんなときにこの表現を使う。

➼ The explorer escaped the wild boar by leaping across a narrow canyon. When he reached the other side, though, he landed on the tail of a giant python and realized that he had jumped out of the frying pan and into the fire.

➼ 探険家はイノシシから逃げるのに、狭い峡谷を飛び越えた。だが、向こう側に着地したところで巨大なニシキヘビのしっぽを踏んでしまい、まさにフライパンから火の中に飛び込んでしまったと天を仰いだ。

A penny saved is a penny earned
「1ペニーの貯金は1ペニーの稼ぎ」

This saying means that when you save money instead of spending it, it is almost the same as earning money, because you'll have extra cash instead of an empty pocket.

このことわざがいおうとしているのは、お金を使わずに貯めるのは、お金を稼ぐようなものだ、ということである。空のポケットの代わりに、いつでも使える現金を持っていることになるからだ。

Read between the lines
「行間を読む」

When you "read between the lines," you go beyond the surface of what someone says or does so you can find out what they really mean.

「行間を読む」というのは、人の言葉や行動が本当はどういうことなのかを理解するために、その奥の意味を考えることである。

Take the bull by the horns
「角をつかんで牡牛を押さえる（困難に体当たりする）」

People use this phrase to mean "stop hesitating and take action."

▸ Norma got to the end of the high diving board and froze. The water was so far down, and it looked as hard and shiny as glass. She was afraid to jump, and she was too scared to turn back and climb down.

"Come on, Norma," her brother called from below. "It's not as scary as it looks. Just take the bull by the horns and jump!"

この慣用句は、「迷っていないで、行動を起こせ」という意味で使われる。

▸ ノーマは高飛び込み台の先端まで行って足が凍りついてしまった。プールの水面ははるか下にあり、ガラスのように硬く光って見えた。とても飛込む勇気はないし、すっかりおびえてしまって戻って降りてくることもできなかった。
「勇気を出すんだ、ノーマ」と兄が下から声をかけた。「見た目ほど恐くはないよ。ええい、やってやれという感じで、一気に飛んじゃえ！」

Time heals all wounds
「時はすべての傷を癒す」

When you scrape your elbow, you know that it will take a week or so to heal. But when people say "time heals all wounds," they are usually talking about feelings. And they mean that sometimes the only thing that can make you feel better after something bad happens is the passing of time.

ひじをすりむいたときは、治るまでに1週間やそこらはかかるものだ。しかし、「時はすべての傷を癒す」というときには、心の傷の話をしているのである。嫌なことを体験した場合、心の回復に役立つのは、ときには時の過ぎ去ることだけだ、というのである。

Vice versa
「逆もまた同様」

When people use this Latin term, they mean, "and exactly the same, but the other way round."

このラテン語の表現は、「そして逆の場合も、まったく同じことがいえる」という意味で使われている。

▸ Martha comes to visit me once a year, and vice versa. That way we get to see each other twice a year.

▸ 年に1度マーサはわたしの所にやってくるし、逆にわたしの方でも行く。そんなふうにして、わたしたちは年に2度会っているのだ。

LANGUAGE ARTS • 国語

Abraham Lincoln's Gettysburg Address

Four score and seven years ago, our fathers brought forth upon this continent a new nation, conceived in liberty, and dedicated to the proposition that all men are created equal.

Now we are engaged in a great civil war, testing whether that nation, or any nation so conceived and so dedicated, can long endure. We are met on a great battlefield of that war. We have come to dedicate a portion of that field as a final resting place for those who here gave their lives that that nation might live. It is altogether fitting and proper that we should do this.

エイブラハム・リンカーン

But in a larger sense we cannot dedicate—we cannot consecrate—we cannot hallow—this ground. The brave men, living and dead, who struggled here, have consecrated it far above our poor power to add or detract. The world will little note, nor long remember, what we say here, but it can never forget what they did here. It is for us, the living, rather to be dedicated here to the unfinished work which they who fought here have thus far so nobly advanced. It is rather for us to be here dedicated to the great task remaining before us—that from these honored dead we take increased devotion to that cause for which they gave the last full measure of devotion; that we here highly resolve that these dead shall not have died in vain; that this nation, under God, shall have a new birth of freedom, and that government of the people, by the people, for the people, shall not perish from the earth.

エイブラハム・リンカーンの
ゲティスバーグ演説

　87年前、われわれの父祖にあたる人々が、この大陸に新しい国家を誕生させました。その国家は自由の精神を母胎として、人間はすべて平等であるという思想に基づいて作られました。

　現在、われわれは酷い内戦を戦っていますが、この国家が、あるいは、かかる母胎と思想から生まれた国家なるものが、はたして長く存続できるのかどうかが験されているのです。今われわれが一堂に会しているのは、その戦争の激戦の地です。われわれは、この国家の存亡を賭けてここで命を犠牲にした人々のための最後の安息地として、この戦場の一部を捧げることにいたしました。われわれがしようとしていることは、まことに正しく時宜を得たものであります。

　しかし、言葉の意味をより大きくとらえてみると、われわれはこの土地を捧げることなどできないのです。また、神聖化することも、聖別することもできないのであります。戦死者と生存者に分かれはしましたが、ここで勇敢に戦った人々自身がこの土地を神聖なものとしたのであって、非力のわれわれにはそれ以上貢献も毀損もできないのです。将来、世界の人々は、われわれがここで何を言ったかなど気にもとめず、長く記憶にとどめることもないでしょうが、彼らがこの地で戦ったことは、決して忘れないでしょう。ここで戦った人々がかくもみごとに前進させてきた未完の仕事のために身を捧げるべきなのは、むしろわれわれ生きている者です。われわれこそが、この地で、われらの前途に託された大きな仕事に、わが身を捧げるべきなのです。その仕事とは、この誉れ高い死者たちが命を賭して最大限の献身をなしとげた大義のために、彼らに劣らぬ献身をすることであります。また、ここに眠る人々の死を無駄にしないと決意することであります。そして、神の庇護のもと、この国家に自由を新たに誕生させることであり、人民の、人民による、人民のための政府を地上から消滅させないことであります。

> **NOTE**
> 第16代大統領エイブラハム・リンカーンは多くの書物を独学で読んで必要なことを学んだ。とくに『聖書』とシェイクスピアを愛読し、力強く深みのある独自の文体を身につけたといわれる。ここに掲げる演説はとりわけ有名で、南北戦争のさなかの1863年、激戦地ゲティスバーグに国有墓地を建立する儀式で行われた。

NOTE 学校施設の英語

gymnasium, gym（体育館）
nurse's office（保健室）
principal's office（校長室）
teachers' room（職員室）
computer room（コンピュータ・ルーム）
laboratory（理科の実験室）
cafeteria（食堂）

NOTE 遊具の英語

tetherball（テザーボール）
＊アメリカではとてもポピュラーな遊具。

swing（ブランコ）
slide（滑り台）
chin-up bar（鉄棒）
＊chin-up とは懸垂のこと。鉄棒競技などの鉄棒は horizontal bar という。

seesaw, teeter-totter（シーソー）
jungle gym, monkey bars（ジャングルジム）
balance beam（平均台）

What American 6th GRADERS Learn in Textbooks

LANGUAGE ARTS • 国語

John F. Kennedy: Inaugural Address

We observe today not a victory of party but a celebration of freedom—symbolizing an end as well as a beginning—signifying renewal as well as change. For I have sworn before you and Almighty God the same solemn oath our forebears prescribed nearly a century and three quarters ago.

The world is very different now, for man holds in his mortal hands the power to abolish all forms of human poverty and all forms of human life. And yet the same revolutionary beliefs for which our forebears fought are still at issue around the globe. . . .

ジョン・F・ケネディ

We dare not forget today that we are the heirs of that first revolution. Let the word go forth from this time and place, to friend and foe alike, that the torch has been passed to a new generation of Americans—born in this century, tempered by war, disciplined by a hard and bitter peace, proud of our ancient heritage, and unwilling to witness or permit the slow undoing of those human rights to which the nation has always been committed, and to which we are committed today, at home and around the world.

Let every nation know, whether it wishes us well or ill, that we shall pay any price, bear any burden, meet any hardship, support any friend, or oppose any foe to assure the survival and the success of liberty.

This much we pledge—and more.

To those old allies whose cultural and spiritual origins we share, we pledge the loyalty of faithful friends. . . .

To those people in the huts and villages of half the globe struggling to break the bonds of mass misery, we pledge our best efforts to help

ジョン・F・ケネディ
「大統領就任演説」

　今日われわれが行うのは党の祝勝会ではなく、自由の祝典であります。この祝典は1つの始まりとともに1つの終わりを象徴し、変化と同時に更新を意味しています。というのも、いま国民のみなさんと全能なる神の前で、175年ほど前のわが父祖たちと同じ誓いを厳粛な気持ちで宣言したからであります。

　今や世界は大きく変わりました。神ならぬ身の人間が、貧困をことごとく消滅させる力と同時に、人間の生活をすべて抹殺する力を持つに至ったのであります。それでもなお、わが父祖たちが闘い取ろうとした革命的な信念が正しいか否かについて、世界中で論争が続いています……

　こんにち、われわれがあの最初の革命の継承者であることを忘れることなどありえません。今この時、この場所から、敵にも味方にも、松明(たいまつ)はアメリカ人の新しい世代に手渡されたのだという声を届けようではありませんか。新しい世代のわれわれは、今世紀になってから生まれました。戦争によって鍛えられ、困難で苦しい平和によって修練を積んできました。われわれは受け継いだ古い遺産を誇りに思い、わが国がつねに守ろうとしてきた人間の諸権利が徐々になし崩しにされるのを、見逃すつもりも、許すつもりもありません。そして今、われわれはそうした権利を、国内でそして世界中で守ろうとしているのです。

　われわれの幸福を願うか不幸を願うかを問わず、ありとあらゆる国家に、こう伝えようではありませんか。われわれは、自由の存続と成就を確かなものとするためには、いかなる代償も支払う。いかなる重荷をも引き受ける。いかなる困難にも臆せず、いかなる同志をも支援し、いかなる敵とも戦う覚悟があるのだ、ということを。

　これだけのことをわれわれは約束します。そして、さらにもっと多くを。

　文化的に、精神的に共通するところのある古い同盟諸国に対してわれわれは、忠実な友人としての信義を約束します……

　地球の半分を占める地域の小さな家、村落に住む人々が、彼らを

> **NOTE**
> 1961年1月、ジョン・F・ケネディ(1917-63)は42歳の若さでアメリカ合衆国大統領に就任した。合衆国大統領としてはいまだに最年少。以下の大統領就任演説では、強いアメリカを継承する新しい世代の責務について熱く語りかける。

them help themselves . . . because it is right. If a free society cannot help the many who are poor, it cannot save the few who are rich. . . .

Finally, to those nations who would make themselves our adversary, we offer not a pledge but a request: that both sides begin anew the quest for peace, before the dark powers of destruction unleased by science engulf all humanity in planned or accidental self-destruction.

So let us begin anew—remembering on both sides that civility is not a sign of weakness, and sincerity is always subject to proof. Let us never negotiate out of fear. But let us never fear to negotiate.

Now the trumpet summons us again . . . as a call to bear the burden of a long twilight struggle, year in and year out . . . a struggle against the common enemies of man: tyranny, poverty, disease, and war itself.

Can we forget against these enemies a grand and global alliance, North and South, East and West, that can assure a more fruitful life for all mankind? Will you join in that historic effort? . . .

The energy, the faith, the devotion which we bring to this endeavor will light our country and all who serve it—and the glow from that fire can truly light the world.

And so, my fellow Americans, ask not what your country can do for you; ask what you can do for your country.

My fellow citizens of the world: ask not what America will do for you, but what together we can do for the freedom of man.

Finally, whether you are citizens of America or citizens of the world, ask of us here the same high standards of strength and sacrifice which we ask of you.

縛っている集団的な貧窮という枷(かせ)を断ち切ろうとしています。わたしたちは彼らが自ら立ち上がれるようできるかぎりのことをすることを約束します……それが正しいことだからです。もし自由な社会が多数の貧しい人々を助けることができないならば、少数の富裕層も救うことはできません……

　最後に、われわれにあえて敵対する国々に対しては、約束ではなく要求をします。どちらの側も、ともに新たに和平を模索しようと。科学によって解き放たれた暗黒の破壊力が、意図的なあるいは事故による自己破壊の淵にすべての人類を呑みこんでしまう前に。

　だからわれわれは新たに始めるのです——双方ともに忘れてはいけないのは、礼節ある行動は弱さのしるしではないということ、誠実さはたえず証明しなければならないということです。決して相手に対する恐れから交渉してはなりません。しかし、決して交渉することを恐れてはならないのです。

　今、ふたたびわれわれを呼ぶラッパが聞こえます。……来る年もまた来る年も、長い薄明の闘いの重荷をになえという合図です……それは人類共通の敵——独裁、貧困、病、そしてまさに戦争との闘いであります。

　これらの敵に対して、われわれは、より豊かな生活を全人類に保証する、南北・東西を結ぶ全地球的な壮大な同盟を作ることができるでしょうか？　その歴史的な努力にみなさんは参加してくれるでしょうか？

　われわれがこの試みにつぎこむ精力、信念、献身が、わが国とそれを支える人々に光明をもたらし、また、その炎の輝きが世界を明るくするのです。

　それゆえ、わがアメリカ国民のみなさん、国があなた方のために何をしてくれるのかを問うのではなく、あなた方が国のために何ができるかを問うていただきたい。

　私の友である世界各国のみなさん、アメリカがあなた方のために何をしてくれるのかと問うのではなく、われわれが力を合わせて人間の自由のために何ができるかを問うていただきたい。

　最後に、アメリカの市民であれ世界の市民であれ、われわれがみなさんに求めるような高い水準の力と犠牲とを、ここにいるわれわれに求めていただきたい。

LANGUAGE ARTS • 国 語

Martin Luther King, Jr.: "I Have a Dream"

Five score years ago, a great American, in whose symbolic shadow we stand, signed the Emancipation Proclamation. This momentous decree came as a great beacon of light of hope to millions of Negro slaves who had been seared in the flames of withering injustice. It came as a joyous daybreak to end the long night of captivity.

But one hundred years later, the Negro still is not free. One hundred years later, the life of the Negro is still sadly crippled by the manacles of segregation and the chains of discrimination. One hundred years later, the Negro lives on a lonely island of poverty in the midst of a vast ocean of material prosperity. One hundred years later, the Negro is still languished in the corners of American society and finds himself in exile in his own land.

So we've come here today to dramatize a shameful condition. In a sense we have come to our nation's capital to cash a check. When the architects of our republic wrote the magnificent words of the Constitution and the Declaration of Independence, they were signing a promissory note to which every American was to fall heir. This note was a promise that all men, yes, black men as well as white men, would be guaranteed the unalienable rights of life, liberty, and the pursuit of happiness. . . . Instead of honoring this sacred obligation, America has given the Negro people a bad check, which has come back marked "insufficient funds." We refuse to believe that there are insufficient funds in the great vaults of opportunity of this nation. And so we've come to cash this check—a check that will give us upon demand the riches of freedom and the security of justice.

We have also come to this hallowed spot to remind America of the fierce urgency of now. . . . Now is the time to make real the promises of democracy; now is the time to rise from the dark and desolate valley of segregation to the sunlit path of racial justice; now is the time to lift our nation from the quicksands of racial injustice to the solid rock of broth-

マーティン・ルーサー・キング牧師「わたしには夢がある」

100年前、1人の偉大なアメリカ人が、奴隷解放宣言(*1)に署名しました。今日、われわれは、その人の象徴的な影の下にいます。このきわめて重要な法的命令は、不正の炎で焼かれて苦しんでいた何百万の黒人奴隷にとって、未来を照らす希望の光でありました。長い、長い、囚われの夜に終わりを告げる、うれしい夜明けでありました。

しかし、100年たった今でも、黒人に自由はありません。100年たった今でも、黒人の生活は、悲しくも人種分離の手かせ、人種差別の足かせで縛られています。100年たった今でも、黒人は、物質的繁栄という大海原のまっただ中で、貧困という孤島での生活に甘んじています。100年たった今でも、黒人はアメリカ社会の片隅で悩み苦しみ、自国にいながら異国に流された思いを味わうのです。

だから、われわれは、今日、屈辱的な状況をはっきりと示すためにここにやって来ました。われわれはわが国の首都に、小切手を換金するためにやってきたのだ、と言ってもいいでしょう。われわれの共和国を設計建築した先人たちが、合衆国憲法と独立宣言にすばらしい言葉を書き記したとき、彼らは、あとに続くすべてのアメリカ人が受取人となる約束手形に署名をしていたのです。この手形は、すべての人間に対して——そう、白人も黒人も含めたすべての人間に対して、生命、自由および幸福を追求する権利を、奪うことのできないものとして(*2)保証するという約束の手形だったのです……この神聖なる債務を指定期日通りに支払うかわりに、アメリカは黒人たちに不渡り小切手を渡してきました。この小切手は、換金しようとすると「残高不足」の判を押されて返されてきました。機会を蓄えておくこの国の巨大な金庫室の残高が不足している——そんなことは信じられるものではありません。それで、われわれはこの小切手を換金しにやって来たのです。この小切手は、われわれが要求すれば、自由の富と正義の保証を与えてくれるはずです。

さらにまた、われわれがこの神聖な場所にやってきたのは、現在がいかに緊急事態であるかをアメリカ国民に認識してもらうためで

NOTE

1963年8月28日、マーティン・ルーサー・キング牧師(1929–68)は、ワシントンのリンカーン記念堂の前で、20万人を超える聴衆を前にこの名演説を行った。

本書の原著監修者であるE. D. ハーシュは、「独立宣言」と「ゲティスバーグ演説」がアメリカの旧約聖書であり、「わたしには夢がある」が新約聖書だと言っている。

NOTE

Five score years ago
scoreとは20の意味。リンカーンの演説 (p.230参照)の冒頭の言い回しを活かしている。

*1 **奴隷解放宣言**：リンカーンは南北戦争のさなかの1862年9月に、翌年1月1日から南部諸州の奴隷を解放するという内容の奴隷解放宣言を発令した。

*2 「生命、自由および幸福を追求する権利を、奪うことのできないものとして」独立宣言からの引用。

erhood; now is the time to make justice a reality for all God's children.

Let us not seek to satisfy our thirst for freedom by drinking from the cup of bitterness and hatred. We must forever conduct our struggle on the high plain of dignity and discipline. We must not allow our creative protest to degenerate into physical violence. Again and again we must rise to the majestic heights of meeting physical force with soul force.

The marvelous new militancy which has engulfed the Negro community must not lead us to a distrust of all white people, for many of our white brothers, as evidenced by their presence here today, have come to realize that their destiny is tied up with our destiny, and they have come to realize that their freedom is inextricably bound to our freedom. . . . We cannot walk alone.

So I say to you, my friends, that even though we must face the difficulties of today and tomorrow, I still have a dream. It is a dream deeply rooted in the American dream that one day this nation will rise up and live out the true meaning of its creed—we hold these truths to be self-evident, that all men are created equal.

I have a dream that one day on the red hills of Georgia, sons of former slaves and sons of former slave owners will be able to sit down together at the table of brotherhood. . . .

I have a dream that my four little children will one day live in a nation where they will not be judged by the color of their skin but by the content of their character. I have a dream today!

マーティン・ルーサー・キング牧師

もあります……今こそ、デモクラシーの約束を現実のものにする、まさにそのときなのです。今こそ、暗く荒れ果てた人種分離政策の谷間から人種間の公平という陽のあたる道へと抜け出す、まさにそのときなのです。今こそ、人種間の不公平という危険な流砂からわが国をすくい上げて、同胞愛という堅固な岩石の上に移す、まさにそのときなのです。今こそ、すべての神の子どもたちのために正義を実現する、まさにそのときなのです。

　自由への渇きを癒すために恨みと憎しみの杯をあおるのはやめようではありませんか。われわれの闘いは、どこまでも高い次元の品位と自制心をもって果たされなければなりません。明日を創り出すわれわれの抗議行動は、肉体的な暴力に堕してはなりません。われわれは何度でも立ち上がり、肉体的な力に魂の力をもって向きあうという、威厳に満ちた高みを目指さなければならないのです。

　最近、驚くほど好戦的な動きが黒人社会を席捲していますが、われわれはそれに引きずられてすべての白人たちに不信をいだくようなことがあってはならないのです。今日ここに多くの白人の同志が参加していることが何よりの証拠ですが、彼らの運命とわれわれの運命が1つに結びついていることを、彼らは認識しているのです。彼らの自由とわれわれの自由とが分かちがたく結びついていることを、彼らは認識しているのです。われわれは、離ればなれに歩んではならないのであります。

　友よ、わたしはこう申し上げたい。今日も明日も難問が次々と立ちはだかるとしても、わたしにはまだ夢がある、と。それはアメリカの夢に深く根ざした夢であって、いつの日かこの国は立ち上がって、「次に掲げる真理は自明であるとわれわれは確信する。すなわち、すべての人間は平等である(*3)」というあの建国の信念が本当に意味するところを実現するであろう、という夢であります。

　わたしには夢がある——いつの日かジョージアの赤土の丘の上で、かつて奴隷だったものの息子たちと奴隷所有者の息子たちが、ともに同志として同じテーブルにつくことができるでありましょう……

　わたしには夢がある——わたしの4人の子どもたちもいつの日か皮膚の色によってではなく人格によって評価される国に住むでありましょう。今、わたしには夢があるのです！

　わたしには夢がある——いつの日か南部のアラバマで……黒人の男の子と女の子が白人の男の子、女の子と兄弟姉妹として手を取り

*3 「次に掲げる真理は自明である……」独立宣言からの引用。この後には、「人間は創造主より一定の奪うことのできない権利を与えられている。その中には、生命、自由および幸福を追求する権利が含まれている」と続く。

I have a dream that one day, down in Alabama . . . little black boys and black girls will be able to join hands with little white boys and white girls as sisters and brothers. I have a dream today! . . .

I have a dream that one day every valley shall be exalted, every hill and mountain shall be made low, the rough places shall be made plain, and the crooked places shall be made straight, and the glory of the Lord will be revealed and all flesh shall see it together.

With this faith we will be able to work together, to pray together, to struggle together, to go to jail together, to stand up for freedom together, knowing that we will be free one day. This will be the day when all of God's children will be able to sing with new meaning—"My country 'tis of thee; sweet land of liberty; of thee I sing; land where my fathers died, land of the pilgrim's pride; from every mountain side, let freedom ring." . . .

So let freedom ring from the prodigious hilltops of New Hampshire.
Let freedom ring from the mighty mountains of New York.
Let freedom ring from the heightening Alleghenies of Pennsylvania.
Let freedom ring from the snowcapped Rockies of Colorado.
Let freedom ring from the curvaceous slopes of California.
But not only that.
Let freedom ring from Stone Mountain of Georgia.
Let freedom ring from Lookout Mountain of Tennessee.
Let freedom ring from every hill and molehill of Mississippi, from every mountainside, let freedom ring.

And when we allow freedom to ring, when we let it ring from every village and hamlet, from every state and city, we will be able to speed up that day when all of God's children—black men and white men, Jews and Gentiles, Catholics and Protestants—will be able to join hands and to sing in the words of the old Negro spiritual, "Free at last, free at last; thank God Almighty, we are free at last."

合うことができるようになるでありましょう。今、わたしには夢があるのです！……

　わたしには夢がある——いつの日か「すべての谷底は身を起こし、丘と山並みは身を低くせよ。険しい土地は平らに、曲がりくねった道はまっすぐになれ。神の栄光がこのように明らかになり、すべての人間がともにそれを目撃するであろう」という夢が。

　かかる信仰があれば、われわれはともに働くことができるでしょう。ともに祈り、ともに闘い、ともに牢獄に入り、ともに自由のために立ち上がり、いつの日か自由になることを知るのです。その日にこそ、すべての神の子どもたちが新しい意味をこめてこう歌うことができるのです——「わが祖国よ、これは汝の歌。うるわしき自由の国。汝の歌をわたしは歌う。わが父祖たちの死せる国、巡礼者が誇りとする国。山という山から自由の鐘を鳴らそう」……

　さあ、ニューハンプシャーの巨大な丘の頂から、自由の鐘を鳴らそう。

　ニューヨークの大きな山並みから、自由の鐘を鳴らそう。

　ペンシルベニアの聳え立つアレゲニー山地から、自由の鐘を鳴らそう。

　コロラドの雪を頂くロッキー山脈から、自由の鐘を鳴らそう。

　カリフォルニアの美しくうねる丘陵から、自由の鐘を鳴らそう。

　しかし、まだあります。

　ジョージアのストーン・マウンテンから、自由の鐘を鳴らそう。

　テネシーのルックアウト・マウンテンから、自由の鐘を鳴らそう。

　ミシシッピのすべての山から、どんな小さな山からも、自由の鐘を鳴らそう。すべての山間から自由の鐘を鳴らそう。

　そして、われわれが自由の鐘を鳴らすならば、あらゆる村や集落で、あらゆる州や都市で自由の鐘を鳴らしていけば、待ち望むその日はたちまちやってくるのです。その日、すべての神の子どもたちは——黒人も白人も、ユダヤ教徒もキリスト教徒も、カトリックもプロテスタントも——手を取り合って古い黒人霊歌を口ずさむことでしょう、「ついに自由に、ついに自由に。全能なる神に感謝せん。われらはついに自由に」と。

NOTE
「すべての谷底は……」
聖書からの引用。equality, justice のイメージを託している。

NOTE
「わが祖国よ……」
国歌「星条旗」と同様によく歌われる愛国歌の1つ「アメリカ」からの引用。国土と民衆への愛を歌い、神を讃える「アメリカ」は、戦場の光景を綴った「星条旗」とは対照的な内容だ。

NOTE
ストーン・マウンテン
アトランタ近郊にある山で、山肌の岩に南部連合軍を象徴する3人（デービス大統領、リー将軍、ジャクソン将軍）の巨大な像が彫り込まれている。1915年にこの山でKKK（クー・クラックス・クラン）が再結成の結団式を行った。

NOTE
ルックアウト・マウンテン
垂直に切り立った断崖を持ち、テネシー川を見下ろす位置にある標高648mの山。近くのチャタヌーガ、チカモーガとともに南北戦争の激戦地となった。

WORLD CIVILIZATION • 世界史

JAPAN: The Opening of Japan

In the 1800s most Asian nations were victims of European imperialism. They were either colonized, like India and Africa, or bullied and humbled, like China. One of the few exceptions was Japan. The Japanese beat the Europeans at their own game: like the European countries, Japan became a modern, industrialized nation, and then an imperialist power.

But the Japanese had to scramble to catch up with the Europeans. In the mid-1800s, Japanese society was pretty much as it had been in feudal times. The Japanese had been sealed off from contact with the outside world for almost two centuries. Japanese rulers in the early 1600s had banned all foreigners from Japan because they saw foreign ideas, including the Christian religion, as a threat to their culture. These leaders had said, in no uncertain terms, "So long as the sun warms the earth, any Christian bold enough to come to Japan . . . even if he be the god of the Christians, shall pay for it with his head."

At the same time, the leaders forbid the Japanese people to travel outside Japan, or even to build a ship big enough to sail to another country! Almost all trade with the outside world ground to a halt. You've read before about how countries develop when they exchange

ペリー提督の日本上陸 (ペリー神奈川上陸図・部分)

日本の開国

　19世紀には、アジアの国々のほとんどがヨーロッパ帝国主義の犠牲となっていた。インドやアフリカのように植民地化されるか、中国のように力で脅かされ、屈辱的な地位にあまんじていた。数少ない例外が日本であった。日本人はまさしくヨーロッパの流儀で、ヨーロッパ人を打ち負かした。ヨーロッパ諸国のように、日本は近代的な工業国となり、帝国主義の強国となったのだ。

　しかし日本人はヨーロッパ人に追いつくため、大急ぎで困難を乗り越えなくてはならなかった。19世紀半ばになっても、日本の社会は封建時代とほぼ同様の状態にあった。日本はおよそ2世紀にもわたって、外国との交渉を断ち続けていた。17世紀初頭、日本の支配者は外国人の入国を禁止した。キリスト教を含む外国の思想が、日本の文化を脅かすと考えたのだ。日本の指導者たちの言葉はそのものずばりで、こう言った。「天の日が地を照らし続けるかぎり、日本に来るような命知らずのキリスト教徒は……たとえキリスト教の神であっても、その代償を首で支払うことになるだろう」

　同時に、日本人が国外へ出ることや、外国へ渡航できるような大型の船を造ることさえ禁止された。外の世界との交易にはブレーキがかかり、やがて停止した。国家は品物や知識を互いに交換して発展するということはすでに述べたが、当時の日本には、どんな新しい品物も知識も入ってこなかったのだ。ヨーロッパで産業革命に移行し始めたころ、日本はいまだに中世の工業技術でやっていた。

　1853年のある日、日本の首都に暮らす人々は奇妙な光景を目のあたりにした。湾上に4隻の巨大な船が浮かんでいた。そのうちの2隻には帆があったが、残りの2隻は帆を使わずに動いていた。船には煙突があり、そこからもくもくと煙が出ていた。それは、蒸気機関を動力とした船など聞いたことのない日本人にとって異様で恐ろしいものにちがいなかった。日本人はその船を「悪魔のごとき黒船」と呼んだ。

　船はアメリカの戦艦であることが分かった。アメリカは海軍士官マシュー・ペリー提督を、日本の指導者たちと会談させるために派

goods and ideas, but no new goods or ideas could get into Japan at this time. While Europe proceeded into the Industrial Revolution, Japan still lived with the technology of the Middle Ages.

Then one day in 1853, a strange sight confronted the people in the Japanese capital city. There in the bay floated four large ships: two had sails, but the other two moved without sails. These ships had chimneys that poured out clouds of smoke. They were strange and frightening to the Japanese, who had never heard of ships powered by steam. They called them "the black ships of evil appearance."

They turned out to be United States warships. The United States had sent a naval officer, Commodore Matthew Perry, to meet with Japanese leaders. He was carrying a letter from the American president, which asked that the Japanese open trade with the United States. Perry delivered the letter, then sailed away, saying that he would return in a year for the Japanese response.

The Japanese leaders did not want to open Japan to the outside world. But they had heard of the European conquests elsewhere in Asia. They had seen Perry's steamships. They knew that the Europeans and Americans had the military strength to conquer Japan. So to keep from being colonized, the Japanese gave in. When Perry returned, they agreed to start trading with the United States.

To celebrate the agreement, the Japanese and Americans gave each other gifts. The Japanese gave the Americans beautiful handmade objects: swords, fans, silk robes, porcelain cups. The Americans gave the Japanese guns, a telescope, a clock, and a telegraph. They also gave them seventy feet of railway track and a miniature (one-quarter-size) locomotive. The Japanese studied these gifts carefully.

The Meiji Restoration and the Modernizing of Japan

Within a few years the Japanese had reopened trade with a number of countries. Foreigners were allowed to live in Japan, and even the Christian missionaries returned. These changes opened Japan to the world but also led to the overthrow of the Japanese government.

Japan has always been a monarchy, headed by an emperor or empress who, according to the Japanese religion, is a divine, godlike

遣したのだった。ペリーはアメリカ大統領の国書を携えており、その国書は日本にアメリカとの交易を開始することを要求していた。ペリーは国書を届けると、1年以内に日本の返答を聞きに戻ってくるといって日本を去った。

日本の指導者たちは開国を望まなかった。とはいえ、彼らはヨーロッパがアジアのほかの国々を征服したことを聞いて知っていた。ペリーの蒸気船も目の当たりにした。ヨーロッパとアメリカが日本を征服するに足る軍事力を持っていることは明らかだったので、植民地化を免れるために日本は譲歩した。ペリーがふたたび日本にやって来ると、日本はアメリカとの交易を開始する協定を結んだ。

この協定を記念して、日本とアメリカは贈りものを交換した。日本はアメリカに美しい手工芸品——刀、扇、絹の着物、磁器の茶碗——を贈った。アメリカは日本に銃、望遠鏡、時計、電信機を贈った。また70フィート(およそ21メートル)の線路と、ミニチュア(4分の1の大きさ)の蒸気機関車も贈った。日本人はこれらの贈りものを仔細に研究した。

> **NOTE**
> **ペリー提督**
> ペリー提督(1794–1858)は若いときに、地中海、アフリカ、カリブ海などの海賊討伐で手柄をあげた。軍艦の装備の近代化、海兵の教育などに大きな功績を残した。巨大な蒸気船軍艦と高性能の大砲は彼のトレードマークでもあった。
>
> なお、船全体に黒いタールを塗っていたので日本では「黒船」と呼ばれたが、この呼称はそれ以前から外国の軍艦に対して使われていた。

明治維新と日本の近代化

数年のうちに、日本は多くの国々との交易を再開した。外国人は日本で暮らすことを許され、キリスト教の宣教師さえ再び日本にやって来るようになった。このような変化によって日本は世界へと開かれたのだが、日本の政治体制もまた崩壊することになった。

日本は伝統的に君主制の国であり、天皇や女帝が君臨してきたが、日本人の宗教観によれば、彼らは神聖かつ神のような存在で、女性の太陽神の子孫とされる。ところが、ペリーが来日したとき、天皇は政治的な実権を握っていなかった。数百年にわたって、日本でもっとも政治的な力を持っていたのは、将軍という軍事的独裁者であった。しかし、この体制は日本の開国によって変わった。そのときの将軍は指導者として力に欠け、すでに武士たちの信頼を失っていた。日本が開国すると、外国人に屈服したとして、将軍は臆病者と呼ばれ、ますますその力は弱まった。1868年、結束して天皇の側についた武士たちによって将軍はその地位を追われた。

その天皇は15歳の少年で、その前年に即位していた。彼は明治天皇の名で知られている。(明治というのは彼の名前ではなく、「聡明なる統治」という意味の称号だ)。1868年は明治維新(王政復古)

being, descended from the Goddess of the Sun. At the time that Perry reached Japan, however, the emperor had no real power. For several hundred years, the most powerful man in Japan had been the shogun, or military dictator. But this changed after the opening of Japan. The shogun then in power was a weak leader who had already lost the respect of many of his warriors. After the country was opened, many people called him a coward for giving in to the foreigners, and his power was undercut even more. In 1868 the shogun was overthrown by warriors who rallied around the emperor.

The emperor was a fifteen-year-old boy who had come to the throne in the preceding year. He was known as the Emperor Meiji. (Meiji was not his name, but a title meaning "Enlightened Rule.") The year 1868 is remembered as the year of the Meiji Restoration because the emperor had been "restored," or brought back, to a position of real power as Japan's ruler. Meiji ruled Japan for the next forty-five years with intelligence and great dignity. The Japanese came to admire their Emperor Meiji as much as the English admired their Queen Victoria.

Meiji's first task was to unify the country under his rule. In the 1860s much of Japan was still run by feudal lords, who were like the noblemen of the Middle Ages in Europe. Each lord ruled his own estate, or fief, and had his own private army. Meiji made the lords give up their fiefs and broke up the private armies so that a new, national army could be formed. Now the emperor and his advisers had power over the whole country.

The Emperor Meiji was determined to shape Japan into a modern, industrialized nation. He was convinced that this was the only way Japan could avoid being colonized. When the emperor came to power, he took an oath which declared, "The bad customs of past ages shall be abolished, and our government shall tread in the paths of civilization and enlightenment." The oath continued, "We shall endeavour to raise the prestige and honor of our country by seeking knowledge throughout the world."

So Japanese leaders were sent to Europe and America to learn about Western ideas and Western technology. Meanwhile, Europeans and Americans were brought to Japan to train Japanese engineers and manufacturers. They also trained Japanese soldiers and sailors in the most modern ways of fighting wars.

の年として歴史に残っている。天皇の王政が復古して、日本の統治者として政治的な力をふるう地位に返り咲いた年だからだ。明治天皇はその後45年にわたって、知性と威信をもって日本を治めた。日本人は明治天皇を敬うようになったが、それはイギリス国民がビクトリア女王を敬う気持ちに劣らなかった。

　明治天皇の最初の仕事は、日本全国を統治下に置くことだった。1860年代、日本の大部分は封建領主によって支配されていた。封建領主とは、中世ヨーロッパの貴族に似ている。領主たちは、それぞれみずからの土地、領地を治め、独自の軍を持っていた。明治天皇は領主たちに領国を放棄させ、軍を解体させて、新しい国の軍隊を組織した。こうして天皇とその側近たちは全国を統治下に置いた。

　明治天皇は日本をどうしても近代産業国にしたいと考えていた。そうすることが植民地化を免れる唯一の道だと信じていたのだ。権力の座につくと、天皇は次のような誓文を発表した。「過去の悪い習慣を捨て、われわれの政府は文明化と啓蒙の道を進まなければならない」。誓文はさらに続く。「広く世界に知識を求めることによって、わが国の威信と名誉を高めるよう努めなければならない」

　かくして日本の指導者たちは、西洋の思想やテクノロジーを学ぶため、ヨーロッパやアメリカに派遣された。一方、ヨーロッパ人やアメリカ人が、技術者や製造業者を指導するために日本に招かれた。彼らはまた、陸軍や海軍の兵士を、最先端の軍事戦略に基づいて訓練した。

> **NOTE**
> **五箇条の誓文**
> 「過去の悪い習慣は……」：五箇条の誓文の一部である。これに該当する誓文の日本語原文は、「旧来ノ陋習ヲ破リ、天地ノ公道二基クベシ。智識ヲ世界二求メ、大二皇基ヲ振起スベシ」である。

明治天皇

Japan Becomes a World Power

During the 1870s and 1880s, Japan steadily became an industrialized nation. By 1890 the country had more than two hundred steam-powered factories. It also had railways, steamships, and telegraph lines and was building a powerful army and navy. Japan was catching up to Europe. Now, like the European nations, it wanted new sources of raw materials and new markets for its goods. It wanted to expand overseas.

The first place into which Japan expanded was Korea, a nation located on a peninsula between China and Japan. For a long time Korea had been partly independent and partly controlled by China. The Japanese decided to drive the Chinese out, so in 1894 they went to war with China. With their more modern army, the Japanese easily defeated their larger neighbor. The peace treaty that was signed between China and Japan recognized the independence of Korea. As time went on, however, Japan took increasing control of Korea.

Ten years later, in 1904, Japan again fought a war over Korea, this time against Russia. The Russian empire was expanding in Asia, and it seemed about to spread into Korea. To prevent this, the Japanese declared war. They knew this would be a tougher fight than their war with the Chinese. Russia was a huge and powerful Western nation with a modern army and navy. Japan appeared to be the underdog. People in England and the United States admired "gallant little Japan." But the Russians looked down on the Japanese. Russian soldiers sang a song that said, "A Japanese is nothing but a mosquito"—just waiting to be squashed.

It is true that the Japanese had a smaller army and navy than the Russians. But they also had determined, well-trained soldiers, led by a group of brilliant generals and admirals. One of these leaders was Admiral Heihachiro Togo. Admiral Togo was skilled in the latest ways of naval warfare. For seven years he had studied under the British, who had the world's most powerful navy. Now he sailed out to meet the Russians, who had sent their European fleet halfway around the world to attack the Japanese.

Before the battle, Togo sent a message to his sailors: "The country's fate depends upon this battle. Let every man do his duty with all his

日本が世界の強国になる

　1870年代から1880年代にかけて、日本は着実に近代産業国への道を歩んでいった。1890年までには、蒸気機関を利用した工場の数は200を超えていた。また鉄道、蒸気船、電信網を持ち、強力な陸軍と海軍を作っていた。日本は急速にヨーロッパに追いつきつつあった。いまやヨーロッパ諸国のように、日本は原料資源の新たな供給源と、製品の新たな市場を必要としていた。日本は海外へ領土を拡大することが必要だったのだ。

　まず日本が領土拡大を図って進出したのは、中国と日本のあいだの半島に位置する国、朝鮮であった。朝鮮では長らく中国からなかば独立しなかば支配されているという状況が続いていた。日本は中国を排除しようと考え、1894年に中国との戦争を開始した。より近代的な軍隊を持つ日本は、隣の大国をやすやすと打ち負かした。中国と日本のあいだで結ばれた講和条約は、朝鮮の独立を認めるものだった。ところが、しだいに日本は朝鮮に対する支配力を強めていった。

　10年後の1904年、日本は朝鮮をめぐって、こんどはロシアと戦争をした。ロシア帝国はアジアへと領土を拡大しており、朝鮮にも侵攻する勢いだった。これを阻止するため日本は宣戦布告した。こんどの戦いは中国との戦争より厳しいものになると日本は考えていた。ロシアは巨大で強力な西洋の国であり、近代的な陸軍と海軍を持っていた。日本に勝ち目はなさそうだった。イギリスやアメリカでは「勇敢な小国日本」に感心していたが、ロシア人は日本人を見下していた。ロシアの兵士たちはこんな歌詞の歌をうたった。「日本兵なんて蚊も同然」──叩き潰されるのをじっと待っているというのだ。

　たしかに、ロシアに比べると日本の陸軍と海軍は小規模だった。しかし日本には戦闘意欲の高い、よく訓練された兵士がおり、多くの優秀な将軍や提督が兵士たちを率いていた。そのような指揮官の1人に海軍大将、東郷平八郎がいる。東郷は海戦の最先端の戦略に精通していた。彼は7年にわたって、世界でもっとも強力な海軍をもつイギリスから戦略を学んだ。今や東郷はロシア軍との会戦に向けて出港し、そのロシアは日本軍を攻撃するために、世界を半周してヨーロッパ艦隊を日本へ向かわせていた。

　開戦に先立って、東郷は兵士たちに訓令を発した。「わが国の命

might." The great Battle of the Sea of Japan began in the morning and raged until sunset. By the time it was over, the Russians had lost nearly all of their ships and almost five thousand men, whereas only one hundred and sixteen Japanese had been killed. The Russian navy was crippled. The Japanese had won one of the greatest sea battles in history.

The Japanese had meanwhile won several tough victories on land against the Russians. By late 1905 the war was over. Russia and Japan signed a peace treaty, which gave the Japanese control over Korea. Even more important, it gave the Japanese a tremendous sense of pride. In only fifty years, a "backward" Asian nation had risen to beat one of the major powers of Europe. From then on, Japan would be respected as a world power.

With their new sense of pride, Japanese leaders set out to build their own empire. Eventually that empire included much of eastern Asia and the South Pacific. It continued to expand until the Japanese were defeated in a war with the United States.

1905年当時の
日本の領土

運はこの戦いにかかっている。各自全力をつくしておのれの義務を全うするように」。日本海海戦は朝に始まり、激しい戦いは日没まで続いた。戦いが終わるころには、ロシア軍はほとんどすべての戦艦を失い、5000名にものぼろうという戦死者を出した。一方、日本軍の死者はわずか116名であった。ロシアの海軍は大きな打撃をうけた。日本は歴史上屈指の大海戦に勝利をおさめたのである。

その一方で、日本は陸地でもロシア軍とのいくつかの激戦に勝利を収め、戦争は1905年の終わりごろには終結した。ロシアと日本は講和条約を結び、それによって日本は朝鮮の支配権を得た。さらに重要なことに、この勝利は日本人にたいへん大きな自尊心を与えることとなった。わずか50年のあいだに、「後進的な」アジアの1国が、ヨーロッパの強国の1つを打ち負かすまでに成長したのだ。これ以降、日本は世界の強国として重視されることになる。

新たな自尊心を得て、日本の指導者たちは帝国を築くことに着手した。最終的には、その帝国は東アジアと南太平洋の大部分を支配下にとりこんだ。帝国日本は、日本軍がアメリカとの戦争に敗れるまで膨張しつづけたのである。

WORLD CIVILIZATION • 世界史

Capitalism and Socialism

As the Industrial Revolution spread and laissez-faire economic ideas grew more popular, England and other nations grew wealthier. But that wealth was not equally shared. An English politician and novelist named Benjamin Disraeli wrote that England was becoming "two nations, between whom there is . . . no sympathy"; these two nations, said Disraeli, were "the rich and the poor."

Many people began to argue about what kind of economic system would be best for the industrialized nations with their growing wealth and inequality. Most people argued for one of two economic systems: either the existing system, called "capitalism," or a very different system, called "socialism."

カール・マルクス

What is the "capital" in capitalism? Capital is wealth, either in the form of money or what money can buy: land, ships, factories, works of art, etc. A capitalist economic system is built upon the idea of "private property," meaning that individuals or groups of individuals can own capital, and can decide how they want to use their wealth. Those who believe in laissez-faire capitalism say that people should be free to do whatever they want with their wealth, without any government control. In a capitalist system, people often use their wealth to try to make more wealth: they are driven by what is called the "profit motive," a desire to acquire more wealth.

In a capitalist economy, people are free to buy and sell just about anything. What will people buy and sell? How much will a buyer pay? How much profit can a seller make? These and other questions depend upon what is called "the law of supply and demand." Imagine, for

資本主義と社会主義

産業革命が波及し、自由放任主義的な経済観が浸透していくにつれて、イギリスとその他の国はどんどん豊かになっていった。しかし誰もが等しくその富を受け取ったというわけではなかった。イギリスの政治家にして小説家であったベンジャミン・ディズレーリは、イギリスが「2つの国に分かれ、たがいに相手を思いやる気持ちのない」状態になりつつあると書いている。その2つの国とは、ディズレーリによれば、「裕福な者と貧しい者」である。

経済的に豊かになり、貧富の差が広がりつつある工業国にとって、どのような経済システムがもっともふさわしいかがさかんに議論されるようになった。多くの場合、2つの経済システムのいずれかを支持した。すなわち、現存する「資本主義」というシステムか、あるいはそれとはまったく異なる「社会主義」というシステムのいずれかであった。

資本主義の「資本」とはなんだろうか。資本とは富のことで、金もしくは金で買うことのできる土地、船、工場、芸術作品などを指していう。資本主義の経済システムは、「私有財産」という考え方を基盤にしている。私有財産とは、個人もしくは個人の集合であるグループが資本を所有し、富をどのように使うか自分で決めることができるというものだ。自由放任資本主義を信条とする人たちは、自分の富をどのように扱うかは自由であり、政府が制限すべきではないという立場をとる。資本主義のシステムにおいては、人々はより多くの富を得るために富を使おうとする。人々をつき動かすのは、「利潤動機」と呼ばれる、より多くの富を得たいという欲望である。

資本主義経済では、どんなものでも自由に売買できる。人々は何を売り何を買うのか？ 買い手はどのくらい支払うつもりがあるのか？ 売り手が得る利益はどのくらいなのか？ このような問題は、「需要と供給の法則」に左右される。たとえば、あなたが綿を紡ぐための新しい機械を供給する最初の製造業者の1人であるとしよう。そのような機械を買おうという需要はたくさんあるので、高い値段をつけて大きな利益をあげることができる。ところが、その

> **NOTE**
> **マルクス**
> カール・マルクス(1818–83)はプロイセン(現在のドイツの北東部)で、ユダヤ教のラビ(律法の教師)の家系に生まれた。過激な思想の持ち主として追われ、ドイツ、フランス、ベルギーなどを転々とするが、最後はロンドンで亡くなるまで執筆を続けた。

example, that you were one of the first manufacturers to supply new machines to spin cotton. Many people were demanding to buy such machines, so you could charge a high price and make a big profit. But as more people bought the machines, the demand for them would go down; as other manufacturers offered similar machines for sale, the supply would go up—and soon, you would be making smaller profits, and probably looking for another way to gain wealth.

In a capitalist economy, people sell more than machines and products: they also sell their labor. They offer their skills and time in exchange for pay. How much pay? That depends on supply and demand. How did the law of supply and demand affect the thousands of laborers who flooded English cities like Birmingham in the 1800s? (How does it affect many teenagers today who are out of school during the summer and looking for summer jobs?)

You can trace the beginnings of capitalism back to the towns that developed in the Middle Ages, and to the growth of trade in countries like Italy during the Renaissance. The United States today is a capitalist country, though our capitalist system is not completely laissez-faire: some laws, for example, control the ways people can use their money, or the minimum wage that employers can pay, or the precautions manufacturers must take to ensure workers' safety or to decrease pollution from factories.

Compared to our current capitalist economy, the capitalist system in England during the 1800s was more laissez-faire. The system was attacked by many people. Critics of capitalism argued that as long as economic decisions were left to individuals rather than the government, then the rich would get richer and the poor would get poorer. To stop this growing inequality, some people offered an alternative to capitalism, called "socialism."

Socialists believed that the government should take over the economy and run it for the benefit of all people. Socialists said the workers or the government should own the factories and fairly distribute the factories' products, and that the country's wealth should be more fairly divided among all its citizens.

One of the most important socialist thinkers was a German writer named Karl Marx. He believed that society was divided into two main

機械を買う人がどんどん増えていくと、機械に対する需要は減ることになる。また、ほかの製造業者が同じような機械を販売することで供給は増し、まもなく利益は少なくなり、おそらくあなたは富を得るために別の手段を探すことになるだろう。
　資本主義経済では、機械や製品だけが売られるわけではない。労働もまた売られるのだ。人々は自分の技術や時間を提供し、そのかわりに賃金を得る。賃金はどれくらいか？　それは供給と需要の法則に左右される。供給と需要の法則は、19世紀のバーミンガムのようなイギリスの都市にあふれた何千もの労働者たちに、どう影響したのだろうか。（その法則は、学校が休みになる夏のあいだに仕事を探すこんにちのティーンエイジャーたちに、どう影響しているのだろうか）
　資本主義の始まりは、中世に発達した都市や、ルネサンス期のイタリアのような国で起こった商業の発達にまで遡ることができる。こんにちのアメリカは資本主義の国だが、わたしたちの資本主義システムはまったくの自由放任ではない。たとえば法律によって、どのように金を使うかが制限され、雇用者が払う最低賃金が決められている。また、製造業者が労働者の安全を確保したり、工場による環境汚染を減らすように予防策がとられている。
　わたしたちの現行の資本主義経済に比べると、19世紀イギリスの資本主義システムはずっと自由放任であった。このシステムは多くの人から強い非難をあびた。資本主義に批判的な人たちは、経済活動が政府ではなく個人に委ねられるかぎり、裕福な者はますます裕福に、貧しい者はますます貧しくなるばかりだと主張した。このような貧富の差の拡大を止めるため、資本主義に替わるものとして、「社会主義」が唱えられた。
　社会主義者は、政府が経済を管理して、すべての人々の利益になるよう運営すべきだと考える。労働者や政府が工場を所有し、工場の生産物を公平に分配し、国の富がすべての国民に、より公平に分け与えられるべきだと社会主義者は主張した。
　社会主義の思想家でもっとも重要な人物の1人に、ドイツ人の著述家カール・マルクスがいる。彼は社会が大きく2つの階級に分かれていると考えた──ブルジョワジーとプロレタリアートだ。ブルジョワジーは中流と上流階級によって構成され、プロレタリアートは下層階級、労働者によって構成される。マルクスによれば、ブルジョワジーに属する人間はあらゆる財産と権力を独占している。彼

classes—the bourgeoisie and the proletariat. The bourgeoisie was made up of the middle and upper classes; the proletariat was made up of the lower classes, or workers. According to Marx, members of the bourgeoisie had all the property and all the power. They oppressed and exploited the proletariat. For example, factory owners took advantage of their workers by paying them much less than their labor was worth.

Marx believed that the proletarian class was constantly struggling to win its rights from the bourgeoisie. Marx referred to this conflict as the "class struggle." He predicted that the class struggle would end in a great revolution, in which the proletariat would overthrow the bourgeoisie and take over the government. The new proletarian government would establish a society completely based on socialism. Private property would be abolished, and society's wealth would be equally distributed.

Marx's version of socialism was called "communism." In 1848 he published a book called The Communist Manifesto (a "manifesto" is a statement of beliefs or principles). Marx called for workers all over Europe to rise up and overthrow the bourgeoisie. He ended his call to arms with these famous words: "Workers of the world, unite! You have nothing to lose but your chains, and a world to win."

The Communist revolution did not occur as Marx had hoped. As the late 1800s wore on, European workers did begin to win more rights, not through violent revolutions but by joining labor unions or electing leaders who supported their cause. It was not until the 1900s, long after Marx's death, that Communists forcefully seized power in certain countries. And the major Communist revolutions did not occur in industrialized Europe, as Marx had predicted, but in underdeveloped Russia and China.

らはプロレタリアートを抑圧し、搾取している。たとえば、工場の所有者は、労働者の弱みにつけこんで、労働に見合う額よりも少ない賃金しか払っていない。

　プロレタリアートはみずからの権利を勝ち取るため、たえずブルジョワジーと闘争しているのだとマルクスは考えた。マルクスはこの争いを「階級闘争」と呼んだ。この階級闘争は大きな革命につながり、プロレタリアートがブルジョワジーを打ち倒し、政府の実権を手に入れるとマルクスは予言した。新たなプロレタリアートの政府は、完全に社会主義に基づいた社会を築きあげるだろう。私有財産の権利は廃止され、社会の富は平等に分配されるのだ。

　マルクスの考えた社会主義は「共産主義」と呼ばれる。1848年、彼は「共産党宣言」という本を出版した（「宣言」というのは、信条や行動指針を述べたものだ）。マルクスはヨーロッパ全土の労働者に、蜂起してブルジョワジーを打倒するよう呼びかけた。彼は闘争への呼びかけを、次の有名な言葉で締めくくっている。「世界の労働者よ、団結せよ！　失うものは束縛する鎖だけだ。そして世界を勝ち取るのだ」

　共産主義革命は、マルクスが望んだようなかたちでは起こらなかった。19世紀の終わりには、ヨーロッパの労働者はより多くの権利を手に入れるようになったが、それは暴力的な革命によってではなく、労働組合に加入したり、彼らの言い分を支持する指導者を選んだりすることによってなされた。共産主義者が力ずくで政治的な力をいくつかの国でつかんだのは、マルクスの死からずいぶん後の20世紀になってからのことであった。大きな共産主義革命は、マルクスが予言したようなヨーロッパの工業国ではなく、発展途上のロシアや中国で起こった。

MATHEMATICS・算数

Large and Small Numbers
大きな数と小さな数

Numbers Through Millions
億までの数

Place Value
数の単位

10 hundred thousands equal 1 million. We write the number one million in digits as 1,000,000.

10万が10で100万になる。100万という数は、数字では1,000,000と書き表す。

A group of three digits is called a period. Beginning at the right, the first three digits are the ones' period, the next three digits are the thousands' period, and the next three digits are the millions' period. Each period is separated by a comma.

3桁を1つの組みとして、ピリオド[点で区切られた1組の数字]と呼ぶ。右から、最初の3桁は1のピリオド、次の3桁は1000のピリオド、その次の3桁は100万のピリオドである。各ピリオドは点で区切られる。

millions 100万				thousands 1千				ones 1		
hundreds 100	tens 10	ones 1		hundreds 100	tens 10	ones 1		hundreds 100	tens 10	ones 1
		4	,	3	1	5	,	8	2	5
4	6	2	,	9	7	7	,	0	0	3
millions' period 百万のピリオド				thousands' period 千のピリオド				ones' period 1のピリオド		

In each period, the pattern of ones, tens, and hundreds repeats itself. Beginning at the right, the values of the places are: ones, tens, hundreds; thousands, ten thousands, hundred thousands; millions, ten millions, hundred millions. Each place has a value 10 times greater than the place to its right. This system of writing numbers is called the decimal system.

それぞれのピリオドの中で、1、10、100というパターンが繰り返される。位の単位は、右から1、10、100、そして1千、10千(1万)、100千(10万)、それから1百万、10百万(千万)、100百万(1億)となる。それぞれの位の単位はすぐ右にある単位より10倍大きい。数をこのように表記する方法を十進法という。

When you read a number, always begin

数はつねにいちばん大きな単位から

with the largest place value. The commas let you know the value of the largest place.

$$4,315,825$$

The four is one digit to the left of the millions' comma. It is in the millions' place. 4,315,825 is read, "four million, three hundred fifteen thousand, eight hundred twenty-five."

Commas and Place Value

You can write the numbers from 1000 to 9999 with a comma or without a comma. You can write 9,672 or 9672. Either form is correct. However, whenever you write numbers ten thousand or greater, always write them with commas, to mark off each period.

Always 10,403   Never 10403

Billions

After millions, the next period is billions.

10 hundred millions = 1 billion

billions 10億			millions 100万			thousands 1千			ones 1		
hundreds 100	tens 10	ones 1	hundreds 100	tens 10	ones 1	hundreds 100	tens 10	ones 1	hundreds 100	tens 10	ones 1
1	5	1	8	7	4	0	0	0	0	0	0

Over the course of one year, the U.S. Government spent $151,874,000,000 more than it received. You read 151,874,000,000: "one hundred fifty-one billion, eight hundred seventy-four million." Learn to read and write numbers in the billions. In digits, twenty billion, four hundred million is written 20,400,000,000. In words, 1,157,000,000 is written "one billion, one hundred fifty-seven million."

Trillions

The period after billions is trillions. 10 hundred billions equal 1 trillion. You read the number 314,506,000,000,000 as "three hundred fourteen trillion, five hundred six billion."

Instead of writing the zeros in large numbers, we often use a shortened word form. 586,000,000,000 can be written as "586 billion." 3,700,000 can be written as "3.7 million." 2,998,810,000,000 can be written as "2 trillion, 998 billion, 810 million."

Rounding

Remember that sometimes you do not need to know an exact value for a number. In these cases you can round numbers. You have learned to round numbers to tens, hundreds, and thousands. Now you can learn to round a number to any place value.

When rounding a number to a certain place value, you must always think: should I round down, to the value of the digit that is in this place, or round up, to the value of the next highest digit?

As an example, we'll round 543,417 to the nearest hundred thousand. When you look in the hundred thousands' place, you see 5 hundred thousands. So your two choices are to round the number down to 500,000 or up to 600,000.

500,000 < 5<u>4</u>3,417 < 600,000

To decide which way to round, always look at the place just to the right of the one to which you are rounding. If the digit to the right is 4 or less, you round down, because the number is closer to the lower round number. If the digit to the right is 5 or greater, you round up because the number is halfway, or more than halfway, between the two round numbers. When a number is exactly halfway between two numbers, you always round up.

In 543,417, the digit to the right of the hundred thousands' place is a 4. You know that 543,417 is closer to 500,000 than it is to 600,000. So you round 543,417 down to 500,000.

Let's round 675,802 to the nearest ten thousand. The digit to the right of the ten thousands' place is a 5. So you know that 675,802 is at least halfway between 670,000 and 680,000. You round 675,802 up to 680,000.

切り上げるか切り捨てるかを決めるときには、つねに概数を得ようとしている位の右側をみる。そして、右の数字が4以下であれば切り捨てるのだが、それは、その数がより小さい方の概数に近いからだ。もし右にある数字が5以上であれば切り上げる。それは、その数字が、2つの概数の間の半分かそれ以上だからだ。数字が2つの概数のちょうど半分であるときには、かならず切り上げるのである。

543,417という数では、10万の位の右側にある数字は4である。当然543,417は600,000よりも500,000に近いから、543,417を概数にすると500,000になる。

675,802を万の位で概数にしてみよう。万の位の右側にある数字は5である。ということは、675,802は少なくとも670,000と680,000の半分には達しているということだ。675,802は切り上げて、680,000とすればよい。

Decimals

Decimals: Tenths

You can write the fraction 1/10 as the decimal 0.1. You read both the same way: you say, "one tenth."

The period to the left of the 1 is called a decimal point. The decimal point shows that the value of the digits to its right is anywhere between 0 and 1, like a fraction. A decimal is any number that uses places to the right of the decimal point to show a fraction.

小数

小数：小数点第1位／10分の1の位

1/10という分数は小数で0.1と書くことができる。どちらも同じく「10分の1」と読む。

1の左側にある点は小数点と呼ぶ。小数点は分数と同じく、その右側にある数字の値が0から1の間のどこかにあることを示している。小数というのは分割された数を表すためのもので、小数点の右側の位を使う数すべてをいう。

The first place to the right of the decimal point is the tenths' place.

小数点の右側の第1番目の位は10分の1の位である。

ones 1の位		tenths 10分の1の位
1	.	7

You can write the mixed number 1 7/10 as the decimal 1.7. You read both the same way: you say, "one and seven tenths."

帯分数1 7/10は小数では1.7と書く。読み方はどちらも同じで、「1と10分の7」である。

Decimals: Hundredths

The second place to the right of the decimal point is the hundredths' place. 1/100 can also be written 0.01.

小数：小数点第2位／100分の1の位

小数点の右側の第2番目の位は100分の1の位である。1/100は0.01とも書く。

ones 1の位		tenths 10分の1の位	hundredths 100分の1の位
0	.	0	1

You read both in the same way: "one hundredth."

どちらも同じく「100分の1」と読む。

$2\frac{47}{100} =$

ones 1の位		tenths 10分の1の位	hundredths 100分の1の位
2	.	4	7

You read both as, "two and forty-seven hundredths."

どちらも「2と100分の47」と読む。

Notice that when there are both tenths and hundredths in a decimal, you read the tenths and hundredths together in terms of hundredths. Also remember to put an "and" between the whole number part and the fractional part of a decimal, just as in mixed numbers.

注意をしておきたいのは、10分の1の位と100分の1の位の両方を含む小数は、100分の1の位の数として読むということである。また、整数と小数点以下の部分との間には「と」を入れることを忘れてはいけない。これは帯分数とまったく同じである。

Decimals: Thousandths

The third place to the right of the decimal point is the thousandths' place. You can write 1/1000 as 0.001.

ones 1の位		tenths 10分の1の位	hundredths 100分の1の位	thousandths 1000分の1の位
0	.	0	0	1

小数：小数点第3位／1000分の1の位

小数点の右側の第3番目の位は1000分の1の位である。1/1000は0.001とも書く。

You read both in the same way: "one thousandth."

Notice that as you move from left to right, each place value gets 10 times smaller: first tenths, then hundredths, then thousandths. In the decimal system (the "ten" system), each place has a value ten times smaller than the one to its left.

どちらも同じく「1000分の1」と読む。

左から右へ行くにつれて単位が10分の1ずつ小さくなることに注意しよう。最初は10分の1で、次は100分の1、そして1000分の1と続く。十進法（「10」の方法）においては、それぞれの単位は、左側にある単位よりも10分の1ずつ小さい。

$$3\frac{857}{1000} = 3.857$$

You read both as "three and eight hundred fifty-seven thousandths." Notice that, because there are thousandths in the decimal, you read the tenths and hundredths in terms of thousandths.

どちらも「3と1000分の857」と読む。小数の中に1000分の1の位があるから、10分の1の位も100分の1の位も1000分の1の位の数として読むことに注意しよう。

Way of Writing Multiplication

掛け算の書き表し方

There are ways of showing multiplication besides using the "×" sign. When variables are being multiplied, the multiplication sign is usually omitted.

×という記号を使う以外にも掛け算の書き表し方はある。変数の掛け算では、ふつう掛け算の記号を省略する。

$8 \times a$ can be written $8a$. $z \times w$ can be written zw.

8 × a は 8a とも書く。   z × w は zw とも書く。

When two numbers are being multiplied, a dot placed between them is sometimes used to show multiplication.

2つの数を掛けるときに、数字の間に中点を打って掛け算であることを示すことがある。

6×8 can be written $6 \cdot 8$.

6 × 8 は 6·8 と書いてもよい。

You can also omit the multiplication sign between two numbers. Then you have to use parentheses to show that you mean 6×8, not 68.

また、2つの数の間の掛け算の記号を省略することもできる。そのときには、68ではなく6×8であることをはっきりさせるためにカッコを使うことになっている。

6×8 can be written $6\,(8)$ or $(6)\,8$ or $(6)\,(8)$.

6 × 8 は 6(8)と書いても、(6)8 や (6)(8) のように書いてもよい。

Exponents

指数

An exponent is a small, raised number that shows how many times a number is used as a factor in multiplication. For example, 3^4 is $3 \times 3 \times 3 \times 3$, or 3 used as a factor 4 times. You read 3^4 as "three to the fourth power." The number that is being used as a factor is called the base. In 3^4, 3 is the base and 4 is the exponent.

指数とは、数字の右肩に小さく記す数で、掛け算の中でその数字が何度因数として使われたかを示す。たとえば、3^4は3×3×3×3であり、3を因数として4回使ったということである。3^4は、「3の4乗」と読む。因数として使われている数字を基数という。3^4では、3が基数で4 が指数である。

Here are some examples of how you read and evaluate expressions with exponents.

指数を使った式の読み方と値の求め方の例をいくつか見てみよう。

5^2 is read as "five squared" (or "five to the second power").

5^2 は 「5 平方」(あるいは「5 の 2 乗」)と読む。

$$5^2 = 5 \times 5 = 25$$

4^3 is read as "four cubed" (or "four to the third power").

4^3 は 「4 立方」(あるいは「4 の 3 乗」)と読む。

$$4^3 = (4)\,(4)\,(4) = 16\,(4) = 64$$

2^5 is read as "two to the fifth power."

$$2^5 = 2 \cdot 2 \cdot 2 \cdot 2 \cdot 2 = 32$$

2^5 は 「2 の 5 乗」と読む。

When a number is raised to the second power, we usually read it as "squared." When a number is raised to the third power, we usually read it as "cubed."

ある数を2乗するとき、「平方」と読むのが一般的である。3乗するときには「立方」と読むことが多い。

Powers of Ten

10の累乗

Powers of ten are very important in working with place value because the decimal system is based on powers of ten.

10の累乗は数の単位を扱うときにはとても重要であるが、それは十進法が10の累乗に基づいているからだ。

$10^1 = 10$
$10^2 = 10 \times 10 = 100$
$10^3 = 10 \times 10 \times 10 = 1,000$
$10^4 = 10 \times 10 \times 10 \times 10 = 10,000$
$10^5 = 10 \times 10 \times 10 \times 10 \times 10 = 100,000$
$10^6 = 10 \times 10 \times 10 \times 10 \times 10 \times 10 = 1,000,000$

The number of zeros in each of the numbers 10, 100, 1000, 10,000, … tells you what power of ten it is. Because 10,000 has 4 zeros, it is 10^4. Furthermore, the exponent in a power of ten tells you the number of zeros the number has when it is multiplied out. 10^9 has nine zeros. 10^9 equals 1,000,000,000, or 1 billion. Examples: 10^3 has three zeros and equals 1000; 100,000 has five zeros and equals 10^5.

10、100、1000、10,000…という数字の中にある0の数から10の何乗であるかがわかる。10,000には0が4つあるので、これは10^4である。さらに、10の累乗の指数から、掛け算して得られる値の0の数がわかる。10^9という数には0が9個ある。10^9は1,000,000,000、すなわち10億である。例：10^3という数には0が3個あり、1000に等しい。100,000には0が5個あり、10^5に等しい。

LANGUAGE ARTS • 国語

Can You Analyze a Poem and Enjoy It Too?

About two hundred years ago, an English poet by the name of William Wordsworth wrote that "we murder to dissect." He meant that in order to study and analyze a living thing, first we have to kill it.

Some people feel that what Wordsworth said applies to more than what goes on in a laboratory. They think that Wordsworth, as a poet, saw a poem as a living thing. And they worry that to analyze a poem—to study it in detail, to look closely at specific lines and words—is to dissect the poem, which would mean, unfortunately, to take all the life out of it. These people feel that poetry is something you should read (and write) not with your mind but with your heart. Poetry, they say, is more a matter of emotions than of thinking.

In some ways, that's true. When you first read a poem, you probably read it for enjoyment. When you first start to talk about it, probably the questions that come to mind are "Do I like this poem? How does it make me feel?"

But then another question often occurs, a question that moves you from feeling into thinking: "What does the poem mean?" As soon as you start thinking about that question, you have to go back to the poem itself. You have to linger over certain lines and words. You begin to wonder why the poet used those particular words, in that particular order. For example, you might wonder why Robert Frost repeated the same line at the end of "Stopping by Woods on a Snowy Evening." (page 274) Here are the last four lines of that poem:

>   The woods are lovely, dark, and deep,
>   But I have promises to keep,

分析しても詩は楽しめる？

　200年ほど前に、ウィリアム・ワーズワースというイギリスの詩人は、「解剖するとは殺すこと」と書いている。ワーズワースは、生きているものを研究し分析するためには、まずそれを殺さなければならない、と言いたかったのだ。

　ワーズワースの言葉は生物実験室で行われること以外にも当てはまるのでは、と考える人もいる。詩人としてのワーズワースは詩を生き物としてとらえていたというのだ。そして、詩を分析すること、すなわち詩の細部を研究し、ある特定の行や言葉を一字一句考えることは詩を解剖することであり、不幸にもそれは詩からすべての生命を奪うことにほかならない、と彼らは危惧する。彼らの感じ方からすれば、詩は頭ではなく心で読む（そして書く）べきものなのだ。詩は思考よりも感情にかかわるというのである。

　いくつかの点でこれは正しい。あなたがはじめて詩を読もうというときには、おそらく楽しみを求めているはずだ。はじめてその詩について話してみようと思ったときに心に浮かぶのは、たぶん「自分はこの詩が好きなのかな」とか、「自分はこの詩を読んでどんなふうに感じるのだろう」といった問いだろう。

　だが、そのあとで、違った問いがやってくることもよくあることだ。それはあなたを感情から思考へと導くような、「この詩は何を言おうとしているのだろうか」といった疑問だ。その疑問について考え始めたら、あなたはもう1度詩を読み返さなければならない。その詩のある1節、ある表現を読みながら、あれこれ考えることになる。詩人はどうしてその言葉にしたのか、どうしてこの語順にしたのかということが気になってくる。たとえば、ロバート・フロストが「雪の夕暮れ、森の近くで馬車を停め」（274頁参照）という詩の最後で同じ行を2度繰り返しているのはなぜだろうとふと思ったりする。その詩の終わりの4行はこうなっている。

　　　森は凛として、暗く、そして深い、
　　　だが、私には約束したことがある、

> **NOTE**
> **ワーズワース**
> ワーズワース（1770–1850）はイギリス・ロマン派の詩人。カンブリアの湖水地方と呼ばれる土地に生まれ、生涯の大半をそこで暮らした。詩人コールリッジと『叙情バラッド集』（1798年）を出版してロマン派の時代の幕を開けた。

> **NOTE**
> **フロスト**
> 革新的・実験的な詩が主流を占めた20世紀前半、フロスト（1874–1963）はニューイングランドの農場で暮らし、その自然を背景にした叙情的な詩、鋭い人生洞察に満ちた詩を書いた。ピューリッツァー賞を4度受賞。詩を定義して「翻訳で失われるもの、それが詩である」と言っている。

And miles to go before I sleep,
And miles to go before I sleep.

There are good reasons that Frost repeats a line. And the place to look for those reasons is in the poem, in specific words and lines.

But wait a minute—now you're analyzing the poem. Does that mean you've murdered it to dissect it? No, not if you don't go overboard. Instead, it means that you are being respectful to the poet. You are acknowledging that he didn't just slap any old words down on a page but carefully chose and arranged certain words, just as a painter would carefully choose certain paints or a furniture maker would carefully choose the right pieces of wood—or just as you would carefully choose exactly the words you want in writing a poem of your own.

You'll find that you can enjoy many poems even more if you look at the craft that went into making them. You might even find that this kind of study, far from killing a poem, breathes life into it, because it brings you closer to the poet who shaped its words.

In looking at the craft of making a poem, you will find it helpful to know a few terms that describe some of the specific ways in which poets structure their words.

Structure in Poetry

• **Stanza**

When you hear a song on the radio, you might notice that often the vocalist sings a group of related lines, then pauses for some instrumental music, then sings another group of lines, often in the same form as the first group.

Similarly, in poetry, related lines are grouped together in stanzas. Usually one stanza is separated from another by a space on the page. Like most poets of the past, some modern-day poets write poems in which each stanza is of equal length, which gives the poem a definite shape and

眠りにつく前に、もう少し行こう、
　　　眠りにつく前に、もう少し行こう。

　フロストが同じ行を繰り返すのにはそれなりの理由があってのことだ。そしてその理由を探るには、詩にもどって、具体的な言葉や表現を見るほかない。

　しかし、ちょっと待っていただきたい——こうなるともう詩を分析していることになる。ということは、あなたは詩を解剖しようとしてすでに詩を殺してしまったのだろうか。いや、そうではない。極端に走らなければいいのだ。むしろ、こうした分析は詩人の仕事に敬意をもって接していることになる。詩人がいかにも陳腐な言い回しをページの上にペタペタ貼りつけたのではなくて、細心に言葉を選んで配列を決めたのだということをあなたが受けとめていることになるのだ。それは、画家がよく考えて絵の具を選ぶとか、家具職人がよく考えて正しい部材を選ぶといったことと同じだ。つまり、あなたが詩を書こうとするときに、自分の気持ちにぴったりと合う正確な表現をよく考えて選ぶということと同じことなのだ。

　詩を書くときに使われた技法に注意を払えば、たくさんの詩を前よりずっと楽しめることに気づくだろう。さらに、このように詩を分析することは、詩を殺すどころかむしろ詩に生命を吹き込むことではないかとさえ思えてくるだろう。それは、分析することで、言葉に形を与えた詩人に近づいていくからだ。

　詩を作る技法を考えるときには、詩人が言葉を組み立てていく独特の方法を説明する用語をいくつか知っておくと役に立つ。

詩の構造

● スタンザ

　ラジオで歌を聞いていると、たいていは歌手が意味のまとまりのある何行かの歌詞を歌い、楽器による演奏が挟まれ、また最初と同じような形式の歌詞を歌うという形になっていることがわかる。

　詩でも同様で、ひとつながりの詩行はスタンザ（連）としてグループ分けされている。印刷するときには、たいていスタンザとスタンザの間を1行あける。現代でも、昔の詩人の多くにならって、スタンザを同じ長さにした詩を書く詩人がいるが、そうすることで詩にはっきりとした形とリズムが生まれる。たとえばロバート・フロス

rhythm. For example, if you look at Robert Frost's "Stopping by Woods on a Snowy Evening", you'll notice it has four stanzas. If you're discussing this poem, you can help others understand your way of reading it by saying something like "I think the first stanza starts out bright and cheery, but by the last stanza the mood has changed."

There's a special kind of stanza that is generally not separated from the others. This kind of stanza is called a couplet, and consists of only two lines that rhyme with each other. Maya Angelou's "Woman Work" begins with a series of couplets:

> I've got the children to tend
> The clothes to mend
> The floor to mop
> The food to shop
> Then the chicken to fry
> The baby to dry . . .

Many poems written in England during the seventeenth and eighteenth centuries consisted almost entirely of couplets. The rhyming lines in a couplet often tend to tie together a thought in a nice neat package. Many couplets are still remembered and quoted today, such as this one by the English poet Alexander Pope:

> Hope springs eternal in the human breast:
> Man never is, but always to be blest.

• **Rhyme Scheme**

Not all poems rhyme, but those that do will often repeat rhymes in a regular pattern within each stanza. This pattern of rhyming words makes up a poem's rhyme scheme. In some poems, the rhyme scheme is very regular and predictable. For example, look at the first two stanzas of "Father William," by Lewis Carroll:

> "You are old, Father William," the young man said,
>   "And your hair has become very white;
> And yet you incessantly stand on your head—

トの詩「雪の夕暮れ、森の近くで馬車を停め」を見ると、4つのスタンザがある。この詩について論じ合っているときに、たとえば「最初のスタンザは明るく快活に始まるが、最後のスタンザにきたときには、感じは変わってしまっているよね」というふうに言えば、うまく自分の読み方を人に伝えることができる。

スタンザとスタンザの間が切り離されていない特殊な形式のスタンザもある。その種のスタンザはカプレット（2行連句）と呼ばれ、行の末尾が同じ音で終わる2行からなる。マヤ・アンジェロウの「働く女」はカプレットの連続で始まっている。

> 子どもたちの面倒をみて
> 服をつくろい
> 床をふき
> 食べ物を買い
> それからフライドチキンを揚げ
> 赤ちゃんのおむつを取りかえ

17世紀から18世紀にかけてのイギリスの詩は、詩全体がほぼカプレットで書かれているものが多い。韻を踏んだカプレットの2行にすると、ある想念をすっきりとひとくくりにまとめることができる。今日でもなお記憶され引用されるカプレットも数多くあって、たとえばイギリスの詩人アレクザンダー・ポープにはこんなカプレットがある。

> 希望は人間の胸中に湧き出る永遠の泉、
> 人間に祝福などない、だがかならずいつの日にか。

● **韻律形式**

すべての詩が韻を踏むわけではないが、押韻詩では各スタンザの中で規則的なパターンに従って韻を踏むことが多い。この押韻のパターンが、その詩の韻律形式を作りあげる。中には韻律形式がきわめて規則的ですぐわかってしまう詩もある。1例として、ルイス・キャロルの「ウィリアム父さま」の最初の2つのスタンザを見てみよう。

> 「もう年なんだから、ウィリアム父さま」と言う息子、
> 　「髪の毛だってまっ白け。
> なのにのべつ幕なし、逆立ち三昧——

NOTE

アンジェロウ
マヤ・アンジェロウは黒人の作家・俳優で1928年にミズーリ州のセントルイスに生まれる。8歳のときにレイプされ、そのショックで5年間声が出ない苦しみを体験した。1970年に出した自伝『歌え、翔べない鳥たちよ(I Know Why the Caged Bird Sings)』はベストセラーになった。

NOTE

ポープ
ポープ(1688–1744)はイギリスの詩人。人間の問題を簡潔で凝縮した詩句にまとめる才能に秀でていた。「過つは人の常、赦すは神の業 (To err is human; to forgive, divine.)」はよく知られている。

Do you think, at your age, it is right?"

"In my youth," Father William replied to his son,
   "I feared it might injure the brain;
But now that I'm perfectly sure I have none,
   Why, I do it again and again."

To describe the pattern in a rhyme scheme, we use the letters of the alphabet, and assign a new letter to each rhyme within a stanza. Let's assign a letter to the rhyming words in the first stanza of "Father William":

    A said   B white
    A head   B right

Now, if you look at the rhyming words in the second stanza, you'll see that the same pattern is repeated.

    A son   B brain
    A none   B again

So we say that the rhyme scheme of "Father William" is A-B-A-B.

Now let's look at a poem by Robert Frost, "Stopping by Woods on a Snowy Evening," in which the rhyme scheme varies from stanza to stanza. Notice how the last word in the third line of one stanza sets up the rhyme in the following stanza.

   Whose woods these are I think I know   A
   His house is in the village, though;   A
   He will not see me stopping here   B
   To watch his woods fill up with snow.   A

   My little horse must think it queer   B
   To stop without a farmhouse near   B
   Between the woods and frozen lake   C

年甲斐もないとは、思わない？」

「若いころには」ウィリアム父さま、答えて言った。
　「脳ミソいかれちまうかも、と怖くもあった。
　じゃが、いかれるほどのミソもなし、とわかったからには
　ほれ、何度も何度もやったるわ」

　韻律のパターンを説明するときにはアルファベット文字を使い、スタンザの中に新しい韻が現れるたびに別のアルファベットを当てる。「ウィリアム父さま」の最初のスタンザの韻にアルファベットをつけてみよう。

　　　　　A　said　　　　B　white
　　　　　A　head　　　　B　right

　そこで第2スタンザの押韻を調べてみると、同じパターンが繰り返されていることがわかる。

　　　　　A　son　　　　B　brain
　　　　　A　none　　　　B　again

　これで「ウィリアム父さま」の韻律形式はA-B-A-Bだということになる。
　次にロバート・フロストの詩「雪の夕暮れ、森の近くで馬車を停め」を見てみると、韻律形式はスタンザごとに異なっている。先行するスタンザの3行目の末尾の語の音が次のスタンザの最初の韻として引き継がれている。

　　　ここが誰の森かはわかっている。
　　　だが、地主の家は村里にあって、
　　　ここで馬車を停め、雪の降り積む
　　　森を見つめるわたしを、彼は知らない。

　　　馬は首をかしげているはずだ。
　　　停めたところに農家はなし、
　　　片や大きな森で、片や凍りついた湖、

NOTE
キャロル
ルイス・キャロル(1832-98)は筆名。オクスフォード大学で数学を教えた。知人の娘たちのために書いた『不思議の国のアリス』や『鏡の国のアリス』はノンセンス文学の古典となり、20世紀のジェイムズ・ジョイスなどにも影響を与えた。
　引用の「ウィリアム父さま」は、健康や時間を浪費する若者を戒めたロバート・サウジーの教訓詩のパロディ。

The darkest evening of the year.	B
He gives his harness bells a shake	C
To ask if there is some mistake.	C
The only other sound's the sweep	D
Of easy wind and downy flake.	C
The woods are lovely, dark, and deep,	D
But I have promises to keep,	D
And miles to go before I sleep,	D
And miles to go before I sleep.	D

If you read Frost's poem aloud, it might sound almost like casually spoken words. But by noticing the rhyme scheme, you can see that Frost was not writing casually at all: he carefully chose and arranged every word. You can enjoy just reading Frost's poem aloud and hearing the simple words and pleasing rhymes. And you can enjoy thinking and talking with others about questions like why Frost chose to end the poem with four repeated rhymes.

• **Free Verse**

Many modern poems, including perhaps some of your favorites, do not have a regular meter or rhyme scheme. These poems are written in what is called free verse. Most poets who write in free verse choose their words as carefully as those who write in regular meter and rhyme. In the opening lines of Langston Hughes's free verse poem "The Negro Speaks of Rivers," you can see and hear how the length and rhythm of the lines vary.

> I've known rivers:
> I've known rivers ancient as the world and older than the
>   flow of human blood in human veins.
>
> My soul has grown deep like the rivers.

一年でもっとも暗いこの夕暮れに。

馬は、どうかしたのかと
馬具につけた鈴を振り鳴らす。
ほかに聞こえるのは、羽毛の雪が
風に吹き舞う音ばかり。

森は凛として、暗く、そして深い、
だが、わたしには約束したことがある、
眠りにつく前に、もう少し行こう、
眠りにつく前に、もう少し行こう。

　フロストの詩を声に出して読んでみると、まるで何気なく語られた言葉を聞いているかのようだ。しかし、韻律形式を調べると、フロストが決して何気なく言葉を書き連ねたのではないことがわかる。彼はどの言葉も、細心の注意を払って選んで組み合わせている。フロストの詩を声に出して読み、単純な言葉と心地よい韻律を耳で聞くだけでも快感がある。そして、なぜフロストは同じ韻を4回繰り返して詩を終えているのかといった問題について考え、人と話してみるのも面白いだろう。

● 自由詩
　おそらくあなたの好きな詩にも現代詩がいくつかあるだろうが、その多くは規則的な韻律や押韻の形式を持っていない。そうした詩は自由詩と呼ばれる体裁で書かれている。自由詩の形式で書く詩人の大部分も、深く考えて言葉を選ぶという点では、規則的な韻律や押韻の形式で書く詩人と変わらない。ラングストン・ヒューズの自由詩形式の詩「黒人は川について語る」の最初の数行を読むと、長さもリズムも行によって変わることを目と耳で確かめることができる。

　　　　わたしはいくつもの川を知っている。
　　　　わたしは、世界と同じくらい年老いた川を、人の血管の、
　　　　人の血液の流れよりも古くからある川を知っている。

　　　　わたしの魂は、そうした川のように深くなった。

LANGUAGE ARTS • 国語

Sayings and Phrases ことわざと熟語

All's well that ends well
「終わりよければすべてよし」

This saying from Shakespeare means that if something finally succeeds, then the difficulties or mistakes along the way can be forgotten.

このことわざはシェイクスピアの作品からで、結果的に成功を収めるならば、途中の困難や失敗は忘れられてしまうものだ、という意味だ。

Pot calling the kettle black
「鉄鍋が鉄瓶を黒いという」

Since most pots and kettles were once made of the same black metal, this phrase is used when you criticize someone for having a fault that you yourself possess.

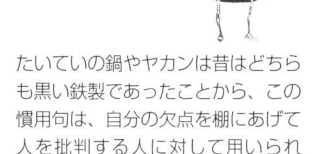

たいていの鍋やヤカンは昔はどちらも黒い鉄製であったことから、この慣用句は、自分の欠点を棚にあげて人を批判する人に対して用いられる。

Tempest in a teapot
「ティーポットの中の大嵐」

A tempest is a very large storm, and a teapot is quite small. We use this expression when a large commotion is made over something pretty little.

暴風雨というのは大きな嵐であり、ティーポットはきわめて小さい。とてもささいなことで大騒ぎになったときなどにこの表現を用いる。

The proof of the pudding is in the eating
「プディングの味は食べてみなければわからない」

This saying means that you can't judge something until you try it.

このことわざは、試してみるまではものの良し悪しの判断はできない、という意味だ。

A fool and his money are soon parted
「馬鹿者と金はたちまち別れる」

This saying means that a person who is foolish with his money won't hold on to it for very long. People usually say it as a warning.

このことわざは、愚かな使い方をすれば、お金は身につかないものだ、という意味だ。たいていは戒めの言葉として使われる。

A friend in need is a friend indeed
「困った時の友こそ真の友」

Some people are your friends when you are happy but avoid you when you are having trouble. This proverb explains that a true friend is the one who sticks around when you are in need of help, comfort, or anything else.

順調にいっているときは友だちだが、困ったときにはしらんぷりをするような人がいる。この格言は、助けや慰めなどを必要としているときにそばにいてくれる人が本当の友だちだと言っている。

He who hesitates is lost
「迷った者が負ける」

If you wait before you do something, it may be too late. People use this saying to urge someone into action or to comment on a lost opportunity.

何かをしようというときに待ったりすると、間に合わなくなることがある。このことわざは、行動を起こすようけしかけたり、逃した機会をふりかえるときなどに使われる。

Good fences make good neighbors
「しっかりした柵が隣人との仲をよくする」

This saying suggests that by clearly marking the boundaries between yourself and other people, you can stay on better terms with them. It comes from a poem by Robert Frost.

このことわざが言おうとしているのは、自分と他人の間にはっきりと境を設けることで、よりよい関係が保てるということだ。もともとはロバート・フロストの詩にあった表現である。

He who laughs last laughs best / To have the last laugh
「最後に笑うものがもっともよく笑う／最後に笑う」

People often ridicule new projects or ideas. But in the end, when something works, the person who took it seriously gets the best laugh of all—one that proves him right.

新しい企画だとか発想はよく笑いものにされる。しかし、最後になってうまくいったりすると、それに本気で取り組んでいた人が誰よりも気持ちよく笑うことになる——その人が正しかったことを証明する笑いだ。

Money is the root of all evil
「金銭は諸悪の根源である」

This proverb means that greed for money can sometimes motivate people to do things that they wouldn't otherwise do.

この格言は、人は金銭欲にとりつかれて、ふつうならしそうもないようなことをしてしまうことがある、という意味である。

Necessity is the mother of invention
「必要は発明の母である」

People often come up with new ideas, new ways of doing things, or new things because they need to solve a problem.

新しい発想や新しいやり方、新しいものを生み出す人はよくいるが、それは問題の解決に迫られて出てくるものだ。

Once bitten, twice shy
「1度噛まれたら、2度目は用心」

If a dog bites you, you will probably be very careful to stay clear of dogs after that. This saying means that people tend to protect themselves from being hurt, especially if they've been hurt before.

1度犬に噛まれたら、その後は犬のそばに近寄らないよう、とても用心深くなるものだ。だれでも痛い思いをしないよう気をつけているが、とくに1度そういう経験があればなおさらだという意味のことわざ。

Wolf in sheep's clothing
「羊の皮をかぶったオオカミ」

This phrase describes someone who appears to be harmless or friendly but who is really dangerous or untrustworthy. It comes from a fable by Aesop.

見かけはおとなしく人がよさそうだが実は危険で信用できないという人を指してこう言う。イソップの寓話から来ている表現だ。

Rome wasn't built in a day
「ローマは1日にして成らず」

Do you remember the story of ancient Rome? It took many people many decades to build that imperial city. People use this expression to mean that it takes a long time to achieve great things. They often use it to counsel patience.

古代ローマについて覚えているだろうか。あの帝国の都市を作るには、多くの人と多くの歳月を要した。大きなことを成し遂げるには長い時間がかかるということを言おうとしてこの表現を使うが、忍耐を言い聞かせるときなどによく用いる。

Truth is stranger than fiction
「事実は小説より奇なり」

Things that happen in real life can be more unusual or surprising than things that people make up in stories.

➡ When I read that the same couple had been married three times, once in an airplane, once in a hot-air balloon, and once in an elevator, I decided that truth really is stranger than fiction!

現実に起きる出来事は、人々が想像でこしらえた話よりも異常で驚くようなことであったりする。

➡ 同じ夫婦が、1度は飛行機で、次には熱気球に乗って、さらにエレベータの中でと、3度も結婚したという記事を読んで思った。まさに事実は小説よりも奇なり！

Give the devil his due
「悪魔でも認めるべきところは認める」

This proverb means that even if you don't like someone, you can still give that person credit for his or her good points.

この格言は、たとえ嫌いな人であっても、美点はそれなりに評価するという意味だ。

6th GRADE 281

Readableな教科書を——後書にかえて

　日本語の中で「知識」という言葉が輝きを失い始めたのは、受験競争の過熱が言われるようになったころかもしれない。「偏重」という言葉をくくりつけられた「知識」の評判は、いつしかガタ落ちになった。かつて知識は「身につける」ものだったのだが、ある時期から「頭に詰め込む」ようになり、その後ろめたさから知識を日陰に追いやってしまったようだ。原著の各学年のタイトル *What Your . . . Grader Needs to Know* のKnowが「頭に詰め込む」ではなく「身につける」ほうの知識であることはいうまでもない。系統的に知識を身につけることは子どもにとって必須である。原著では宗教、神話、古代文明から始まって、元素の周期表や原子の構成要素の説明までがゆるやかに繋がって語られている。大げさに言えば、大宇宙（マクロコズム）から小宇宙（マイクロコズム）まで、子どもが出会う世界の全体を6冊の中に収めている。教科書についての発想が明らかに違うのだ。それでも日本の子どもの方が成績は優秀だ、という人もいるだろう。むろんそういう問題ではない。

　原著の編者E.D.ハーシュの考え方の一端をかいつまんで言えば、こういうことだ。アメリカでは、子どもの自主性を育て創造力・批判力を養うといったカリキュラム目標（それ自体は間違っていないが）のもとに、知識を処理するskillの習得を優先する教育が行われてきた。多くの市民が共有すべき基本的な認識や文化的な知識の習得よりも、知識の利用法や選別の仕方に重きが置かれた。その結果、たとえば知識不足で新聞の文脈が十分に追えない、社会的な問題の議論がかみ合わないということが起こった。こういう事態は、市民の社会的関心が不可欠のデモクラシーを危うくする、とハーシュは危惧する。彼は教育エリートを問題にしているのではない。公教育の荒廃の拡大を恐れているのだ。私達にとってこれは対岸の火事ではない。

日本の読者にとって本書の魅力は、全体が語りかける説明のスタイルをとっていることではないだろうか。教科書全体に流れがあって、知識は断片化されることなく、リンクを形成していく。本書には入れていないが、原著は章ごとになぜ学ぶのか、これまで学んだこととどう繋がるのかを丁寧に説明している。これは日本の教科書と大きく異なる点だ。要するに、基本的に独習ができるようになっている。読む力をつければ、授業で理解できなかったところを自分でゆっくり補うことができる。自分でできるという可能性は、子どもにゆとりと積極性を与えるに違いない。読んで独力で学べるということはとても大切なことなのだ。独学はアメリカの隠れた伝統でもあった。フランクリンとマーク・トウェインにとっては印刷工の仕事が最良の教育になった。リンカーンは仕事の後で、借りた本を懸命に読んだ。刑務所を出たマルコムXの学校は公立図書館であった。独学は貧困や人種という壁を乗り越えてしまう。

　小学校の場合、算数・理科・社会もある意味で国語の授業の延長上にある。授業での説明を聴き取る力、教科書の説明を読み解く力が科目の理解に大きく影響する。要するに学ぶ力は日本語能力と切り離せないのだ。それだけを考えても、読む力をつけることがいかに重要かわかる。しかし、日本の教科書は基本的に独習書にはなっていない。そのことを性急に批判するつもりはないが、独習書のスタイルはいいヒントを与えてくれるように思う。少なくとも教科書に感じる子どもの不安はずっと軽減されるにちがいない。親も先生方も口をそろえて本を読めと子どもにいう。それならば、どの子どもも教科書は読むのだから、まず教科書をreadableにすべきではないだろうか。本書ができるだけ多くの英語の独習者に届くよう願っている。

　　2006年2月

　　　　　　　　　　　　　　　　　　　　　　　　村田　薫

ILLUSTRATION AND PHOTO CREDITS

Courtesy of Core Knowledge Foundation

Courtesy of Dover Publications, Inc.
    3,800 Early Advertising Cuts
    Bible Illustrations
    Gods and Deities
    Hope's Greek and Roman Designs
    Lively Advertising Cuts of the Twenties and Thirties
    Old-Fashioned Children Illustrations
    Plants

Orion Press
アフロ・フォトエージェンシー
共同通信社
世界文化フォト
東京国立博物館 (Image: TNM Image Archives)

TEXT CREDITS

"I Have a Dream" by Martin Luther King, Jr.
Copyright © 1963 Martin Luther King, Jr.,
copyright renewed 1991 Coretta Scott King.
Reprinted by arrangement with the Estate of Martin Luther King, Jr.,
c/o Writers House as agent for the proprietor New York, NY.

"Fog" from CHICAGO POEMS by Carl Sandberg, copyright 1916
by Holt, Rinehart and Winston and renewed 1944 by Carl Sandberg,
reprinted and translated by permission of Harcourt, Inc.

"Dreams" "The Negro Speaks of Rivers" from THE COLLECTED POEMS
OF LANGSTON HUGHES by Langston Hughes, copyright © 1994
by The Estate of Langston Hughes. Used by permission of Alfred A. Knopf,
a division of Random House, Inc.

"Woman Work," copyright © 1978 by Maya Angelou, from AND STILL I RISE
by Maya Angelou. Used by permission of Random House, Inc.

Excerpt from "Stopping by Woods on a Snowy Evening" from
THE POETRY OF ROBERT FROST, edited by Edward Connery Lathem.
Copyright 1923,1969 by Henry Holt and Company. Copyright © 1951
by Robert Frost. Reprinted by permission of Henry Holt and Company, LLC

編者紹介

ジェームス・M・バーダマン　James M. Vardaman, Jr.
　1946年、米国テネシー州生まれ。ハワイ大学でアジア研究専攻、修士。1976年来日し、いくつかの大学で教鞭を取る。早稲田大学名誉教授。
　著書に『アメリカ南部』（講談社現代新書）『わが心のディープサウス』（河出書房新社）『黒人差別とアメリカ公民権運動』（集英社新書）『アメリカ黒人の歴史』（NHKブックス）、編著に『アメリカの小学生が学ぶ歴史教科書』（ジャパンブック）など多数。

村田　薫　Murata Kaoru
　1953年、福島県いわき市生まれ。早稲田大学大学院文学研究科修了。早稲田大学名誉教授。専門はアメリカ文学。
　著書に『マージナリア──隠れた文学／隠された文学』（共著、音羽書房鶴見書店）、J. M. シング『アラン島ほか』（共訳、恒文社）、編著に『アメリカの小学生が学ぶ歴史教科書』（ジャパンブック）など。

アメリカの小学生が学ぶ国語・算数・理科・社会教科書
What American Elementary School Students Learn in Textbooks

2006年　3月15日　　第1刷発行	
2022年10月28日　　第9刷発行	
編　　者	ジェームス・M・バーダマン 村田　薫
発行者	齋藤民樹
発行所	株式会社ジャパンブック 〒101-0061 東京都千代田区神田三崎町3-1-8天野ビル3階 TEL: 03-5211-2625 FAX: 03-5211-2648 http://www.japanbook.co.jp
印刷所	株式会社シナノ
製本所	株式会社シナノ

　落丁本、乱丁本は、株式会社ジャパンブック宛にお送りください。
　送料小社負担にてお取替えいたします。

　定価はカバーに表示してあります。

ISBN978-4-902928-02-0

アメリカの小学生が学ぶ歴史教科書

EJ対訳

ジェームス・M・バーダマン

村田 薫 [編]

120点の図版でアメリカ史を身近に

レキシントンの戦い――ここで独立戦争の第1弾が発射された。思想家〔ラルフ・ウォルドー・エマソン〕は "Concord Hymn"（コンコード賛歌）という詩の中いうし野中で、この銃声をと表現した。ここから6年にもおよぶ長い独立戦争が始まった。

キャプションで史実をさらに詳しく

While most of the British soldiers ...Concord, minute men attacked and scattered a small group of Redcoats left to defend a bridge. The British in Concord, finding no large store of supplies, turned back to Boston. And all along their way, they were fired on from every side by angry colonists hiding behind trees and walls along the road. When the day was over, 273 British and 90 colonists had been ki... ...nded. The American Revolution had begun.

American Nov

We can start thinki... ...erican than British after the fighte... ...A month after the fighting in Massachu... ...tts, the Continental Congress met in Philadelphia for second ti... It named George Washington as commander in chief of ...ental army and sent him to help Boston. Even before he arrived, the British and Americans had fought again in a battle called ...the minutemen were so low on ammunition ...fire until you see the

1年から6年用のテキスト使用

今やアメリカ人

コンコードとレキシントンでのイギリス人というより、アメリカしょう。マサチューセッツでの戦いで2回目の大陸会議が開かれまし軍総司令官に指名され、ボストンの到着前、イギリス軍とアメリカていました。その際ミニットマある指揮官は彼らに「相手の白ました。こんな状態でも、訓練をはるかに熟練したイギリス兵だたえ、負けたのは3度目、弾薬カナダやサウスカロライナがあまりに多かったので、ジ　　　多くのアメリカの言葉に従するようになりそ決別のとき」。ペインは2.かりでしたが、イギリスと決モン・センス」という有名な小さな国が北アメリカの

英軍の進撃開始を疾駆するポール

JapanBookの本

真珠湾攻撃、日系アメリカ人の強制収容、原爆投下、朝鮮戦争、ベトナム戦争──。
アメリカ人の歴史観と考え方が分かる本。

アメリカの小学生が学ぶ歴史教科書
What Young Americans Know about History
ジェームス・M・バーダマン
村田薫[訳]
EJ対訳

定価:本体1,500円+税
ISBN978-4-902928-00-6

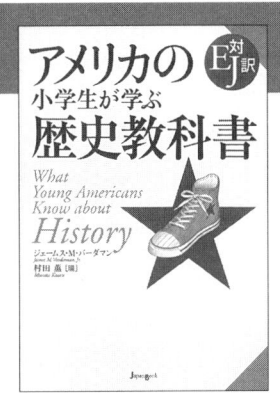

「これが教科書?」──迫真の記述

本書の特長

1　「これが歴史教科書?」と思わせるドキュメンタリー・タッチの記述。

　南北戦争の終わり、南軍のリー将軍が北軍のグラント将軍に降伏を申し出た「アポマトックスの降伏」。西部の無法者、ビリー・ザ・キッドの最期。そして「真珠湾攻撃」の戦闘シーンなど、まさにドキュメンタリー・ノベルを読んでいるような面白さです。

2　日本人が身に付けるのにふさわしい英語がここにあります。

　簡単な単語と優しい構文でありながら、ネイティブ感覚いっぱいの英語に触れることができます。先生が小学生に語りかける口調の英語は日常会話にも最適な英語で、日本人が目指す理想の英語がここにあります。

3　真珠湾攻撃、原爆投下、ベトナム戦争etc.──アメリカ人の考え方のスタンダードが分かります。

　「世界の自由」のために第1次、第2次世界大戦に参戦、朝鮮戦争、ベトナム戦争に突入したアメリカ。こうした経緯をどのように小学生に説明しているのでしょうか。アメリカ人の考え方のスタンダードが分かります。

4　アメリカの人たちとの会話を弾ませるトリビアの宝庫です。

　歴史を知るということは、その国への敬意を表すこと。ホームステイ、留学、ビジネスなどでアメリカ人とお付き合いするとき、知っておきたいエピソード満載です。

- ポカホンタスはどんな顔をしていた?
- あの有名なリンカーンの演説は何分?
- 世界中で愛されるテディ・ベアの起源は?
- 大統領を3期以上務めた唯一の大統領は?

ポール・リビア

アメリカ独立戦争最初の英雄となった工芸職人。フランス系の移民で、熱心な愛国派だった。民兵仕官でもあり、ボストン茶会事件にも参加した。1775年4月18日、英軍の進撃を知ると、ボストンから、英軍のフラに、コンコードまで馬を駆って、暗く寒い夜更けを飛ばし、英軍の襲撃を触れ回った。700人の英軍に、わずか77人の民兵で構えていたのは、この夜明けの空に、「一人のポール・リビア」Paul Revereが描かれ、建国神話の1つとなった。

コラムはアメリカ雑学がいっぱい

Paul Revere (1735-1818)